DD29

Monastic Wisdom

The Letters of
Elder Joseph the Hesychast

© 1998 St. Anthony's Greek Orthodox Monastery
4784 N. St. Joseph's Way
Florence, Arizona 85232

Monastic

Wisdom

The Letters of
Elder Joseph the Hesychast

St. Anthony's Monastery

Dedication

We humbly dedicate this volume to all the divinely illumined ascetics of the Holy Mountain who have left us as an inheritance their monastic wisdom.

The Panagia of Arizona

Elder Joseph the Hesychast

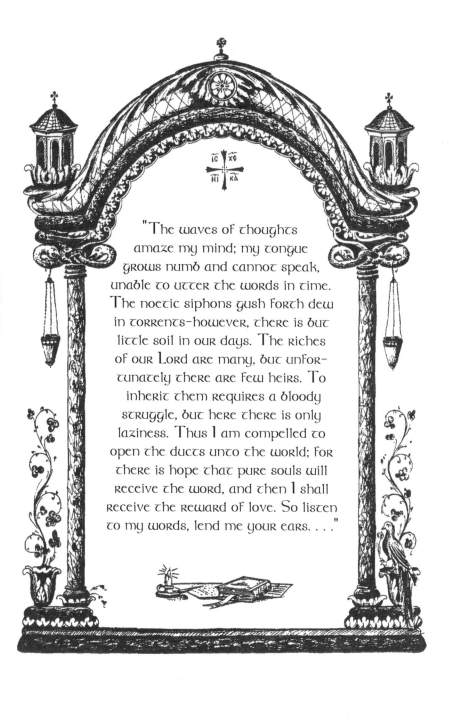

"The waves of thoughts
amaze my mind; my tongue
grows numb and cannot speak,
unable to utter the words in time.
The noetic siphons gush forth dew
in torrents-however, there is but
little soil in our days. The riches
of our Lord are many, but unfortunately there are few heirs. To
inherit them requires a bloody
struggle, but here there is only
laziness. Thus I am compelled to
open the ducts unto the world; for
there is hope that pure souls will
receive the word, and then I shall
receive the reward of love. So listen
to my words, lend me your ears. . . ."

Contents

Contents 15

Part II: An Epistle to a Hesychast Hermit

Preface

 was nineteen years old, I remember, when I followed the path that took me to the garden of the *Theotokos*,* the *Holy Mountain*.* The road that lead me to the monastic life was shown to me by my philomonastic mother, now Nun Theophano of blessed memory.

During the first years of hardship during the German Occupation, when for the sake of work I had to stop going to high school, a *hieromonk** from the Holy Mountain came to be the parish priest in one of the two old-calendar churches in Volos, Greece. He was a *disciple** of an elder known as Elder Joseph the *Hesychast*,* and he became my spiritual father. This hieromonk from the Holy Mountain was for me at that time a precious advisor and helper in my spiritual journey. With the many stories he told me about the Holy Mountain and with his spiritual counseling, I soon began to feel my heart drifting away from the world and cleaving to the Holy Mountain. Especially when he would speak about the life of Elder Joseph, I would burn with the ardent desire for the day that I would meet him.

When the time finally came—September 26, 1947—a small boat brought us slowly one morning from the world to the Holy Mountain as if from the shores of the ephemeral to the other side of eternity.

At the dock of St. Anne's, a venerable old man, *Geronda** Arsenios, was waiting for me.

---

* Terms found in Glossary are marked with an asterisk and written in italics the first time they appear.

"Aren't you Johnny from Volos?" he asked.

"Yes," I replied, "but how do you know me?"

"Oh," he said, "The Honorable Forerunner appeared to Elder Joseph last night and said to him, 'I am bringing you a little lamb. Put it in your sheepfold.'"

My thoughts were fixed on the Honorable Forerunner, my patron saint, on whose birthday I was born. I was very grateful to him for looking out for me in this way.

"So, Johnny, let's go," said Arsenios, "for Geronda is waiting." We started up the narrow cobblestone path. What feelings! Try as one might, they cannot be described.

That night within the small chapel of the Honorable Forerunner that was built in a cave, I did my metanoia of obedience† to my Elder. It was within that dimly lit chapel that my soul became acquainted in its own way with the luminous countenance of my holy Elder.

Spiritually and physically, I was the youngest in the *synodia*,* and Elder Joseph was one of the greatest Hagioritic†† spiritual personages of our times. I stayed by his side, learning from him for twelve years—that was how long he lived thereafter. The Lord made me worthy of serving him until his last holy breath. And he was worthy of being served because of his many spiritual toils and holy prayers that he left to us as a precious spiritual inheritance. When I met him, he was a true God-bearer, a spiritual general par excellence, most experienced in the battle against the passions and the demons. It was impossible for a person to come and stay with him and not be cured of his passions, regardless of how many and how strong they were, as long as he was obedient to him.

The elder always taught his monks that Christ-like obedience was more important than anything else. He permitted the Christians in the world who knew him to practice *noetic*

---

† Once a person has chosen his spiritual father and is accepted by him, he does a *metanoia** symbolizing his submission.

†† Hagioritic means of or relating to Hagion Oros—the Holy Mountain.

prayer,* but always under the guidance of those who were experienced, for he had seen much delusion and had become fearful of it. He would often tell us, "If you see a person not asking for advice or not heeding advice given to him, expect to see him deluded soon."

As for our ascetic struggles, he was most strict. With all his soul he loved fasting, vigils, and prayer. His food was always in moderation. He did not eat freshly cooked food if he knew that there were some leftovers from the day before or even three days before.†

Concerning the diet of us younger members of the brotherhood, however, he was more moderate. Seeing our many physical weaknesses, he deemed this necessary. But it was as if this concession used up all his lenience; beyond that he was extremely demanding. Not that he didn't know how to forgive mistakes or put up with weaknesses, but he wanted us to employ all our spiritual and physical powers in our ascetic endeavors. He would say, "Whatever we do not give to God to use in our ascetic struggles will be used by the other one (i.e., Satan). Our Lord gives us the commandment to love Him with all our soul and all our *heart*,* so that the evil one cannot find a place of rest within us."

We would stay awake all night in prayer. This was our *typikon*.* He demanded that we struggle—shed our blood—against sleep and carnal *thoughts*.* He kept vigil in the darkness of his tiny cell with his inseparable companion, unceasing noetic prayer. Even though he was secluded in his cell, he knew what was going on outside and how we were doing. With a simple glance he could read our thoughts. Whenever he saw that we were in need of spiritual toning he would relate to us the various wondrous and ascetic feats of the Fathers of the Holy Mountain. He was very captivating in his narrations.

---

† One must keep in mind that no electricity for refrigerators was to be found on the Holy Mountain at that time.

When he would start talking, you would not want him to stop. Despite his natural gift of narrating, many times it would seem that he was having difficulty when he would try to speak to us about divine *illumination** and the various states of grace, because human vocabulary was poor and insufficient for him to express those deep meanings. He would become silent and distant, unable to communicate to us those things which exist in the utterly unknowable, superbrilliant apex of mystics— where the simple and absolute, the immutable and ineffable mysteries of theology lie.

My elder did not study academic theology, but he theologized with profound depth. He writes in one of his letters: "When through obedience and *hesychia** a monk's senses have been purified, his *nous** has been calmed, and his heart has been cleansed, he then receives grace and enlightenment of *knowledge.** He becomes all light, all nous, all lucid. He overflows with so much theology that even if three people were to start writing down what they were hearing, they could not keep up with the current of grace coming out in waves, spreading peace and utmost quiescence of passions throughout the body. The heart burns with divine love, and he cries out, 'Hold back, my dear Jesus, the waves of Thy grace, for I am melting like wax.' Truly he melts, unable to bear it. His nous is caught up into *theoria.** A mixing occurs; he is transformed and becomes one with God to the point that he cannot recognize or distinguish himself, just like iron in a furnace becomes one with the fire." (Forty-eighth Letter)

From these words we see that the divine "cloud," which is illumined by the uncreated light, was not something unknown or inaccessible to him, but he knew it as a place and a manner of God's presence, as an ineffable mystery, as resplendent light. And all this was because the Elder knew how to pray.

Many times we saw him after hours of *prayer of the heart** with his face changed and bright. It is not at all strange that the light in which his soul continuously bathed would at times also visibly bathe his body. Besides, the halos on saints and angels we see depicted on *icons** are simply a reflection of the uncreated light of grace which shines within them.

The Elder's purity was truly astonishing. I remember that when I would enter his cell at night, it was all fragrant. I felt the fragrance of his prayers imbue everything that surrounded him, affecting not only our internal senses, but our external senses as well. Whenever he talked to us about the purity of soul and body he always used the All-holy Mother of God as an example.

"I cannot describe to you how much *Panagia** loves chastity and purity. For she is the only Pure Virgin and that is how she wants us and loves us all to be. . . .There is no sacrifice more fragrant to God than purity of body and soul which is obtained through the shedding of blood and a dreadful struggle." He would then conclude, "So struggle forcefully in purifying the soul and body; do not allow any carnal thoughts to enter the nous at all."

As for silence, he would not utter a single word unless it was necessary. Especially during Great Lent, when he was alone with Elder Arsenios, they were silent the whole week. They spoke only when necessary from Vespers on Saturday until Sunday evening Compline, and then remain silent again throughout the following week, using hand signals to communicate when necessary. Because he had found this practice very salutary, he forbade us to talk as well, except when absolutely necessary. When he would send us away from the hermitage on a task, we were not allowed to talk to anyone. I remember that when I returned, he always interrogated me thoroughly to see if I had been obedient and had kept absolute silence. For a minor transgression of two or three words, my first penance was two hundred metanoias.

But this heavenly man was truly a master at curing his disciples from their passions. If they managed to stay beside him in obedience, they experienced spiritual rebirth. Many came to him to learn by his side, but only a few stayed. It was not easy to live with him. Some would find it hard to believe how he would rebuke my unworthiness as an expression of his paternal love and care for my soul. For example, in those twelve years that I lived with him, rarely did I hear him call me by name. To call me or address me, he used all kinds of insults with appropriate adjectives. But the driving force behind all that masterful verbal abuse and insult was true paternal affection and a sincere interest in the cleansing of my soul. How grateful my soul is now for that paternal affection!

We stayed in the wilderness for a number of years. But because of the many hardships almost all of us grew ill. The Elder was informed in his prayers that we should move down from the crags where we were in Small Saint Anne's *Skete*,* so we moved down to New Skete. There the climate was milder, we toiled less, and we all regained our health—all except the Elder. He was ill throughout his entire life. Due to his fasting, the toils of his lengthy vigils, the sweat of his prayers, and even from the tempter, his body became one great sore. One day I asked him, "Geronda, why after so much exhaustion do you still fast?"

"I fast now, my child, so that our good God may give His grace to all of you."

In spite of his physical ailments and pains, he would feel so much bliss and serenity within his soul that he found it hard to describe. He would only say that he felt something like paradise within him.

Finally, the time came for his departure. He had awaited death all his life, for his sojourn here was nothing but trials and afflictions. His soul longed for rest and so did his body. And even though he had firmly implanted within us the remembrance of death, his familiarization with "that most dreadful mystery"—death—made a very strong impression on us. It seemed as though he was getting ready for a festal celebration. That was how much his conscience informed him of the divine mercy that awaited him. But even so, during his last few days he wept more than usual. To console him, Elder Arsenios said, "Geronda, you have toiled and prayed so much all your life, you have cried for your soul so much, and you are still weeping?"

"Eh, Geronda Arsenios, that is true—but I am only human. How can I know whether or not my deeds are pleasing to God? He is God and does not judge as we humans do. Besides, it is not as if I am coming back to weep again; this is my last opportunity. The more one mourns and weeps for his sins, the more he will be consoled."

His love towards the Mother of God was beyond any description. As soon as he mentioned her name, his eyes would shed tears. He had been beseeching her for some time to take him from this life so that he could rest, and the Queen of all hearkened to his supplication. She informed him one month before his departure that his time had come. The Elder then called me and told me what to prepare. We waited.

On the eve of the Dormition of the Theotokos—the fourteenth of August, 1959—Mr. Sotiri Skoinas from Volos passed by to see him. They were very good friends.

"How are you, Geronda? How is your health?"

"Tomorrow, Sotiri, I am leaving for the eternal Fatherland.

Remember my words tomorrow when you hear the bells toll."

That night, during the vigil of the Dormition of the Theotokos, the Elder chanted along with the rest of the Fathers as much as his ailing body permitted. During the Divine Liturgy, right before he was to partake of the immaculate Mysteries, he said, "Provision for life eternal." It was early in the morning, the fifteenth of August. The Elder was sitting in his martyric little chair in the yard of our hesychasterion.† He was awaiting the hour and moment of his departure. He was sure of the Panagia's promise. As time passed and the sun began to rise, though, it seemed that he was starting to worry about the delay. It was the last visit of the evil one. He called me and asked, "My child, why is God slow in taking me? The sun is rising and I am still here!"

"Geronda, don't worry. We shall say *the prayer** for you now, and then you will leave." His tears stopped. All the fathers were saying the prayer intensely with their *prayer-ropes*.* Not more than fifteen minutes had passed before the Elder said, "Call the fathers of the synodia to come and do their last metanoia because I am leaving." We all did our last metanoia and received his blessing. Shortly thereafter, he started to stare up in the sky for about two minutes. Then, turning to us full of serenity and indescribable spiritual amazement, he said to us, "Everything is finished; I am leaving. I am departing. Bless!" He then bent his head down to the right, opened and closed his eyes and mouth calmly for two or three times, and that was it. He gave up his soul to Him Whom he longed and worked for since his youth.

His death was truly holy. To us, it brought a feeling of resurrection. In front of us we had a dead person, and mourning was appropriate, yet within us we were living the resurrection. This feeling has never left me. It is this feeling that

---

† A hesychasterion is a place where hesychasts live.

always accompanies my memory of my ever-memorable holy Elder.

Elder Joseph was unlettered as far as his secular schooling was concerned. He had only completed his second year in elementary school. But he was wise in things divine, for he was tutored by God. The University of the Wilderness taught him what we basically need: the divine.

We know that monastics will benefit from the Elder's letters. We also know that many lay people who are "fighting the good fight"[6] in the world will also be benefited. God only knows who else will benefit from the Elder's letters. However, these things are not readily assimilated without a brave spirit, nor can they be applied in our lives without a spiritual struggle and much toil.

We thank everyone, and call upon the Elder's prayers for those who contributed to this publication. We humbly ask forgiveness for all our mistakes.

† Archimandrite Ephraim
Former Abbot of the Holy Monastery
of Philotheou on the Holy Mountain

⸭⸺the holy monastery of philotheou ⸻

---

[6] cf. 1 Tim 6:12

Prolegomena

by Dr. Constantine Cavarnos

ince the appearance of my book *Anchored in God* (1959), where I devote a chapter to my 1958 meeting with Blessed Elder Joseph the Hesychast and his disciple Hieromonk Ephraim, both of New Skete, Mount Athos, readers of that book have been asking me from time to time for more information about Father Joseph. Some want to learn more about my meeting with him; others, to know if any of his writings have been published in English translation.

Such questions increased since the publication of my second book on Athos, entitled *The Holy Mountain*, in 1973. In it I devote several pages to Father Joseph, presenting his biography, deriving my data from a 75-page Greek manuscript entitled *The Life of Our Ever-memorable Father Joseph the Hesychast*. This work was written in 1962 by his disciple Joseph the Younger, then a monk at New Skete and now a Spiritual Father at the great Athonite Monastery of Vatopedi.

The present book constitutes the best response to the questions raised by the readers of my above-mentioned books. And I am sure it will be received with great joy by all persons who are sincerely interested in authentic Orthodox spirituality. It is comprised of eighty-two letters, most of them addressed to monks and nuns who sought the Elder's spiritual guidance. Taken together, they constitute a great treasury of teachings on the spiritual life. They provide valuable instruction on many phases of it. This instruction is based on the Holy Scriptures, the writings of the Holy Fathers of the Orthodox Church, the lives of saints, and on the Elder's own life as a spiritual striver and guide at the Holy Mountain.

In order to properly understand his teaching, it is best to begin by taking note of the written sources of his teaching and some of his exemplars among the saints of the past. As far as writings are concerned, Father Joseph mentions here and there the following:

(1) *Holy Scripture*
(2) *The Ascetical Homilies of Saint Isaac the Syrian,*
(3) *The Spiritual Homilies of Saint Macarios the Egyptian,*
(4) *The Contrite Discourses of Abba Dorotheos,*
(5) *The Evergetinos,*
(6) *The Philokalia,*
(7) *The Sayings of the Desert Fathers,*
(8) Books of Lives of Saints,
(9) *The Way of a Pilgrim,* and
(10) *The Salutations of the Theotokos.*

About the *Holy Scriptures,* he says: "Always have the *New Testament* in your pocket, and when you find a brief opportunity, read an excerpt. Thus Christ gives you light and guides you towards His commandments. He completes your love and guides you to imitate Him" (Letter 78). About the *Old Testament,* he says: "Piously read the *Old Testament* and you will extract the divine nectar of faith and love. In it God spoke directly to men, and angels guided them" (ibid.). In the Letters there are innumerable quotations from the *Holy Bible.*

About the *Ascetical Homilies of Saint Isaac the Syrian* and *The Spiritual Homilies of Saint Macarios the Egyptian,* Father Joseph remarks: "Purchase these books and you will greatly benefit" (Letter 2). Recommending Abba Dorotheos's book, he says that it "is very contrition-evoking, well written, and of great spiritual benefit" (Letter 16).

Speaking of the *Evergetinos*, he says: "There you will find many stories that will benefit you greatly" (ibid.). This monumental Byzantine work of the eleventh century presents teachings and instructive incidents of hundreds of early Desert Fathers and some Desert Mothers. (I discuss it in Vol. 1 of my *New Library*, pp. 46-49.)

From *The Sayings of the Desert Fathers* the Elder quotes this striking statement: "An angry and irritable man is not accepted in the Kingdom of God, even if he raises the dead!" (Letter 6).

He recommends again and again reading the lives of Saints. In one of his Letters he remarks: "The lives of Saints and the writings they left us warm up the fervor of your soul and incite it to desire ardently our sweetest Jesus, just as officers in the army tell their troops about the feats of the brave and thus make them fight valiantly" (Letter 11). In another Letter he says: "Read the lives of Saints and see how many hardships they endured against their 'old man'" spoken of by Saint Paul in Romans 6:6 (Letter 23). And in still another Letter he says: "If you read the lives of saints and toil (pray) a little at night, you will quickly obtain what you seek, and your soul will rejoice that Christ loves you so much" (Letter 77).

About the book *The Way of a Pilgrim*, the Blessed Elder advises one of his spiritual children to acquire copies of it and distribute them to Christians, that they might benefit spiritually (Letter 78). It is worth nothing that in my meeting with him which I describe in *Anchored in God*, Father Joseph said to me: "I suggest strongly that you read *The Way of a Pilgrim*. This book shows the importance of mental prayer, or

prayer of the heart, and the manner in which it is to be practiced. The first part of this work is more valuable than the
sequel, which seems to have been added by another author."

With regard to *The Salutations of the Theotokos*, he advises: "Read them, and she will always guard you from every
evil" (Letter 78).

All reading of edifying writings, he emphasizes, "should
be done *with much attention*, so that with all this the soul may
increase and grow. Thus the 'old man' fades away and dies,
whereas the new man is renewed and overflows with the love
of Christ. And then a person is no longer pleased at all with
earthly things, but continuously hungers for the heavenly"
(Letter 5).

Also important for properly understanding the Elder—
besides the writings he recommended for reading—is taking
note of some of the Saints he particularly admired. He mentions Saints Isaac the Syrian, Andrew the "fool for Christ,"
Anthony the Great, Arsenios the Great, Lukas of Steirion,
Macarios the Egyptian, Mary the Egyptian, Nectarios of
Aegina, Onouphrios, and Peter the Athonite.

He calls Abba Isaac the Syrian "the boast of hesychasm
and the consolation of ascetics, who assures and encourages
spiritual strivers more than all the other Fathers do" (Letter
82, Chapter VI).

He calls Nectarios a great Saint, and notes that he read
Nectarios's Letters and learned from him the need of paying
attention to doctors and medicines. "During my earlier period," remarks Father Joseph, "I wanted to heal only through
faith. But now I, too, am learning that both medicines and
grace are necessary." From Saint Nectarios he also learned the
importance of watching one's diet. Thus he tells one of his
spiritual children: "Take control of your appetite: don't eat

things that you know are harmful to your health: fried foods, salty foods, sauces, pork, meats, salted fish, alcoholic beverages in general" (Letter 49).

About Saints Anthony the Great, Onouphrios, Mary the Egyptian, and Luke of Steirion, he remarks that they were highly gifted mentally and "were taught by God, receiving teachings from God without a teacher" (Letter 3). However, he emphasizes that generally, a spiritual striver needs a wise and experienced guide, in order to tread safely and successfully the path that leads to purity and spiritual perfection.

The *beginning* of the path is *self-examination* with a view to *self-knowledge*. "Know thyself" is a phrase that appears in several of the Letters. "The first and foremost step" that one must take, says Father Joseph, "is to 'know oneself.' That is, to know who you really are in truth, and not what you imagine you are. With this knowledge you become the wisest man. With this awareness, you reach humility and receive grace from the Lord. However, if you don't obtain self-knowledge, but consider only your toil, know that you will always remain far from the path" (Letter 3). Knowing yourself consists in knowing "your weaknesses, passions, and shortcomings" (ibid.).

The Elder place great emphasis on the need of becoming *aware* of your "passions" and proceeding *to struggle to overcome them*, to *free* yourself from them to attain *passionlessness*, which means *purity*. This high spiritual state can only be attained, he stresses, by *persistent struggle* and *Divine grace*.

"Passion" (pathos) in Orthodox Patristic writings, is a term used in two senses: (a) to denote *bad thoughts charged with emotion*, and (b) *vices* (kakiai), that is, such thoughts become *habits*, settled dispositions of the soul, bad traits of character All the "passions" are viewed by Father Joseph as *diseases* of the soul in need of *therapy*. Removing them from the soul is a process he calls—as do the Holy Fathers of the past—*purification*. This restores the soul to a state of health and peace. "The more you are purified from the passions, the more peace you have, the wiser you are, the more you understand God" (Letter 65).

Success in this is attained when the striver is helped by Divine grace, called by the Elder "purifying grace." This "mystically helps the struggling penitent to be purified from sins and to be in the state *according to nature*. . . . For the passions entered the nature of man after Adam's disobedience, whereas the *natural state* in which man was created by God was passionless" (Letter 82, Chapter XI).

Blessed Father Joseph distinguishes *three stages of the spiritual life*: (1) the stage of *purification*, which has already been discussed, (2) the stage of *illumination*, and (3) the stage of *perfection*. The second and the third stages lift man to a state *above nature*.

During the stage of *illumination*, the mind is illuminated by "*illuminating grace*" and *perceives everything clearly*. "One receives *the light of knowledge* and is raised to *the vision of God*. This does not mean seeing illusory lights, fantasies, and images; it means radiance of the mind, clearness of thoughts, and depth of ideas. . . . The mind receives Divine illumination and becomes entirely Divine light, by which one mentally perceives the truth and discerns how he must proceed until he reaches Love, which is our sweet Jesus" (Letters 2 and 82.XI).

"The third stage of the spiritual life is that of the *grace of perfection*" (Letter 2). This grace perfects the spiritual striver. It wipes out all the passions and preserves all the virtues as parts of one's nature, without one needing to use his own devices and methods to do this (Letter 82.XI). The virtues, adds the Elder, render the possessor of them "in the likeness of God" (Epilogue).

With regard to the last point, it should be explained that following the great Holy Fathers of Orthodoxy, he distinguishes between being "in the likeness of God" from being "in the image of God." The latter expression denotes the possession of a rational soul; "in the likeness of God" refers to the possession of the totality of the virtues in highly developed, permanent form.

At the stage of perfection, of "perfecting grace," there is a blossoming of the virtues of obedience, wisdom, discernment, humility, patience, chastity, courage, gentleness, temperance, spiritual love, and the other virtues.

The orientation of the Letters assembled in this book is manifestly what is called "otherworldly." The goals set by Blessed Father Joseph the Hesychast are all spiritual. They are set by one who sees human life *under the aspect of eternity*. Man's most precious possession is his *soul*, which is *immortal*; he *must take care of it*. The Elder writes in one of his Letters: "I earnestly entreat you: take care of your souls" (Letter 29). And he explains throughout his 82 Letters what he means by "taking care of the soul." It means preeminently striving to *purify* it of all the passions, and to *adorn* it with all the virtues, which *perfect* it as far as is possible during our life on the earth.

He who cares for his soul in such a manner will abide in peace and contentment in this world and may justly expect to fare well in the life beyond death. Thus, Father Joseph says: "When the hour of death comes, as soon as these eyes close, the inner eyes of the soul will open. And as it contemplates the things 'there,' suddenly it finds itself in those things it longs for, without realizing how. It passes from darkness to light" (Letter 38). "As from sleep we shall wake up into the other life. Then we will see parents, brothers, relatives. Then we will see angels and saints. . . . We shall converse with them as with brothers, giving one another a divine embrace, and continuously wondering at the heavenly choirs, until we reach our Master and Savior, and thenceforth remain inseparable." (Letters 40,47).

The divine ladder of St. John leading to heaven

the treasure of a miser

all-devouring Hades

He who has united his heart to prayer
will not easily be raided by spiritual thieves

Part One

Letters to Monastics and Laymen

Part I: The Letters

First Letter

To a youth asking about "the prayer"

 y beloved brother in Christ, I pray that you are well. Today I received your letter and shall answer all your questions. The information you seek does not require time and effort for me to think and respond. For noetic prayer is to me as any other man's trade is to him, because I have been working at it now for more than thirty-six years.

When I came to the Holy Mountain, I immediately sought out the hermits who practiced prayer. Back then, forty years ago, there were many who had life in them—men of virtue, elders of the past. We chose one of them as our elder and received guidance from several of them.

Now then, to start mastering noetic prayer you must constantly force yourself to say the prayer without ceasing. In the beginning quickly: the nous must not have time to form any distracting thoughts. Pay attention only to the words: "Lord Jesus Christ, have mercy on me." When the prayer is said orally for a long period of time, the nous becomes accustomed to it and eventually takes up saying it. Then it becomes sweet to you as if you had honey in your mouth, and you want to keep saying it all the time. If you stop it, you feel greatly distressed.

When the nous gets used to it and has taken its fill—when it has learned it well—then it sends it to the heart. Since the nous supplies food for the soul, the task of the nous is to send whatever good or evil it sees or hears down to the heart, which is the center of man's spiritual and physical powers, the throne of the nous. So, when someone saying the prayer keeps his nous from imagining anything, and pays attention only to the words of the prayer, then, breathing gently with a certain compulsion and volition of his own, he brings his nous down to his heart; he holds it within as if in confinement, rhythmically saying the prayer:

"Lord Jesus Christ, have mercy on me!"

In the beginning he says the prayer a few times and takes a breath. Later, when the nous has become accustomed to remaining in the heart, he says one prayer with each breath: "Lord Jesus Christ" breathing in, "have mercy on me" breathing out. This happens until grace overshadows the soul and begins to act within it. Beyond this is theoria.

So, the prayer is said everywhere: seated, in bed, walking, and standing. "Pray without ceasing. In everything give thanks,"[1] says the apostle. However, it is not enough to pray only when you go to bed. It takes a struggle: standing and sitting. When you get tired, sit. Then stand up again so that you are not overcome by sleep.

This is called *"praxis."** You show your good intention to God, but everything depends on Him, on whether or not He gives to you. God is the beginning and the end. His grace is the driving force that activates all things.

As for how love is activated, you will realize how when you keep the commandments. When you get up at night and

[1] 1 Thes. 5:17-18

pray; when you see someone ill and sympathize with him; when you see a widow, orphans, or the elderly and you are charitable to them, then God loves you. And then you also love Him. He loves first and pours out His grace, and we return to Him what is His; "Thine own of Thine own."

Well, if you seek to find Him only through the prayer, do not let a single breath pass without it. Just be careful not to accept any fantasies. For the Divine is formless, unimaginable, and colorless; He is supremely perfect, not subject to syllogisms. He acts like a subtle breeze in our minds.

Compunction comes when you consider how much you have grieved God Who is so good, so sweet, so merciful, so kind, and entirely full of love; Who was crucified and suffered everything for us. When you meditate on these and other things the Lord has suffered, they bring compunction.

So, if you are able to say the prayer out loud without ceasing, in two or three months you can get used to it. Then grace overshadows you and refreshes you. Only say it out loud, without a break. When the nous takes it up, you stop saying it orally; and then when the nous loses grip of the prayer, let the tongue resume saying it out loud. All the forcefulness is needed with the tongue until you get used to it in the beginning. Afterwards, all the years of your life, your nous will say it without exertion.

When you come to the Holy Mountain, as you mentioned, come and see us. But then we shall talk about other things. You will not have time for the prayer. You will find the prayer wherever your mind is at rest. Here you will be visiting the monasteries and your mind will be distracted by the things you hear and see.

I am certain that you shall find "the prayer." Have no doubts. Only straightaway knock at the door of divine mercy, and surely Christ shall open unto you. It is impossible for Him not to. The more you love Him, the more you will receive. The size of His gift, be it great or small, depends on your love, whether it is great or small.

Second Letter

To the same person about the prayer, and a reply to questions.

 he eagerness you have to benefit your soul delighted me. I also thirst to benefit every brother who seeks salvation. Therefore, my dearly beloved brother, open your ears.

Man's purpose, from the moment he is born, is to find God. However, he cannot find Him unless God finds him first. "In Him we live and move."[1] Unfortunately, the passions have shut the eyes of our soul and we cannot see. But when our very loving God turns an affectionate eye towards us, then we awake as if from sleep and begin to seek salvation.

As for your first question, God has now seen you; He has enlightened you and is guiding you. Keep working where you are. Say the prayer incessantly, both orally and noetically. When the tongue gets tired, resume saying it noetically and when the nous is weighed down, let the tongue begin—just don't stop. Do many metanoias; keep vigil at night as much as you can. And if a flame is lit in your heart with love towards God, if you seek hesychia and can no longer remain in the world because the prayer is igniting within you, then

---

[1] Acts 17:28

write to me and I shall tell you what to do. But if grace does not act like this and your zeal is limited to keeping the commandments of the Lord towards your neighbor, then be at peace as you are, and you will be fine. Do not seek anything more. You will discover the difference between thirty, sixty, and one hundred[2] when you read the *Evergetinos*. There you will find many more stories that will benefit you greatly.

Now then, in response to your other questions: the prayer must be said with the *inner voice*.* But since initially the nous is not accustomed to it, it forgets to say the prayer. This is why you say it at times orally and at other times noetically. This happens until the nous gets its fill and grace begins to act within.

This "action" of grace is the joy and delight you feel within yourself when you say the prayer, and you want to say it continuously. So when the nous takes over the prayer and this joy that I am writing about occurs, the prayer will be said unceasingly within you, without any effort on your part. This is called perception of the action of grace, because grace acts without man's volition. He eats, walks, sleeps, awakes, while internally he cries out the prayer continuously. And he has peace and joy.

Regarding the hours of prayer: since you are in the world and have various cares, pray whenever you find time. But constantly force yourself so that you do not become negligent. As for "theoria" which you asked about, it is difficult there, for it requires absolute stillness.

The spiritual life is divided into three stages, and grace acts in a person accordingly. The first stage is called *purification*,* during which a person is cleansed. What you have now is called the grace of purification. This form of grace leads one to *repentance*.* All the eagerness that you

---

2 cf. Mt. 13:8

have for spiritual things is due to grace alone. Nothing is your own. It secretly acts upon everything. So when you exert yourself, this grace remains with you for a certain period of time. If a person progresses with noetic prayer, he receives another form of grace which is entirely different.

As we mentioned earlier, this first form of grace is called "perception of the action of grace," and is the grace of purification. That is, one who prays feels the presence of divine energy within him.

The second form of grace is called the grace of illumination. During this stage, one receives the light of knowledge and is raised to the vision of God. This does not mean seeing lights, fantasies, and images, but it means clarity of the nous, clearness of thoughts, and depth of cognition. For this to occur, the person praying must have much stillness and an unerring guide.

The third stage—when grace overshadows—is the grace of perfection, truly a great gift. I shall not write to you about this now, since it is unnecessary. However, if you wish to read about it, I have written, despite my illiteracy, a small hand-written pamphlet entitled "A Spirit-moved Trumpet" while I was undergoing these transformations. Search for it. Also purchase the book by St. Makarios from Mr. Schoinas, as well as *The Ascetical Homilies of Saint Isaac the Syrian*, and you will greatly benefit. In addition, write to me about any transformation you encounter, and I shall answer you with great eagerness.

These days I am constantly writing to those who ask questions. This year people came from Germany solely to learn about noetic prayer. From as far as America, people write to me with much eagerness. There are also many from Paris who are earnestly seeking. But we who have everything right here at our feet, why are we negligent? Is it really hard labor to cry out continuously the name of Christ so that He may have mercy on us?

Furthermore, a sinister notion from the evil one prevails today: that there is danger of delusion in saying the prayer. On the contrary, this in itself is a delusion.

Whosoever desires, let him try it. Once the prayer has acted for a long time, he will feel paradise within himself. He will be freed from the passions; he will become a new man. And if he happens to be in the desert, then—oh! oh!—there is no telling of the bounties of the prayer!

𝔗hird 𝔏etter

To a monk entering the arena of combat.

ejoice in the Lord, beloved child, whom the grace of my Jesus has enlightened and delivered from the world; who has flown to the wilderness and dwelt in a monastery with a holy synodia, and now glorifies and thanks God with all his soul.

Divine grace, my child, is like bait which enters the soul and without coercion attracts a person toward higher and superior things. It knows how to catch us rational fish and to pull us out of the sea of the world. But then what?

Once God takes the monastic aspirant out of the world and brings him to the wilderness, He doesn't immediately show him his passions and the temptations, until he becomes a monk and Christ binds him with His fear. Then the trial, the struggle, and the fight begin.

If a novice exerts himself from the beginning and lights his torch of asceticism with his struggles before it is too late, it will not go out when grace withdraws and temptations come. Otherwise, when grace does withdraw, he will return to his previous state. Then, corresponding to the passions he had in the world, temptations will arise and will revive his former habits which used to enslave him because he used to cater to them.

First of all, my child, know that there are great differences from man to man and monk to monk. There are souls with a soft character that are very easily persuaded. There are also souls with a tough character that are not subordinated so easily. They are as different as cotton is from iron. Cotton needs only to be rubbed with words, but iron requires fire and a furnace of temptations to be worked. Such a soul must be patient during temptations to be purified. When a monk does not have patience, he is like a lamp without oil: soon it will burn out.

So, when a person with a nature harder than iron comes to be a monk, as soon as he enters the arena, he rebels against obedience. Immediately he breaks his promises and gives up the battle. Then you see that as soon as grace withdraws a little to test his intentions and patience, at once he throws away his weapons and starts regretting that he came to be a monk. Then he passes his days full of disobedience and bitterness, always talking back arrogantly.

Then, through the prayers of his elder, grace disperses the clouds of temptations somewhat so that he comes to his senses a little and mends his ways. But soon afterwards he returns once more to his own will, to disobedience, agitation, and annoyance.

You write about the brother you see there and are amazed that although he works so hard at his *diakonema*,* his ego within still overcomes him. But do you think it is easy for man to conquer a passion?

Good deeds and almsgiving and all other external good things do not subdue the haughtiness of one's heart. But mental work, the pain of repentance, contrition, and humility are what humble the unsubmissive spirit. An insubordinate person is unbearable and toilsome to deal with. Only with utter patience can he be handled. Only with utter patience on behalf of the elders and with the forbearance and love of the brethren can stiff-necked disciples come to their senses. But behold: many times they, too, are as useful as your right hand. Almost always such people, who are in some way more gifted than the others, humble themselves with difficulty. They think highly of themselves and look down on others.

So a great deal of hard work and patience are needed until this old foundation of pride is dug up, and another foundation is set with Christ's humility and obedience. But the Lord, seeing their efforts and good intentions, allows another trial to come upon them which counteracts their passion, and by His mercy, He "Who will have all men to be saved"[1] saves them too. As for you, emulate whomever you want.

It would be wonderful if everyone had a good character, humility, and obedience. But if one's nature happens to be tougher than iron, he should not despair. He needs to struggle, and by the grace of God he can win. God is not unjust in His expectations. He seeks repayment according to the gifts He has given.

For from the beginning of creation He separated men into three classes: He gave five talents to one, two to another, and one to the other. The first one has the highest gifts: he has greater mental capacity and is called "taught by God," because he receives teachings from God without a teacher, just like St. Anthony the Great, St. Onouphrios, St. Mary of Egypt, Cyril Phileotes, Luke of Steirion, and thousands of others in the old days who became perfect without a guide. The second type of person has to be taught what is good in order to do it. And the third one, even if he hears,

---

[1] 1 Tim. 2:4

even if he learns, he hides it in the ground: he doesn't do anything.

So that is why there is such a big difference among the people and monks that you see. And that is why first and foremost you must "know thyself." That is, know who you really are in truth, and not what you imagine you are. With this knowledge you become the wisest man. With this kind of awareness, you reach humility and receive grace from the Lord. However, if you don't obtain self-knowledge, but consider only your toil, know that you will always remain far from the path. The prophet does not say, "Behold, O Lord, my toil," but says, "Behold my humility and my toil."[2] Toil is for the body, and humility is for the soul. Moreover, the two together, toil and humility, are for the whole man.

Who has conquered the devil? He who knows his own weaknesses, passions, and shortcomings. Whoever is afraid of knowing himself remains far from knowledge, and he doesn't love anything else except seeing faults in others and judging them. He doesn't see gifts in other people, but only shortcomings. And he doesn't see his own shortcomings, but only his gifts. This is truly the sickness that plagues us men of the *eighth millennium*:* we fail to recognize one another's gifts. One person may lack many things, but many people together have everything. What one person lacks, another person has. If we acknowledged this, we would have a great deal of humility, because God, Who adorned men in many ways and showed inequality in all of his creations, is honored and glorified; not as the unbelievers say, who toil trying to bring equality by overturning the divine creation. God made all things in wisdom.[3]

Therefore, my child, now that it is still the beginning, see to it that you know yourself well, so that you set humility as a

---

[2] Ps. 24:18 (All quotes from the Old Testament are from the Septuagint)
[3] cf. Ps. 103:24

firm foundation. See to it that you learn obedience and acquire the prayer.

May "Lord Jesus Christ, have mercy on me," be your breath.

Do not leave your mind idle, so that you aren't taught evil things. Don't let yourself look at the faults of others, because without knowing it, you will become the evil one's partner without any progress in virtue. Do not out of ignorance ally yourself with the enemy of your soul.

The cunning enemy knows very well how to hide behind passions and weaknesses. So in order to strike him, you must fight and mortify yourself—all your passions, that is. When the "old man"[4] dies, the strength of your hostile enemy is abolished.

We are not battling with a man, whom you can kill in many ways, but with the powers and rulers of darkness. They are not fought with sweets and marshmallows, but with streams of tears, with pain of soul until death, with utter humility, and with great patience. Blood must flow from overexhaustion in saying the prayer. You have to collapse from exhaustion for weeks as if gravely ill. And you must not give up the fight, until the demons are beaten and withdraw. Then you will receive freedom from the passions.

And so, my child, force yourself from the beginning to enter the narrow gate, because only it leads to the spaciousness of paradise. Cut off your own will every day and hour, and seek no other path besides this one. This is the path that the feet of the Holy Fathers trod. Reveal your path unto the Lord and He will guide you, too. Reveal your thoughts to your elder, and he will heal you. Never hide a thought, because the devil conceals his cunning within it: as soon as you confess it he disappears. Do not reveal another

---

[4] cf. Rom. 6:6

person's fault to justify yourself, because at once grace, which had covered you until that point, will reveal your own faults. The more you cover your brother with love, the more grace warms you and guards you from the false accusation of men.

As for the other brother you mentioned, it seems that he has some unconfessed sins, because he is ashamed to tell them to the elder. And this is why that temptation takes place. But he must correct this improper behavior, for without frank confession, one cannot be purified. It is a shame to be ridiculed by the demons. Deep down his ego is hiding. May the Lord enlighten him to come to his senses. And you should pray and love him as well as everyone; yet guard yourself from all.

In any case, now that you have entered the arena, you will undergo many kinds of temptations, so prepare yourself to be patient. Say the prayer constantly, and the Lord will help you with His grace. Temptations are never stronger than grace.

Fourth Letter

My child, if you pay attention to everything I write to you. . .

y child, if you pay attention to everything I write to you and compel yourself, you will find great benefit. All these things are happening to you because you are not forcing yourself to say the prayer. So force yourself to say the prayer unceasingly; don't let your mouth stop at all. In this way you will grow accustomed to it within yourself, and then the nous will take over. Do not become overconfident with your thoughts for you will be weakened and defiled. If you pray and continuously force yourself to pray, you will see how much grace you will receive.

My child, man's life is full of sorrow because he is in exile. Do not seek perfect rest. Since our Christ bore His Cross, we shall bear ours, too. If we endure all afflictions, we shall receive grace from the Lord. The Lord allows us to be tempted, so that He can test the zeal and love we have for Him. Therefore, patience is needed. Without patience a person does not obtain experience, acquire spiritual knowledge, or attain any measure of virtue and perfection.

Love Jesus and say the prayer unceasingly, and it will enlighten you on His path.

Be careful not to judge, because then God will allow grace to withdraw and will let you fall and be humbled so that you can see your own faults.

Everything that you wrote about is good. The first things that you are feeling are due to God's grace; when it comes, it makes a man spiritual and makes everything seem fine and beautiful. Then he loves everyone and has compunction, tears, and a fervent soul. However, when grace withdraws to test a man, everything becomes carnal and the soul falls. Do not lose your eagerness at this point, but force yourself to cry out the prayer continuously with distress, with might and main, "Lord Jesus Christ, have mercy on me!"

Say the same thing continually, over and over again. And as if you were noetically gazing at Christ, say to Him, "I thank Thee, my dear Christ, for all the good things which Thou hast given me and for all the hardships that I suffer. Glory to Thee, glory to Thee my God." And if you are patient, grace and joy will come once more. However, temptations, sorrow, agitation, and irritability will come again; then struggle, victory, and thanksgiving follow. This recurs until little by little you are cleansed from the passions and become spiritual. With time, as you grow older, you attain *dispassion*.*

However, you must struggle. Don't expect good things to come by themselves. One does not become a monk through luxury and comforts. A monk must be insulted, derided, tested. He must fall and then get up so that he can become a true person. He must not be cuddled in his mother's arms. Who ever heard of someone becoming a monk by his mother's side? As soon as he cries out, "Oh!" she would say, "Eat, so you don't get sick!"

Ascesis, * my son, requires deprivation. You cannot obtain virtues through luxury and the easy life. It takes a struggle and much labor. It takes crying out to Christ day and night. It takes patience in all temptations and afflictions. It takes supressing your anger and desires.

You will fatigue greatly until you realize that prayer without attention and *watchfulness** is a waste of time; work without pay. You must set attention as a vigilant guard over all your inner and outer senses. Without attention, both the nous and the powers of the soul are diffused in vain and ordinary things, like useless water running down the streets. No one has ever found prayer without attention and watchfulness. No one was ever counted worthy to ascend to the things above without having despised the things below. Many times you pray and your mind wanders here and there, wherever it pleases, to everything that attracts it out of habit. It takes considerable force and a struggle to break the mind away from there so that it pays attention to the words of the prayer.

Many times the enemy craftily creeps into your thoughts, your words, your hearing, your eyes, and you are unaware of it. When you do realize it later on, you need to struggle greatly to be cleansed. However, don't give up fighting against the evil spirits. By the grace of God, you will be victorious, and then you will rejoice for all you had suffered.

In addition, be careful—and tell the others, too—not to compliment one another in each other's presence, for if compliments harm the perfect, how much more harmful they will be to you who are still weak.

There was once a saint who had a visitor. Three times he told the saint that he was doing his handicraft well. After the third time, the saint replied, "Since you came here, you have driven God away from me!"

Do you see how precise the saints were? For this reason, great caution is necessary in everything. Only reproaches and insults benefit a man spiritually, because they give birth to humility. He gains crowns, and by enduring, he crushes his egotism and vainglory. Therefore, when they insult you, "You arrogant egotist, you impatient hypocrite," etc., it is a time for patience. If you respond, you lose.

So always have the fear of God. Have love for everyone and be careful not to sadden or hurt anyone in any way, because your brother's grief will serve as an obstacle when you pray. Be a good example to everyone in word and deed, and divine grace will always help you and protect you.

And be careful, my child; don't ever forget throughout your entire life that a monk must be a good example to lay people and not behave scandalously, just as angels are an example to him.[1] Therefore, it is his duty to be very careful lest Satan cheat him.

If it is necessary for a monk to go out into the world, let him go. However, he must be all eyes and all light: he must see very clearly, so that he doesn't suffer any harm while trying to benefit others. Young monks and nuns, who are still in the prime of life, are particularly endangered when they go out into the world, since they are walking in the midst of many snares. As for those who have somewhat matured in age and have become withered through ascesis, there is not so much danger. They are not harmed so much as they benefit others, if they have experience and knowledge. But in general, a monk does not obtain any benefit from the world—only praises and glory, which clean him out and leave him bare. And woe to him, if divine grace does not protect him according to the need and purpose for which he went out.

---

[1] vid. *The Ladder of Divine Ascent,* step 26:31

Fifth Letter

Do not clothe yourself only with leaves.

y beloved child in the Lord, offspring of the Divine Spirit, I rejoice when you rejoice. Dominions and Principalities rejoice along with the Cherubim and Seraphim, the angelic Hosts, the choirs of Martyrs and Righteous, and our All-pure Mother, the Queen and Lady of all.

Today you gladdened my soul with what you wrote with paper and pen. I shall greatly rejoice and be exceedingly delighted if you faithfully complete what you wrote.

The war of the enemy begins after three or four years, because grace withdraws to test a person, and your torch goes out. Things that seem beautiful now—which truly are beautiful—will then seem repulsive, black, and dark. Therefore, don't even think that the things that are happening to you now are real temptations, because someone else is protecting you. And since, my beloved child, you sought advice from me the lowly one, listen:

Do not clothe yourself only with leaves, but spread your roots deep to find a spring, as the sycamore tree does, so that you may constantly draw water and continuously grow. Thus, when a drought comes upon you, you will suffer no harm, because you have found your own spring. When the torch you now have goes out, you will have another one lit through your works, and you will never suffer from darkness. The method of obtaining these blessings is as follows:

First of all, perfect and unquestioning obedience to all. From this arises humility. The distinctive mark of humility is profuse tears, which for three or four years flow like a stream. From them is born ceaseless prayer, called noetic prayer. So that as soon as you say, "My sweetest Jesus!" tears run. As soon as you say, "My Panagia!" you are unable to control yourself. Then, from them is born tranquillity throughout the body and perfect peace.

Once a brother wanted to control himself—because the tears had started and someone had knocked on the door—but he was unable to until the tears had ceased of their own accord. That is how much power they have.

So, if you obtain them, there is no danger of suffering any harm, since you have become a different type of person. Not that your nature changes, but grace changes its properties through the divine energies of God.

The services should contain substance, just as the leaves on a tree cover fruits. Chanting should be done with humility. The nous should hunt out the meaning of the hymn. The *intellect** should be sweetened by the thoughts of the nous and should be led up to their *contemplation*.*

Likewise, reading should be done with much attention, so that with all this the soul may increase and grow. Thus the "old man" fades away and dies, whereas the new man is renewed and overflows with the love of Christ. And then a person is no longer pleased at all with earthly things, but continuously hungers for the heavenly things.

The body, too, must struggle with all its might. It should always be subservient to the spirit. Don't feel sorry for it at all. And whether you are eating or working, don't stop the prayer.

And in all prayers, the nous should follow and understand what you are praying and saying. For if you yourself don't understand what you are saying, how will you communicate with God so that He grant what you seek?

If you do as I tell you, you will do yourself good. You will be saved forever and also make me happy. But if you disobey out of negligence, you will make many grieve.

Sixth Letter

You write about anger in the heart of a fool.

 o listen to me once again. Lay a solid foundation. Build a beautiful little palace in the heavens. Clean the inside of the cup, as the Lord instructs us, so that the outside becomes clean as well, because everything done with the body resembles leaves which merely decorate the outer man. Those works are well and good, but everything I have written to you about previously is what cleanses a person internally. These things will open the eyes of the soul. It is through them that the heart is purified to see God on that day. For without noetic work, there is little benefit from outer works.

If you do not see tears pouring forth every time you remember God, you suffer from ignorance, which leads to pride and hardness of heart. So let humility serve as a garment in all your actions, and become a sponge in the brotherhood that mops up every reproach and abasement. Do not water your soul with honors and praises but with reproaches and accusations, even if you are innocent.

Never seek to find what is just, because then you are unjust. On the contrary, learn to endure temptations bravely, regardless of what kind the Lord permits. Without a lot of excuses, just say, "Forgive me!" and without actually being at fault, repent as if you were. Do so with conviction of soul; not just outwardly admitting to be at fault for the sake of praise, while inwardly judging.

During times of affliction, do not seek human consolation, so that God may console you.

The bridge we must all cross is to forgive the transgressions of others. However, if you don't forgive them, you destroy the bridge that you should have crossed. So become a good model and example to the others through your good and God-pleasing deeds, and do not wish to defeat everyone with your words.

Do not think that you will find rest when you speak out seeking justice for yourself. Justice is to endure with bravery the temptation that comes so that you emerge victorious, whether or not you were at fault. But if you say, "But why?" you are fighting against God Who sent the afflictions because of your *passionate** condition. God disciplines us so that we reach dispassion. Thus, if you do not endure it, truly you are fighting against God.

You write about anger in the heart of a fool. Anger in itself is natural. Just as the body has nerves, the soul has anger. Everyone should use it against the demons, heretics, and anyone who hinders us from the path of God. However, if you get angry with your fellow brothers, or get in a rage and ruin the works of your hands, know that you are suffering from vainglory and are abusing the nerve of your soul. You are delivered from this passion through love towards all and true humility.

Therefore, when anger comes, close your mouth tightly, and do not speak to him who curses, dishonors, reproaches, or bothers you in any way without reason. Then this snake will writhe around in your heart, rise up to your throat, and (since you don't give it a way out) will choke and suffocate. When this is repeated several times, it will diminish and cease entirely.

Since man was created rational and gentle, he is corrected far better with love and gentleness than with anger and harshness. After much and thorough testing, I have also found that with goodness and love you can pacify many. And if someone is of good intentions, you can quickly make him comply and become an angel of God.

So this is what I would say to you and to everyone: never seek to correct each other with anger, but only with humility and sincere love, because one temptation does not cast out another temptation. When you see anger ahead, forget about correcting for the moment. Once you see that the anger has passed, that peace has come, and that your powers of discernment are functioning properly, then you can speak beneficially.

I have never seen anyone corrected through anger, but always through love; and then, he will even make sacrifices. Therefore, this is how you should act. Take yourself for example: how are you pacified—with curses or with love?

Don't you marvel at the words of that saint in *The Sayings of the Desert Fathers*, "An angry and irritable man is not accepted in the kingdom of God even if he raises the dead!"?

You say that you respect my words. If this is really true, try out my advice, and choke the passion when it comes to choke you. Over and over again, keep the serpent locked up inside, and you will immediately find the path to joy and victory. Then the prayers I say for you will take effect right away. And once the mother is defeated, the entire swarm of daughters born of anger is vanquished, because the principal passions that give birth to all the rest are anger and desire.

Therefore, supress anger with all your might every time it is aroused, and you will find it weaker the next time. Continually strike at it and cut off its head whenever you see it rising. Then composure, the fruit of forbearance, will soon blossom. Thenceforth you will have peace and grace, and all good things will follow.

Desire, the *appetitive aspect** of the soul, is the second such mother that hurls the rider[1] [i.e., the nous]. When abstinence is applied in everything and there is no increase of fat, there will be no excess of blood. And then the *flesh** cannot hurl the person, but it only fights.

So resist with *rebuttal** of thoughts. Don't let thoughts enter, but fight them off with prayer. Fight valiantly, not torpidly, and the passions will be paralyzed immediately. By doing so, the flower of purity and chastity will blossom, whereby your soul will rejoice with an unspeakable joy and be assured that henceforth a place of rest has been prepared for you. And in this manner, you will paralyze the wickedness of this passion along with the wickedness of all its daughters.

---

[1] cf. Ex. 15:1

Seventh Letter

Listen to something that happened to me.

ust this moment I received your letter and saw what you wrote. I am glad that you are healthy but am sorry for your afflictions.

Everything you mentioned, my child, is happening because you lack patience.

You, my child, are seeking Christ. You are seeking to enter the heavenly city. The elder and the fathers are praying for this, and I, too, the poor one, am praying out here on the crags. So the Lord heard all of us, and in order to crush your proud soul, to humble and defeat your anger, wrath, temper, and ego, He sent you a flea—this small temptation—to keep biting you, so that you learn to bear it. He sent it to bother you, so that you learn to be patient. In this way, your anger, wrath, and agitation are gradually soothed. He sent it so that you learn to choke temptations inside you and not let harsh words come out. And then, once that power of Satan has been stifled inside you repetitively, he goes away and leaves the person meek and calm like a little lamb.

Listen to something that happened to me: When I was in the world, I could take on thousands. I had a lion's heart. And the love of Christ exhausted me. If I wanted to relate everything I went through on a daily basis with this passion of anger, I would have to write a book. Since God wanted to free me from it, He would bring about everything appropriate: people would bother me unjustly, they would insult me, they would annoy me. And they would not just simply tempt me, but they would do things that would make you commit murder. But by enduring and choking Satan within me with extreme patience, I was delivered from the evil.

So the tempter stored up all his best wiles for a severe winter day, as he knows how to tempt and as God allows one to be tested. He made three or four attempts to tempt me, but he saw that his attacks were futile. Then suddenly a gush of wind burst through the door and blew off the roof with all the pilasters, along with thousands of kilos of stones on top of it—it flew through the air like an airplane—and tossed it across the crags into the snow. After that, we were left under the open sky in the snow.

But if you hear also the kinds of temptations I had, you wouldn't be able to bear it without being harmed, because you would judge the culprits. Anyway, by enduring your trials, you will receive so much grace instead, in proportion to your temptations, that you won't be able to measure it. So don't think that if you shy away from this one, no other temptation will come. One will necessarily come. And if you prove to be unmanly with it, that is how you will be with all temptations as well.

For the tempter is within us. Don't you see him, my child? Take a look! He ascends from the navel of the belly to the heart and heats it up. He burns it. He heats up the blood and ascends to the throat. He strikes the head. He darkens the nous. He stands in the larynx like a knot and obstructs the air and chokes a person.

The one who causes the temptation might well be the worst person, or rather the tempter pushes him, too, to disturb and upset you. However, the Lord allows him so that you become more experienced every day and reach dispassion. For when you prepare yourself and expect temptations, you are not confounded, you are not troubled; you do not lose control of yourself.

You write that if you knew that you would receive grace, you would endure thousands of temptations like that one. But how do you know that if you endured, you wouldn't receive grace? I am telling you and all the brethren that there is no shorter road than enduring one's temptations, no matter how they come. One's spiritual state and the grace he has are testified by his patience. How does the elder endure all of you? He has patience. This bears witness to the fact that he has grace. He is virtuous.

Virtue does not have a bell so that you can recognize it by its ring. The bell of virtue is forbearance, long-suffering, patience. These are the ornaments of a monk and of every Christian.

When a struggler foresees the reward from above and the grace that he is about to receive from the Lord, he endures everything. See how the elder assigned that strong brother to bear and endure that person who is suffering from the devil. To you who are weak he gave this little thorn. So show patience so that you may also become strong enough to put up with that possessed person. You should bear with him, serve him, and be patient with him. What a great virtue! Do you know what it's like to endure and put up with a lunatic?

Once a lunatic came to us, and I didn't have the heart to turn him away. Everywhere they had kicked him out. Well, I kept him so he could rest a little, so his heart could be warmed, because he is a human being too. And so what happened next? I made him keep an extremely strict fast, as the Lord said, "This kind can come forth by nothing, but by prayer and fasting."[1]

And so one day while we were all outside, he locked all the doors and windows of the cell and left us outside. He wouldn't open up even with many entreaties. What could we do? Finally, we found a screwdriver and took apart the hinges and opened the door, and then he went outside.

"Hey you!" I said. "Why did you lock the doors and leave us outside?"

"Because," he said, "there were potatoes and onions inside, and I wanted to be an ascetic by myself and eat onions and potatoes!"

He got well in a little while, but he left and got possessed again. He came three times, and as soon as he got well, he would leave and then go crazy again, and the demons would overcome him. He is hospitalized now.

As for you, be careful not to despise one of the least of these who are scorned and sick in this world. For this contempt and affront of yours doesn't stop at those unfortunate fellows, but ascends through them to the presence of the Creator and Fashioner, whose image they bear. You will be greatly astonished in that day, if you see the Holy Spirit of God resting in them more than in your heart.

As for me, I am constantly ill. I am like a paralytic. I can't take ten steps. Because of this and everything else, I am dead tired. Please, I ask that you pray for me, because I have many souls that seek my help. And believe me, my fathers and

---

[1] Mk. 9:29

brethren, for every single soul that is helped, I go through the warfare he has.

This is also why your elder is constantly ill. He is debilitated by the mental strain and the temptations which he suffers because of all of you. Therefore, my child, don't repeat what the devil is telling you: that the elder is supposedly indifferent to you and overlooks your toil and your needs. How is it possible for him to be indifferent, since he suffers for all of you?

Be careful! Cast away this thought and be patient, so that God sees your intention and lightens your hard work. Accept the temptation and don't blame the others. For when you don't endure temptations and blame the others—since the Lord gives them to us—then He Himself will lash us, which is much harsher and exceedingly more severe. For no man can punish as the Almighty can. Therefore, my child, "lay hold of instruction, lest at any time the Lord of all be angry."[2] Love His will, and accept what befalls you as your own due, lest He deliver you over to faintheartedness and blasphemy.

And whenever you err and fall, repent once more. Don't despair. Give yourself courage and hope. Say, "Forgive me, my Christ, once again I am repenting!" Don't say, "The wrath of God is upon me. Isn't it a shame? We're only human."

Don't be indignant with the brethren, but bear their faults, so that they bear yours. Love them so that they will love you, and endure them so that they will endure you. Become good, and all will become good along with you. Subdue your passions, and you will see many respecting not just your words, but even the wink of your eyes.

As for your diakonemas which you mentioned, if there are too many and you don't have time for them, and it vexes you,

---

2 cf. Ps. 2:12

I shall also ask the elder to reduce them so that you won't do them with grumbling.

And as for the other things you wrote, they show that you have a great deal of vainglory. Therefore, become a corpse that everyone walks over. Become like mud. Beat, hit, and hate yourself like a bitter enemy. Hate your evil side with perfect hatred, because if you don't knock him down, he will knock you down. Be brave, don't feel sorry for him! By the grace of God, I support you. But I shall also remind you of the saying of the Holy Fathers: "If you do not shed blood, you shall not receive Spirit."

Don't consider yourself to be a man, if you haven't received grace. If we don't acquire grace, in vain have we been born into the world.

The more purified and illumined our soul becomes here, the closer and clearer we shall enjoy Christ's fragrance there, and we shall rejoice and leap for joy more than the others.

So don't consider yourself to be a man, if you haven't received grace.

Take, eat,
this is
my body

Drink of
it, all of
you, this
is my
blood

Eighth Letter

Will you not endure everything for My love?

here is nothing else that can help appease anger and all the passions as much as love for God and for every fellow man. It is with love rather than with other struggles that you can win easily. In addition, when love reigns in your nous you feel no pain while struggling. For this reason, "love never faileth,"[1] as long as you constantly steer the soul's rudder towards it. And no matter what happens, you shout your maxim: "For the sake of Thy love, Jesus, my sweet love, I will endure curses, disgraces, injustices, toils, and all afflictions that I might encounter!" And at once, while you are pondering these words, the burden of pain is lightened, and the demons' bitterness ceases.

Let me tell you a true story. Once, because of my continual and frightful temptations, I was overcome with sadness and faintheartedness, and I presented my case to God as if I had been treated unjustly. I was complaining because He kept allowing so many temptations to befall me without curbing them even a little, that I couldn't even catch my breath. In this time of bitterness, I heard a very sweet and clear voice within me say with extreme compassion, "Will

---

[1] cf. 1 Cor. 13:8

you not endure everything for My love?" As soon as I heard that voice, I broke out into many tears and repented for being overcome with faintheartedness. I shall never forget that voice, which was so sweet that the temptation and all my faintheartedness immediately disappeared.

"Will you not endure everything for My love?"

"O truly sweet Love! For Thy love, we are crucified and endure everything!"

That same brother told me that once he was upset with another brother. He would give him advice, but the latter kept disobeying, and this saddened him greatly. Then while he was praying, he fell into *ecstasy*.* He saw the Lord nailed to the Cross all bathed in light. Then Christ turned towards him and said, "Behold how much I have suffered for your love! What have *you* endured?" And with these words his sadness vanished. He was filled with peace and joy, and shedding fountains of tears he marveled and continues to marvel at the condescension of the Lord, Who permits afflictions but also consoles us when He sees us losing heart.

So don't lose heart. Don't worry during times of affliction and temptation, but with the love of our Jesus, alleviate the anger and faintheartedness. Furthermore, give yourself courage, saying, "My soul, don't lose heart! A small affliction can cleanse you from a chronic illness." The truth is that it will soon go away anyway.

When we lack patience, our temptations seem greater than they really are. The more a person grows accustomed to enduring them, the smaller they become, and he passes through them effortlessly. Thus he becomes as solid as a rock.

So be patient! After many years have passed, what seems difficult to achieve now will fall into your hands for you to possess as your own, without your realizing how it happened.

Therefore, struggle now during your youth without asking "why" and losing heart. And when you grow old you will reap sheaves of dispassion. Then you will wonder how such beautiful crops grew, since you did not cultivate anything! You will be astonished how you got rich—you who are worth nothing! You will be amazed at how your grumbling, disobedience, and faintheartedness sprouted such beautiful fruits and fragrant flowers! Therefore, exert yourself.

If a righteous person falls even ten thousand times, he does not lose his courage, but he rises up once more and gathers his strength, and the Lord registers victories for him. However, He does not show him his victories, so that he will not think highly of himself. Rather, He makes him fully aware of his falls, so that he sees them, suffers, and is humbled. But once he has passed the barracks of the enemy and has amassed unseen victories everywhere, the Lord begins to show him little by little that he is winning and is being rewarded; that his hands are touching something that he was previously seeking but had not been given. And in this manner one is exercised, tried, and perfected, as much as our nature, nous, intellect, and soul's vessel can hold.

Therefore, be brave and strong in the Lord, and don't let your eagerness flag. Rather, keep seeking and crying out constantly, regardless of whether you receive anything or not.

Ninth Letter

**The Creator breathed into you and
gave you a living spirit.**

race is, to put it simply, a small
or great gift from God's infinite,
divine, rich abundance that He
kindly distributes out of His infinite
goodness. He accepts everything we
render to Him in thanks, namely:
wonder, love, worship, hymnody,
and doxology, which proceed from the full knowledge of
God. The benevolent Provider accepts all this from us, and
furthermore rewards us with more of His own—"Thine own
of Thine own."

He distributes out of His own wealth, and we who are poor,
blind, and lame are made rich by Him, while He always
maintains the same wealth: it does not decrease, nor does it
increase. Oh, what inconceivable grandeur! He enriches all!
Thousands upon thousands and myriads upon myriads were
enriched and became saints, while His wealth remains the same.

Therefore, my child, know first of all that every good starts
from God. There is no good thought that is not from God, nor
is there any bad thought that is not from the devil. So

whatever good thing you think, say, or do, all is a gift from God. "Every perfect gift is from above."[1] Everything is a gift from God; we have nothing of our own.

So everyone who desires grace and wants God to give it to him freely, must first properly understand his own existence, "know thyself." This is the real truth, for every object has an origin, and if you don't learn its beginning, it will not turn out to have a good ending for you.

Well, the beginning and the truth is for one to realize that he is nothing—zero—and that everything came into being out of nothing. "He spake, and they came to be; He commanded and they were created."[2] He spake and the earth came to be. And He took clay and formed man. Without a soul, without a nous; just a clay man. This is your own existence. That is what we all are—dirt and mud.

This is the first lesson for him who wants not only to receive grace, but also to have it always abide with him. From this he acquires full knowledge and from this, humility is born. Not just idle words and talking humbly, but with a solid foundation to confess the truth: "I am dirt; I am clay; I am mud." This is our first mother. Well, dirt is stepped on, and you, as dirt, ought to be stepped on. You are mud; you are worthless. You are tossed here and there; they build things with you. As a useless material you are transformed from one thing to another.

All the same, the Creator breathed into you and gave you a living spirit. And behold, at once you became a rational man. You speak, work, write, teach; you have become a machine of God. However, don't forget that your root is earth. And if He Who gave you your spirit takes it away, once again you will be used to build walls. Therefore, "Remember thine end and thou shalt not sin unto the ages."[3]

---

[1] Jam. 1:17

[2] Ps. 148:5

[3] Ecclesiasticus(Wisdom of Sirach) 7:36

This is the first cause that not only attracts grace, but also increases and retains it. Grace raises the nous to the first theoria of nature. Without this beginning, one finds some small amount of grace but loses it after a while because he is not building on solid ground, but is striving with methods and artifices.

For example, you say, "I am a sinner!" But deep down, you consider yourself to be righteous. You are unable to avoid delusion. Grace wants to remain, but since you haven't really found the truth yet, necessarily it has to leave. For without a doubt you will come to believe in your thoughts that say that you are something you are not. Consequently, grace does not stay.

For we have an adversary who is a mighty expert, an inventor of evil, and creator of every delusion. He is vigilant to trip us up. He became darkness from light and knows almost everything. He is the enemy of God and seeks to make all of us become His enemies as well. And finally, he is an evil spirit and easily intermingles with the spirit God bestowed upon us. Thus he takes our little motor and runs it however he wants. He observes where the soul's desire leans, and in what manner God helps it, and at once he contrives things similar to delude us.

There are battles that a person knows and avoids. But there are also others which he is unaware of, because the struggle is noetic and it is difficult to *discern** them. There are changes of the soul, movements of the mind, bodily illnesses and alterations. The Creator, Who fashioned the clay, made our composition out of four elements: dry, wet, hot, and cold. Consequently, it is necessary for a man to suffer constantly according to the change of each element. That is, to get dry, wet, hot, and cold. And if the properties of one element are in excess, the body will of necessity get sick, and therefore the soul will suffer too. The nous is unable to produce its noetic movements because it suffers along with the body.

Is the body dried up by the sun's heat? Then the nous is dried up as well. Is the body affected by humidity and limp when it rains? Then the nous is also limp. Is the body cold when the wind blows? Then bile greatly increases, the nous is darkened, and only fantasies prevail.

So in all these changes, even though grace is present, it is not active because we are too weak. But our enemy the devil knows how to fight us during each change. During dry spells he hardens you to become like a rock, to talk back, to disobey. When it is cold he knows how to cool your zeal, to make you cold and frozen before holy things. When it is hot he knows how to get you angry and agitated, and not let you discern what is true. For, as we have said, the blood is in excess, and with the warmth, it rouses desires and anger—the passionate part of the soul. And when it is humid he causes sleepiness, laxity, languor, and paralysis throughout the body. So in all of these cases the soul suffers along with the body, even though it is spiritual and bodiless.

Grace is similar. When it approaches a person, it does not change his nature, but it fills and overfills—as much as each person's vessel can hold—the same natural properties and good attributes with which his nature is endowed. Also it can reduce and remove natural weaknesses.

Just as man was first fashioned and then breathed into, thus praxis must precede theoria. Everything done by the body is called "praxis," whereas everything done by the mind is "theoria." It is impossible to reach theoria without praxis. So struggle now in everything that praxis requires, and the more spiritual things will come by themselves.

Behold, you have learned that you are clay, poor, and naked. Now, seek from Him Who is able to regenerate nature to make you rich. And whether He gives you a lot or a little, acknowledge your Benefactor. And do not boast of foreign things as your own. You will receive grace with pain and tears. And then with tears, thanksgiving, and fear of God you will keep it. With fervency and zeal is it attracted; with coldness and negligence is it lost.

Christ does not demand anything from you to give you His holy gifts other than to acknowledge that anything good you happen to have belongs to Him. Sympathize with him who does not have gifts. Don't judge him because he doesn't have any, saying that he is a sinner, depraved, evil, a babbler, a thief, a fornicator, a liar. If you acquire this knowledge, you will never be able to judge anyone, even if you see him committing a mortal sin, because you would say right away: "He doesn't have Your grace, my Christ, and that is why he sins. If You leave me, I shall do worse things. If I am standing, it is because You are supporting me. This brother does as much as he can. He is blind. How do You expect him to see without eyes? He is poor. How can You demand riches from him? Give him riches. Give him eyes to see."

If you seek justice in anything—when your neighbor treats you unjustly, dishonors you, reviles you, hits you, persecutes you, or even plots against your life—you are unjust if you consider him to be the cause or passionately criticize him. For you are seeking from him something that God has not given him. If you understand fully what I am telling you, everyone will seem unaccountable for whatever his faults may be, and only you will be accountable for everything.

There are three enemies that fight the human race: the demons, our own nature, and habit. Except for these, there is no other enemy. Take away the devil that tyrannizes all mankind, and all of us would be good. Behold who is to blame: it is him you should hate and condemn and consider to be your enemy until the end.

The other enemy we mentioned is one's nature. As soon as a person realizes what the world really is, his nature resists against the law of the spirit and desires everything that destroys the soul. Behold another enemy that should be hated all your life. This is what you should criticize and blame.

In addition, we have a third enemy: habit. Once we grow accustomed to doing all kinds of evil, it becomes a habit to us and takes the place of second nature with sin as a law. And this also requires a similar struggle for God to change our bad habits and deliver us from them. Behold then the third enemy which deserves complete hatred.

So, if you want your neighbor to be good in everything as you wish, take away from him these three enemies with the grace you possess. This is justice, if you want to find it: pray that God frees him from these enemies. And then you will both be in harmony.

Otherwise, if you seek to find justice any other way, you will always be unjust, and consequently, grace will keep coming and going until it finds rest in your soul. A person is entitled to have only the amount of grace that corresponds to how thankfully he endures temptations and how much of his neighbor's burden he bears without grumbling.

Now then, the previous letters I sent you deal with "praxis." This letter I wrote now contains illumination. A person receives illumination of knowledge from praxis, praxis itself, however, is blind, but illumination is the eyes through which the nous sees what it could not see at first.

So now it has a lamp and eyes, and it views things differently. First was the grace of praxis, but now the nous has received grace tenfold. Now the nous has turned into heaven. It sees far. It has much more capacity than before. Now only theoria is missing. As king, it has found the throne, and only the theater is missing, which we shall talk about another time. Recopy these letters with ink so that they aren't erased—since they are written in pencil—and study them to correct your conduct.

The Creation of Adam

Tenth Letter

Grace always precedes temptations as a warning to prepare.

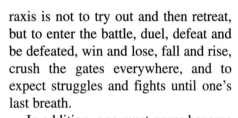

Praxis is not to try out and then retreat, but to enter the battle, duel, defeat and be defeated, win and lose, fall and rise, crush the gates everywhere, and to expect struggles and fights until one's last breath.

In addition, one must never become overconfident before his soul leaves the body. But even when he is ascending to heaven, he must expect to descend into Hades at any moment. I would even say that the descent can occur at that very moment. So one should not be surprised at changes, but should be aware that both conditions are his.

Know that grace always precedes temptations as a warning to prepare. As soon as you see grace, tighten your belt and say, "The declaration of war has come! Watch out, you man of clay, where the malicious one will wage the battle." Many times it comes quickly; other times after two or three days. But it shall definitely come, so your fortifications should be solid: confession every evening, obedience to the elder, humility and love towards all. In this way you alleviate the affliction.

Now, if grace comes before purification, I ask that you be careful and keep a clear mind.

Grace is divided into three stages: purifying, illuminating, and perfecting. Life is also divided into three stages: according to nature, above nature, and contrary to nature. Man ascends and descends within these three stages. There are also three great charismata that one receives: theoria, love, and dispassion.

During "praxis," purifying grace helps a person to purify himself. When anyone repents, it is grace that urged him to repent. And whatever he does, he does with God's grace, even though he may be unaware of it. Nevertheless, it is grace that nourishes and guides him. And according to the progress he is helped to make, he ascends, descends, or remains in the same state. If he has zeal and self-denial, he ascends to theoria, which is followed by enlightenment of divine knowledge and partial dispassion. But if his zeal and eagerness cool, then the action of grace will also withdraw.

Regarding one who prays cognitively, as you mention, this refers to one who is aware of what he is praying for and seeking from God. He who prays cognitively does not use vain repetitions or ask for superfluous things. On the contrary, he knows the place, the method, and the time, and seeks what is suitable and beneficial for his soul. He communicates noetically with Christ. He grasps Him and lays hold of Him, saying, "I will never let you go."

So he who prays asks for the remission of his sins and for the Lord's mercy. And if he asks for grand things before their time, the Lord does not give them to him, because He gives things in due order. But if he keeps burdening Him with his requests, He allows the spirit of delusion to imitate grace and deceive him by showing him nonsense. Therefore, it is not beneficial to ask inordinately. But even if his requests are heard before he is purified, if he did not ask at the right time, they turn into snakes and harm him. So you should have pure repentance and be obedient to all, and grace will come on its own without your asking.

Like a stammering infant, man seeks from God His holy will. And God, as an extremely good Father, gives him grace, but He also gives him temptations. If man endures the temptations without grumbling, he receives additional grace. The more grace he receives, the more temptations he will have.

When the demons approach to begin a battle, they do not attack in a place where you will defeat them effortlessly, but rather they test to see where your weakness is. The place where you least expect them is where they dig through the wall of the fortress. And when they find an ill soul and a weak spot, they always defeat him there and render him accountable.

Do you seek grace from God? Instead of grace, he allows a temptation. Are you unable to withstand the battle and do you fall? Then you are not given any additional grace. Do you seek it again? Again temptation. Again defeat? Again deprivation. This happens your whole life. Therefore, you must emerge victorious. Endure the temptation till death. Fall down like a casualty in battle; cry out like a paralytic on the ground, "I will never leave Thee, sweetest Jesus, nor forsake Thee![1] I will remain inseparable from Thee until the end of time, and I will die in the arena for Thy love." Then suddenly, He appears in the arena and calls out from the whirlwind, "I am here! Gird up thy loins like a man[2] and follow me!" And you reply full of light and joy, "Woe to me the wretch! Woe to me the evil and useless one! I have heard of Thee by the hearing of the ear, but now mine

---

[1] cf. Heb. 13:15

[2] cf. Job 38:1-3

eye seeth Thee. Wherefore I abhor myself and reckon myself dust and ashes."[3]

Then you are filled with divine love and your soul burns as did Cleopas's.[4] And in times of temptation you no longer leave the linen cloth and flee naked,[5] but persevere in afflictions with the thought that just as one temptation passed after another, so, too, will this one pass.

However, when you lose heart and grumble and do not endure the temptations, instead of winning you must continually repent for the faults of the day and the negligence of the night. And instead of receiving grace upon grace, you increase your afflictions.

Therefore, do not be intimidated and do not be afraid of temptations. Even if you fall many times, arise. Don't lose your composure. Don't be discouraged. They are clouds and will pass.

And when you have passed through all of this, which constitutes "praxis" (with the assistance of grace which cleanses you from all the passions), then your nous experiences illumination and is moved to theoria.

The first theoria is of creation: that God created everything for man, even the angels, for his service. How much worth, how much grandeur, what a great destiny man has, who is the very breath of God! That is, he was not created to live the few days of his exile here, but to live eternally with his Creator, to see the heavenly angels, and to hear their inexpressible melody. What joy! What grandeur! As soon as this life of ours reaches its end and these eyes close, immediately the other ones open and the new life begins—the true joy that does not end.

While thinking such things, the nous is plunged into deep peace and extreme tranquillity that spreads throughout the body, and one completely forgets that he exists in this life.

---

[3] Job 42:6

[4] Lk. 24:32

[5] cf. Mk. 14:52

These theorias come one after another. It is not a matter of fabricating fantasies in one's nous, but the state is due to the action of grace which brings thoughts, and then the nous occupies itself with theoria. Man does not fabricate them, but rather they come by themselves and seize the nous into theoria. And then the nous expands and a person is beside himself. He is illumined. Everything is open to him. He is filled with wisdom, and like a son he possesses his Father's belongings. He knows that he is nothing—made of clay—but also a son of the King. He owns nothing, but possesses everything. He is filled with theology. He cries out insatiably, confessing with full awareness that his existence is nothing. His origin is clay, but his vital force is the breath of God— his soul. Immediately his soul flies to heaven!—"I am the inbreathing, the breath of God! Everything has dissolved and remained on earth, out of which it was taken.[6] I am a son of the eternal King! I am a god by grace! I am immortal and eternal! In a moment I am beside my heavenly Father!"

Truly, this is the destiny of man. For this reason he was created and must return whence he came. These are the kinds of theorias that occupy a spiritual person. He awaits the hour when he will leave his earth behind and when his soul will fly to heaven.

So take courage, my child, and with this hope endure every pain and affliction, since in a little while we shall be made worthy of these things. It is the same for all of us. We are all children of God, and day and night we call upon Him along with our sweet, dearest Mother, the Lady of all, who never abandons anyone who entreats her.

---

[6] cf. Gen. 3:19

Eleventh Letter

I found many of the Fathers in "praxis" and "theoria."

 hen the love of our Lord sets a person's soul on fire, he is no longer held down by measures, but transcends limits. That is why it "casteth out fear,"[1] and whatever he writes or says, he tends towards immeasurableness. But at this moment of grace, in the presence of the flaming brilliance of divine love, anything he tries to say is insignificant. Afterwards, once grace recedes and the cloud withdraws, then a pair of compasses comes in and looks for a measure to explain it.

Well, everything I wrote to you was written for one purpose: to warm up the fervor of your soul, to incite it to desire ardently our sweetest Jesus, just as officers in the army tell their troops about the feats of the brave and thus make them fight valiantly.

Likewise, the lives of the saints and the writings they left us have the same purpose. Likewise, if the soul—since God made it like this—does not hear about these lofty and wondrous things often, it is overcome with drowsiness and negligence. And only with such things, with readings and sto-

---

[1] 1 Jn. 4:18

ries of spiritual worth, can one banish forgetfulness and restore the old edifice.

As for me, when I came to the Holy Mountain, I found many of the Fathers in "praxis" and "theoria," ancient holy men.

One of them was Elder Kallinikos, a first-rate ascetic, a recluse for forty years. He practiced the noetic work and thrived on the sweetness of divine love, and became beneficial to others as well. He experienced ecstasy of the nous.

Further down from him was another holy man, Elder Gerasimos, a total hesychast, an amazing ascetic, ninety years old. He practiced noetic prayer. He was from Chios, and spent seventeen years at the peak of Mt. Prophet Elias. Even though he wrestled with demons and was badly battered by the weather, he remained an unshakable pillar of endurance. He had continuous tears. He led his carefree life sweetened by the contemplation of Jesus.

Higher up was Elder Ignatios. He was blind for many years, a spiritual father for years, an elder ninety-five years old, praying noetically without ceasing. The prayer made his mouth give off such a fragrance that you would rejoice talking with him near his mouth.

There was also another even more admirable elder at the cave of St. Peter the *Athonite*,* Father Daniel, an imitator of St. Arsenios the Great. A profoundly silent recluse. He served Liturgy daily until the end of his life. For sixty years he never even thought of omitting the Divine Liturgy. Even during Great Lent, he served Presanctified Liturgies every day. He died in deep old age without ever getting sick. His Liturgy always lasted three and a half or four hours, because he couldn't say the petitions due to his compunction. He always soaked the ground in front of him with his tears. That is why he didn't want any strangers to be present at his Liturgy, so that they wouldn't see his work. But as for me, since I begged him very fervently, he accepted me. And every time I went—after walking three hours at night to attend that truly fearsome and divine spectacle—he told me one or two sayings as he left the altar and immediately hid himself until the next day. He had noetic prayer and all-night vigils throughout his life. It was from him that I also received my schedule and found great benefit. He ate only one hundred grams of bread every day. He was all rapt in his Liturgy; he never finished a Liturgy without the ground turning into mud from his tears.

There were also many others with theoria, whom I was not counted worthy to see, because they had died one or two years beforehand. I asked people to tell me about their wondrous feats, because this is what I occupied myself with. Step by step I wandered the mountains and caves to find people like this, because my elder was good but simple. After I prepared his food, he would give me a *"blessing"** to search for such people who would benefit my soul. After I buried him, I explored all of *Athos.**

There was one in a cave who had to cry seven times a day. This was his work; he would pass the entire night in tears, and his headrest was always thoroughly soaked. His helper went there only two or three times a day. His elder did not want to have him near him, so that he would not interrupt his *mourning.** Once, he asked his elder:

"Geronda, why do you cry so much?"

"My child, when man beholds God, he sheds tears out of love and cannot contain himself."

There were also others of lesser significance such as Father Cosmas and the rest. There were also others of greater significance; if someone would write about them, he would need a lot of paper. All of them have left this life here and live unto the ages there.

But today, you don't hear about such things. For people are so pre-occupied with cares and material worries and have such complete disdain for noetic work, that most of them not only do not want to inquire, to investigate, to do these things, but they immediately rise up adversely against a person if they hear him even talking about it. And they consider him absurd and foolish, because his life is different and he seems ridiculous to them.

It is similar to what happened in the days of idolatry. Back then, if you reviled the idols, they would stone you or put you to a miserable death. Now in our times, every passion has taken the place of an idol. And if you reprove or criticize the passion that you see overcoming each person, they all shout, "Stone him, because he reviled our gods!"

Finally, since without any exception I do not socialize— nor do I want to hear how people in the world and monks are living or what they are doing—I am continually the target of condemnation. Yet I don't cease praying for the fathers day and night and saying that they are right. Only I am at fault because I scandalize them, since they see with whatever eyes God gave them. Wouldn't it be unjust and unfair for me to say, "Why don't they see as I can see?"

May the God of all have mercy on everyone through the prayers of the holy God-bearing Fathers.

ᘓwelfth ᘔetter

Thus the nous becomes all light, all clarity.

My child, since your elder has experience with prayer, there is no danger of being deluded. Do as your elder tells you, and don't feel sad if grace comes and goes. For this is how it trains a person to think humbly and not become arrogant. In the beginning, this is how an infant acts. "Woe to thee, O city, when thy king is a child,"[1] say the Holy Scriptures. "Woe to thee, O soul, when thy nous is a beginner in these things!"

The nous, my child, cannot remain motionless, especially the nous of one who is spiritually weak. One moment he needs reading, another moment chanting, later silence. When a person is silent, the nous finds the opportunity to meditate on various themes from the Scriptures which he had read previously. So when you give the nous whatever it likes that is good, it gains strength, just as the body does when it receives healthy food. But when you give it just anything, then it is darkened instead of being enlightened. Likewise, when it is tired it needs rest.

In this manner, it learns to discern the good from the bad. Thus the nous becomes all light, all clarity. It sees the soul's

---

[1] Eccl. 10:16

purity. It sees the thorns. It endures temptations. Grace increases. The body is cleansed of passions. The soul becomes peaceful. And finally, everything comes in succession as if chained together, quickly and without much toil. This is all the result of perfect obedience. Furthermore, you should know that he who has perfect obedience is totally free from cares.

Now then, the nous is the steward of the soul that carries its food—that is, whatever you give it. So when it is at peace and you give it the good things it wants, it lowers them into the heart. First of all, the nous is cleansed from whatever *predispositions** it was obsessed with in the world. It is disentangled from the cares of life, and by constantly saying the prayer, it completely stops wandering. And then you realize that it has been purified, because it no longer inclines towards the evil and filthy things which it had seen or heard in the world. Afterwards, through the prayer that is going in and out of the heart, the nous clears a path and expels all indecency, evil, and filth from the heart. For the nous declares war against the passions and against the demons, who arouse the passions and who have been lurking in the heart for so many years without anybody seeing or knowing about them. But now that the nous has acquired purity—its original garment—it sees them and, like a watch-dog, barks, howls, and fights with them as lord and guard of the entire intellectual part of the soul. It wields the name JESUS like a weapon and flogs the enemies, who also are barking like wild dogs, until it throws them all out to the periphery of the heart. Then the nous begins to clean up all the filth and dirt with which the demons had defiled us every time we assented to do anything evil and sinful. It proceeds to fight with the demons in order to drive them out and remove them entirely, so that they do not disturb it at all. And it constantly struggles to throw out the filth which they constantly throw in. Then, as a good steward, it carries provisions suitable for the enlightenment and health of soul.

In all of this, purifying grace assists. The one praying is covered under the protection of obedience as if he were in the shade. He is guarded by the grace of him who has assumed the responsibility of his soul before God. And slowly the change of the Most High occurs.[2] In short, once the demons have been completely banished and the inner heart has been purified, the defilement ceases. The nous is enthroned upon the heart as a king and rejoices like a groom with his bride in the bridal chamber. He celebrates with a holy, peaceful, pure joy. He says the prayer effortlessly. And then grace acts freely and shows his nous the promises that he expects to receive as a reward, if he carries out his obligations without fail. Once grace has come upon him, he is henceforth calm and peaceful, and it raises him to theoria in proportion to the foundation's capacity.

So it is primarily the fear of God, faith, perfect obedience, and self-denial that bring all these good things. Then a person attains blessed love and finally dispassion, so that evil is no longer active in his nous; rather, he cries out from the depths of his heart, "My soul thirsted for Thee, my God! When shall I come and appear before Thy holy countenance?"[3] And he awaits death as the greatest joy; he awaits the time when these eyes will close and the other ones will open, whereby he will see everything with joy forever.

Therefore exert yourself, my child, exert yourselves in blessed obedience where all these good things lie, and live as one soul in different bodies. Then the elder is relieved and has time to pray for you with all his soul and is full of joy and delight. Whereas when you are disobedient and deprive

---

[2] cf. Ps. 76:10
[3] cf. Ps. 41:2

yourselves of all these blessings, his soul is continually burdened and weakened from the grief, and slowly he proceeds towards death.

I have tried out all these things through experience, and I have eaten their fruit, and it is very sweet. Personally, I have never seen anything more comforting in my soul than perfect obedience. I buried my good little elder, and I found hesychia through his prayers.[†]

So then, labor now while you are young so that you reap the fruit of dispassion in old age. And not in ripe old age, but in twenty years you will see what I am telling you, if you exert yourselves. But if you don't exert yourselves, even if you live as long as Methouselah,[4] you will never enjoy these gifts.

So exert yourselves and emulate the elder and each other in what is good. And you will see the passions completely immobilized and will enjoy such peace of soul as if you were in paradise.

[†] A disciple who has been completely obedient to his elder partakes in his elder's grace both before and especially after his elder's death.

[4] vid. Gen. 5:27

Thirteenth Letter

The grace of God doesn't depend on one's years.

 I received your letter, my child, and I shall answer all your questions.

Well, you asked who receives grace more quickly: a hesychast or a disciple. Without a doubt, an obedient disciple not only receives grace quickly, but also is always safe. There is no danger of falling or getting lost; only, he must not fall into negligence; that is enough. Once Christ enters a man, he has hesychia both when he is alone and when he is with many people, and has peace everywhere.

The grace of God doesn't depend on one's years, but on the way he struggles and on the mercy of the Lord. Experience through praxis is obtained with the years; but grace—and that is why it is called grace, in other words, a gift—depends on God and is given in proportion to the fervency of faith, humility, and good intentions.

Solomon received grace when he was twelve. Daniel was also the same age. David was a youth tending his father's sheep. And it was the same for all the ancient and recent saints.

When a person truly repents, grace approaches at once, and it increases with zeal. But experience is obtained only with many years of ascesis.

He who seeks grace from the Lord must, above all, endure temptations and afflictions no matter how they come. Otherwise, if he becomes indignant and doesn't show enough patience during a temptation, neither will grace manifest itself, nor will his virtue be perfected or will he be counted worthy of any spiritual gift.

Whoever has learned that afflictions, and in general everything that temptations cause us, are gifts from the Lord, has truly found the way of the Lord. Such a person eagerly waits for them to come, because he is purified through them, and by enduring them he is illuminated and beholds God.

God is not seen in other way except through spiritual knowledge. This knowledge is theoria. That is, when you understand that God is near you and that you move about within God and that He sees whatever you do, and you are careful not to sadden Him—since He sees everything inside and out—then you don't sin because you see Him, you love Him, and you are careful not to sadden Him, "for He is at your right hand."[1]

Therefore, everyone who sins does not see God, but is blind.

---

[1] cf. Ps. 24:18

ℑourteenth ℒetter

Truly great is the mystery of obedience.

 ejoice in the Lord, child of the heavenly Father.

You write, my child, about a thought against the elder. You should greatly fear this thought of yours. Avoid it as if it were a poisonous snake, for it has a frightful influence upon our generation. This is a ruse of the evil one. He brings you thoughts against your elder in order to alienate you from the grace that protects you and to make you accountable. Then he will ravage you mercilessly. Therefore, keep my advice and never let any thought against your spiritual father lurk in your heart. Get rid of it immediately as if it were a poisonous snake.

Furthermore, regarding the book you sought: even if you were about to be saved through it, don't get it without a blessing. For without a blessing, it is considered adultery before God. You should keep so much exactness in small and large matters that without the blessing of your spiritual father, you should neither pray, nor give alms, nor do any other good deed.

Take Saul, for example, whom God chose amongst all the tribes of Israel and anointed king. But since he did not have perfect obedience to Samuel and kept the good animals for the sacrifice, God destroyed him; even as the prophet said, "Obedience is better than a pure sacrifice."[1]

Truly great is the mystery of obedience. Since our sweet Jesus first marked out this path and became a model for us, aren't we obliged to follow Him?

My child, I wish I were also amongst you practicing my truly beloved obedience! For I wholeheartedly confess with all my strength, with complete awareness, that there is no other path of salvation like this one, remote from every delusion and action of the enemy. And if someone truly desires to be saved and find our sweet Jesus soon, he should have obedience. Furthermore, he should look upon his elder as an image of Christ.

So my child, hold on firmly to the whole armor[2] that you received, and fight strongly; aim your arrows well at your enemies with one goal in mind: never to disobey your spiritual father. For if you sadden God, you have as an intercessor your elder who entreats Him on your behalf. But if you sadden your elder as well, who will propitiate the Lord for you?

Struggle in accordance with your strength to lighten your elder's burden, so that you may have relief and patience in your afflictions. For I know through personal experience how much responsibility and how great a burden the elder assumes, and how much he suffers until he makes an unworthy soul worthy and leads it into paradise, especially if it happens to have a tough character.

A very heavy chain is placed around the elder's neck for every soul for which he assumes the responsibility. To lighten his burden, it takes many holy prayers; it takes much unadulterated love—not disobedience and back-talk; it takes

---

[1] cf. 1 Kings 15:22
[2] cf. Eph. 6:11

devotion and grace overflowing from his disciples' lips—not gall and bitterness, bickering and quarrels. Every harsh word you say to him in times of temptation—since it proceeds from the serpent, the devil—waters his soul with poison, and his soul withers like a flower struck by hail. Then he is no longer able to pray for himself until the pain goes away.

Conversely, when the disciples are obedient in everything, then the elder is uplifted: he prays fervently, he is enlightened abundantly, he speaks wisely, he advises in good order, he receives additional grace, and he becomes an ever-flowing spring distributing to everyone the divine grace that he has received from the Lord.

Therefore, my child, if you wish to progress quickly and without much labor, learn to abandon every personal opinion so that it does not become your will. Let your ear be by the mouth of your elder, and accept whatever he tells you as if it were from the mouth of God. Execute his commands without hesitation, and you will always be at peace. In addition, you must always remember that your obedience or disobedience does not stop at the elder, but ascends to God through him.

Never conceal a thought from your elder and never alter your words while confessing before the Lord. Reveal your thoughts forthrightly and at once your heart will be at rest.

Break your neck under the yoke of obedience, and cleave to the breath of your elder. As soon as a word comes out of his mouth, grab it. Grow wings and take off to carry it out, without examining whether it is right or wrong. Blindly and indiscriminatingly do whatever he who is responsible for you orders, so that you will be unaccountable for your actions. Whoever gives orders will be accountable for whether or not he gave good orders. You will be accountable for whether or not you had good obedience.

Obedience is not to carry out this or that order that you were given, while you object on the inside. Obedience is to subordinate your soul's convictions so that you may be freed from your evil self. Obedience is to become a slave in order to become free. Purchase your freedom for a small price. Become unaccountable and joyful. And don't listen to that thought of yours which advises you to abandon your monastery in difficult times.

Know full well that he who is not obedient to one, will be obedient to many [i.e., many passions], and in the end remains insubordinate.

Saint Gregory  of Sinai

Fifteenth Letter

"So, you won't listen to me and go back?"

 od said to Adam, "Who told thee that thou wast naked? Hast thou eaten of the tree, whereof I commanded thee that thou shouldest not eat?"[1]

And I say to you, "Who put into your head all those things you wrote? Have you opened a door to the enemy who has entered with his entire encampment and humbled your soul?"

My child, you should have thought of all these things before you wore the holy garment. Now that you wear the angelic *schema** and Christ has put a seal on all your promises to Him, these thoughts no longer have any place within you. For once the Mystery was performed, relatives and parents and everything became nonexistent.

Now pay close attention to my words.

If afterwards a monk becomes languid and lazy and leaves his elder or synodia without due cause, woe to him, because he will fall into great tribulations and will not escape retribution. He will be paying all his life, and in the end he will still be in debt. He will be considered to be one who broke his vows and a transgressor of the commandment. For the Lord said, "He

---

[1] Gen. 3:11

that loveth father or mother more than me is not worthy of me."[3] And furthermore He said, "No man, having put his hand to the plow, and looking back, is fit for the kingdom."[4] And likewise, "Better is it that thou shouldest not vow than that thou shouldest vow and not pay."[5]

So, when Christ explicitly declares these things—He Who is your Teacher, God, and Father, Who holds in His hands your breath and your life—what place do those things have that you are saying now?—that supposedly you will not have any peace, that your conscience will prick you continually because of the responsibilities you left behind, and other such things. Let God, Who laid down the terms and set the boundaries, think about these things. Let Him be accountable to Himself if He did not say things right. But as for you and me and all who have worn this holy schema, we should at all costs keep the promises we made Him, so that we may become heirs of the blessings He has promised us.

And don't think that your parents will benefit now if you go back. Their souls will be greatly harmed, and those who are at home will head for perdition, since they resist the divine will. But neither shall I ever participate in this sin, nor do I agree with your solution. But even if the elder gets tired in the end and lets you go, he will pay very dearly for this concession.

So completely erase from your memory this evil recollection, in order to stop the warfare of thoughts and to pacify your heart. Otherwise, if you are defeated and go back, not only will I write you no more letters, but I shall also entirely erase you from my heart. I am unable to do more than this, since I see that although you realize that this is a temptation from the devil, you persist in listening to him. So what more can I write?

---

[3] Mt. 10:37

[4] Lk. 9:62

[5] Eccl. 5:5

But listen to me, now that there is still time. For when a person knowingly gives in to a temptation, later there will come a time when he is no longer able to listen to what is healthy and salutary, because the hearing of his soul will already be ruined. After that, he becomes contemptuous and walks towards perdition.

Don't you see that when the Lord was speaking to all, at the end he concluded, "He that hath ears to hear, let him hear"[6]? Therefore, leave aside these thoughts of yours and establish your mind "with a governing spirit."[7] You have no obligation for anything you left behind when you left the world and your family. He Who created the heaven and earth has providence and solicitude for everything and takes care of everyone.

Now listen to something amazing that happened here on the Holy Mountain, since you might not have heard it yet.

There was a monk here at Katounakia in our days, whom I didn't meet because he had died a little before I arrived. He was the disciple of a blind elder. One day, a poor layman passed by his cell. And the young monk asked him:

"Where are you from?"

It turned out that they were from the same village. The monk didn't tell him who he was, he only asked how Mr. X was doing, who was his father. The stranger said that he had died and left his wife and three daughters in the streets as poor orphans. He said that they also had a son who had left years ago, but they don't know what happened to him.

So the monk was immediately wounded as if he had been struck by lightning, and at once he was attacked by a barrage of thoughts.

"I will leave," he said to his elder, "I will leave and go protect them!"

---

[6] Mt. 11:15

[7] Ps. 50:12

He asked for a blessing. His elder didn't give it. He kept insisting. His elder gave him advice, weeping for himself and for his disciple. But it was impossible to convince him. Finally, he let him do his will, and the disciple left.

Once he left the Holy Mountain, he sat down to rest in a tree's shade. Coincidentally, another travelling monk arrived there, too, and also sat down to rest under the same tree. Then the one who showed up started saying:

"I see that you are troubled, my brother. Won't you tell me what's wrong?"

"Don't ask," he said. "I suffered a great misfortune . . ." and he related his whole story in detail. Then his good wayfarer said to him:

"If you would, dear brother, listen: Go back to your elder and God will protect your home. Serve your elder, especially since he is blind."

But he wouldn't listen. He was overcome with thoughts and the words of the other monk seemed like nonsense to him. Even though he was given many examples, as now I am giving you, the disobedient monk got up to continue his trip to the world. Then the other monk who showed up finally asked him:

"So, you won't listen to me and go back?"

"No!" he answered stubbornly.

"Well then!" said the monk who showed up, "I am an angel of the Lord, and as soon as your father died, God commanded me to be by their side to protect them and be their guardian. Well, now that you're going there instead of me, I will abandon them, since you're not listening to me." And he disappeared right in front of him. At that point, the monk came to his senses and returned immediately to his elder. And he found him on his knees praying for him.

Do you understand, my child? That is what happens when

we leave everything to God, since He arranges everything very well as a good Ruler, and there is no error in His good will. Therefore, he who seeks salvation must have patience. But if we demand that God does things the way we like, and according to our discernment, then woe to our wretched condition.

The devil is unable to enter wherever there is the blessing of obedience and the bond of love. So he struggles in every way to make a monk defect and thus isolate him, and afterwards to make him a plaything of his evil wiles. However, if he is prudent, he will listen to his superiors who know the way, and then the devil who sets traps falls, and the evil returns upon his own head.

So have obedience now to those older than you, and in good time you will also become experienced to benefit those who are younger. There will come a time when you will acquire what you don't have now and seems difficult for you to accomplish, and you will wonder how you acquired it, since you had already stopped asking for it. These things will happen, as long as you persevere and keep seeking the purification of your soul, and that is enough. Anger will cease, peace will come, you will find dispassion commensurate to your work, and you will find the prayer. Just seek and exert yourself as much as you can. Everything is not achieved all at once; as with the body, you did not become a man from an infant all at once.

Now all these falls are lessons for you to learn humility. So you shouldn't be distressed, but you should be careful; and brace yourself for the battles which are coming one after another. The lesson of each battle should be a preparation for the next. The preparation is to say, "Whatever happens to me, whatever under the sky the demons are able to do, I will not put forward my own will, I will not express my opinion, and I will not argue. Let the command be wrong, let it be anything, like a cross; I will do it without discrimination. And let God see my heart and alleviate my warfare."

Man should stand like a sentry and wait to see from where the enemy will strike. Then at once he should turn his weapons in that direction. All his life, he should not expect a respite, even though many times the Lord gives one. However, he must never become cocky, but must be constantly vigilant like a soldier during a battle, because a single moment can be worth so much more and can bring so much more benefit to the soul, than an entire year can. The same holds true, however, for spiritual damage, if one is not cautious.

Sixteenth Letter

When you are ascending Golgotha,
it is impossible not to fall.

acred love of my soul, my beloved son in the Lord: I just received your letter today. And behold, once again I cry and mourn, once again I shall lay down my life for you.[1]

So arise. I give you my trembling hand. Do not be frightened. Once again I shall carry you. Weep on my shoulder. I am beside you and weep with you. I sigh, I suffer, my soul grieves, and my heart throbs until I bring you up to Mount Tabor. When you are ascending Golgotha, it is impossible not to fall. The cross is heavy; many times you will fall to your knees. But why do you listen to the tempter? In the end, he will be defeated.

Nevertheless, it is your elder who is right. Twice he called you, and both times you were disobedient! To whom were you obedient at that moment? What were you thinking then?

Anyway, no matter what happened, we shall not despair. We shall beg the elder to forgive us, and we shall do our penance. I shall also repent together with you. Do twenty-five more metanoias daily, and be careful from now on. Make a good start

---

[1] cf. Jn. 10:17

and guard yourself from disobedience. For if a person has been defeated once by a passion, he must be very careful thereafter and fight against the temptation so that he does not fall again.

Therefore, be valiant. Wherever the evil one turns his arrows, we shall turn them back on him. Let him understand that you are not alone, that you have a guardian who watches over you and dismantles the traps that the evil one sets at your feet. Not just for forty days, but for a hundred and forty days shall I gladly fast for you, keep vigil, and toil with you. You, on the other hand, must rise and stand bravely. Receive valor from the Lord, and do not fear the worthless devil that has been unnerved by Christ and no longer has the vigor and strength he once had. He only stirs up fantasies and fears; he only says impudent and foul words. Receive grace from above to step on him, and let there be strength in your limbs. Say to him, "Stop fighting me, O enemy, for my spiritual father is watching out for me and bears my deficiencies. He suffers hardships and fasts for me. Even if I fall seventy times seven,[2] you will still be defeated."

Give courage to yourself by saying such things, and immediately repent for everything that you do wrong as a human. All those fantasies and fears are from the evil one to make you despair and lose heart, to strip you of everything through sorrow. But don't listen to him.

As for the letters that are delayed and lost, it is the devil that is hindering them. He makes others open them. He is responsible for all evil. No one else is to blame except him. Therefore, it is him we must fight all our life; not the brethren, but him who impels them to think or do any evil thing, visible or hidden.

Now then, since I have told you that I am beside you, when you get angry and are ready to lose your temper, say

---

[2] cf. Mt. 18:22

to yourself, "For the love of the elder, who will weep when he finds out, I had better not get angry and disobey. Who has ever benefited from disobedience? So then how shall I be benefited now?"

Regarding the book of Abba Dorotheos that you sought, it is easy for us to find it, but they do not allow books to leave the Holy Mountain if they are old copies. Abba Dorotheos is very compunctious, very graceful, and of great spiritual benefit. I shall ask if they will let me buy and send the *Evergetinos* or the *Philokalia* to you.

As for the brother you wrote about who is suffering, we shall say prayers on his behalf. He must be committing some hidden sin now or in the past, and for this reason God allows him to suffer in this way. Many times a person commits a sin without realizing that he is sinning by doing it. He walks like a blind man in the darkness, without the courage to see himself in the light and to say, "I have sinned, my God!"

The more time passes, the closer the devil comes to his end, so he fights and struggles with extreme rage to condemn us all to hell. Especially now during Great Lent, which is coming, the thoroughly malicious demons incite many temptations and disturbances against us. Since we oppress them more severely with fasting and prayer during this time, they also become more fierce against us. So see to it that you win crowns in this arena of struggling. You must become braver and array yourself face to face against those bodiless enemies. Don't be afraid of them.

You don't see how many of them fall and turn their backs with every prayer you say. You only see how much you are wounded. But they are also thrashed; they also suffer. Every time we are patient, they flee with leaps and bounds, and every time we say the prayer, they are seriously injured. So at the time of battle, when you are firing shots and bullets, don't expect them to throw marshmallows and chocolates.

Do you remember what you used to write back in the beginning? You were saying that you put on the holy schema as a suit of armor to fight the principalities and powers of darkness.[3] Struggle, therefore, so that your actions correspond with your words.

---

[3] cf. Eph. 6:12

Seventeenth Letter

During temptations, do not desert your bastion.

My delightful child with the entire brotherhood in Christ. . . Rejoice with the holy joy of our Lord Jesus Christ. Today is the feast day of St. Haralambos. Yesterday we were informed that the mail came, and a brother who had fasted for three days went to receive the postal order and the registered letter. Please, don't send registered mail, because it is a great inconvenience for us to go to Daphni from here. And the way things are now, it is very costly for us every time.

As for the opening of my letters, this is what is going on: it seems that some people think that I write about their faults to the elder, who is the spiritual father, and that is why they open them to see what I write. But I am not at all worried about this, nor should any of you worry. Let each of you take care of his own soul, because each of us will give an account not only for his lawful and unlawful deeds, but even for an idle word and for ill-conceived thoughts.

Do a metanoia to your elder for me, and thank him for the favor he did us by relieving you from the penance. And from now on be careful, my little child, because sins cause affliction and it is hard work to fulfill a penance. It is extremely contemptuous not to respond or go to the elder when he speaks to you. This is unjustifiable for someone who will face his father again the next day. Only someone who has decided to leave his father and never see him again could do that. Otherwise, if he stays, how will he face his spiritual father again? How will he speak to him and ask for his blessing?

Be careful, my child, because this is callous egotism and a haughty attitude. In the event that, as a human being, you are tired or ill or your diakonema encumbers you, say so to your elder with humility. Candidly explain it with a straightforward conscience, and he knows how to be condescending. He knows how to lighten your burden from time to time, so that your work is not cut short due to illness, and you are thus harmed instead of benefited.

But learn to obey forthrightly without negotiating. And don't burden your elder with deals and concessions, because in the end, either here or there, you will pay the price for all of these concessions. Don't burden your soul's account for trivial things.

And now that you were defeated and fell once, be vigilant from now on with this passion, for the tempter always stands beside us. And in whatever battle a person has been defeated once—even if a hundred years pass—as soon as he encounters that same temptation that had defeated him, he is overpowered once again. Therefore, I am saying to you as well as to all the brethren that in every battle with the enemy, you must emerge victorious. Either die in the struggle, or win with God. There is no other road.

During temptations, do not leave your place; do not desert; do not reveal the other person's error, but in silence let the temptation and the agitation pass. And once the temptation passes and there is perfect peace—whether you are an elder or a disciple—then you should dispassionately show him the harm and the benefit of it. And thus virtue is built up.

All temptations and afflictions require patience to be overcome, and this constitutes their defeat. Note the names of all those who have endured until death during temptations, whose saliva becomes blood in their mouth so that they would not speak. You should have great reverence for them and honor them as martyrs and confessors. These are the people I love and regard with affection, and for them I should shed my last drop of blood in Christ's love every day, because you see that such a person prefers to endure thousands of deaths rather than to let a harsh word slip out of his mouth. And when people oppress him, when thoughts of justice oppress him, when internal thoughts also oppress him, he fights back but becomes weak and collapses as if he were dead. Yet he still fights noetically with the temptation and takes all the burdens upon himself, aching and sighing as if he were at fault. So nothing greater do I love and desire than to hear that you are being patient in your temptations.

For God, as a self-glorified Being, does not need man's work. Nevertheless, he rejoices and loves us when we are tormented and suffer for His love. That is why he crowns us as athletes, and abundantly bestows His grace upon us.

I wanted to write three homilies or even three books. The first one would contain only this: "Man is nothing," and I would shout out constantly that I am nothing. In the other I would write that the self-glorified God is everything in all and for all. And the third: "Have patience in everything until death." Whether you are young, whether you have grown old, or whether you have struggled for years, if you don't have patience until your soul departs, your works are considered to be a rag before God.

Therefore, "know thyself"—know that you are nothing. This is your existence: nothing. Your origin is clay and your vital force is the breath of God, so everything is God's. Know that you are nothing and have patience in temptations, so that you may be delivered from them and become a god by grace; for you are the breath, the inbreathing of God.

So cry out often to your Father Whom you always have beside you and Who is never absent. He is even closer to you than your own soul. He is in your breath, in your nous, in your words. Everything is contained by God. In Him we live, we are carried in His arms; we are wretched and senseless. Your Father is present and He continuously sees you. Why don't you see Him? Why do you sin? Why do you disobey? Why do you sadden the Giver of life? Whereas He, on the other hand, sees you, is grieved, and overlooks your mistakes because you are blind. Entreat Him and endure your temptations, and your eyes will open to see Him, and then together with Job you will cry out, "I have heard of Thee by the hearing of the ear: but now mine eye seeth Thee. Wherefore I abhor myself, and reckon myself dust and ashes!"[1]

---

[1] Job 42:5-6

Eighteenth Letter

Once again I rose and waged war against all the spirits.

hat incident, my child, shows that you have a great deal of vainglory. You have a high opinion of yourself, and this is why you do not have a condescending, humble spirit. You think that you will no longer err or disobey or undergo any change, but will live hereafter without any changes; something not humanly possible.

You have already been told that you suffer from much ignorance, which gives birth to arrogance. So be careful, my child, and flee from ignorance, the mother of all evil. Ignorance of what is good is darkness of soul. And if a person does not ally with Christ, Who is the Light, he cannot free himself from the prince of darkness, the devil.

Behold, the Lord is my witness, Who destroys the liars along with their lies: I have been furiously and bloodily wrestling with the demons for more than twenty-five years in this world. I have descended to the bottom of the sea, devoid of any complacency and self-will, in order to find the pearl of great price.[1] I conquered Satan himself along with all his army, skill, and cunning. Having shackled him through

---

[1] cf. Mt. 13:46

humility, I asked him, "Why do you have so much rage towards us and fight us with so much fury?" And he answered, "So that I may have many companions in Hades and brag to the Nazarene, 'I am not the only transgressor— see how many others are with me?'!'"

Then once again I ascended to the heavens through grace and spiritual theoria and saw the ineffable beauty of paradise, which God has prepared for them that love Him.[2] And after all this, grace was lifted away a little, and my feet were well nigh shaken.[3] Then I fell into a little negligence, and sleep took me captive and deprived me of many blessings. Shortly thereafter, I rose once again and waged war and a bloody battle. But after I won, I fell into drowsiness. And once more negligence, the mother of every evil, began to eat away at my bones. Yet once again I rose and waged war against all the spirits.

In the beginning I battled with the passions of the flesh for eight years. I didn't sleep on my side, but I slept standing in a corner or sitting on a stool. I beat myself two or three times a day, wailing and weeping, so that God would feel sorry for me and take the warfare away. This continued until the All-compassionate One had mercy on me and took away Satan's rage. And now I am only briefly relating to you my countless sufferings, giving you just a drop out of the entire sea.

Every night for eight whole years, legions of demons furiously tortured me with clubs, axes, and anything else destructive. One would grab me by my then small beard, another by my hair, my feet, my hands: with every kind of evil and torture. They would all shout, "Strangle him! Kill him!" And only through the name of Christ and the Panagia would they disappear and their strength disperse like smoke. Finally the Lord had mercy upon me and brought me out of

---

[2] cf. 1 Cor. 2:9

[3] cf. Ps. 72:2

the depth and pit of suffering.[4]

And now, my child, I may be a fool to tell you these things, but since I think it will benefit you, I have related and continue to relate these things to you.

So now, I have grown old as if I were a hundred years of age due to all the sufferings and many changes I went through since my youth, when I was in my prime. First of all, through my handiwork, as you have seen from what I sent you, I toil with sweat to earn my bread. People come from various monasteries and sketes of the Holy Mountain, and by God's grace, we tell them whatever the Lord enlightens us to say.

I also work noetically and fulfill my monastic duties without fail. And for quite a while at night, after my nous has become tired saying the prayer, I write not a few letters, since Christians seek benefit from me in many ways. And after everything you have heard, I fall into despair thinking that I do not do the will of my Lord. I say with tears, "I wonder, who knows if what I am doing is pleasing to my Lord, or perhaps I am deluded, preaching to others while I remain a castaway?[5] For the divine will of my Lord is unknown to me. For who hath known the mind of the Ruler of All?[6] Or who will stand before Him, if He should observe iniquities?[7]"

So my child, have you thrown away all your weapons just because of one disobedience? Are you giving up the fight because of the words of one demon? And when have you ever seen a real winter? When have you ever seen snowstorms? When have you ever seen battalions and regiments of demons intimidating you? Were you frightened by the threats of one demon? But you should never believe things he tells you, because he has always been a liar, and he has no power against us, unless we have ignorance due to our pride. They only

---

[4] cf. Ps. 39:3

[5] cf. 1 Cor. 9:27

[6] cf. Rom. 11:34

[7] cf. Ps. 129:3

threaten and intimidate us, but they cannot do anything. For if they did not even have the power to enter into the swine,[8] how will they harm us without the Lord's permission?

So learn to think humbly, and do not fear the words of a possessed person at all. We have the clear testimony of our Lord: as soon as the demon said, "I know Thee who Thou art,"[9] the Lord silenced him, even though he said the truth, to give us an example so that we would not listen to the words of the possessed, no matter how truthful they may seem, because the demon speaks through the mouth of that person. *Now* he might be saying the truth, but later he will lie again, because he has been a liar since the beginning and he never remains truthful. And if a person lets himself believe these words, he will soon become the mock and laughing-stock of the demons.

So come to your senses and expel those words from your nous. Even if a humble person falls ten thousand times, he will rise once again, and his fall is reckoned as a victory. But as soon as a proud person falls into sin, he also falls into despair and his heart hardens, and then he no longer wants to rise. Despair is a mortal sin, and the devil rejoices in it more than anything. But it disperses immediately through confession.

So then, my child, exert yourself in every good deed. And if we fall down many times while working towards virtue, we should not remain in that fallen state, but should rise, asking for forgiveness from our Savior. And since He told His disciple to forgive his brother seventy times seven in a day,[10] how could the Law-giver Himself not forgive us?

Therefore, do not fear. But rather, as many times as you fall, rise and ask for forgiveness through the priests. And He, as the All-good One, will neither hold anything against you, nor harbor anger. "As far as the east is from the west, so far hath He removed our transgressions from us."[11]

---

[8] cf. Mk. 5:12

[9] cf. Mk. 1:24

[10] cf. Mt. 18:24

[11] Ps. 102:11

Nineteenth Letter

Always do a metanoia when you are wrong and don't lose time.

received your letter, my child, and I saw your anxiety.

But don't be sad, my child. Don't worry so much. Even though you have fallen again, get up again. You have been called to a heavenly road. It is not surprising for someone running to stumble. It just takes patience and repentance at every moment.

Therefore, always do a metanoia when you are wrong and don't lose time, because the longer you wait to seek forgiveness, the more you allow the evil one to spread his roots within you. Don't let him make roots to your detriment.

Therefore, don't despair when you fall, but get up eagerly and do a metanoia saying, "Forgive me, my dear Christ. I am human and weak." The Lord has not abandoned you. But since you still have a great deal of worldly pride, a great deal of vainglory, our Christ lets you make mistakes and fall, so that you perceive and come to know your weakness every day, so that you become patient with others who make mistakes, and so that you do not judge the brethren when they make mistakes, but rather put up with them.

So every time you fall, get up again and at once seek forgiveness. Don't hide sorrow in your heart, because sorrow and despondency are the joy of the evil one. They fill one's soul with bitterness and give birth to many evils. Whereas the frame of mind of someone who repents says, "I have sinned! Forgive me, Father!" and he expels the sorrow. He says, "Am I not a weak human? So what do I expect?" Truly, my child, this is how it is. So take courage.

Only when the grace of God comes does a person stand on his feet. Otherwise, without grace, he always changes and always falls. So be a man and don't be afraid at all.

Do you see how that brother you wrote about endured the temptation? You, too, should do likewise. Acquire a brave spirit against the temptations that come. In any case, they will come. Forget about what your despondency and indolence tell you. Don't be afraid of them. Just as the previous temptations passed by the grace of God, these, too, will pass once they do their job.

Temptations are medicines and healing herbs that heal our visible passions and our invisible wounds. So have patience in order to profit every day, to store up wages, rest, and joy in the heavenly kingdom. For the night of death is coming when no one will be able to work anymore.[1] Therefore, hurry. Time is short.

You should know this too: a victorious life lasting only one day with trophies and crowns is better than a negligent life lasting many years. Because one man's struggle, with knowledge and spiritual perception that lasts one day, has the same value as another man's struggle, who struggles negligently without knowledge for fifty years.

Without a struggle and shedding your blood, don't expect freedom from the passions. Our earth produces thorns and

---

[1] cf. Jn. 9:4

thistles after the Fall. We have been ordered to clean it, but only with much pain, bloody hands, and many sighs are the thorns and thistles uprooted. So weep, shed streams of tears, and soften the earth of your heart. Once the ground is wet, you can easily uproot the thorns.

Twentieth Letter

Don't despair! These things happen to everyone.

y soul grieves and a heavy cloud covers my heart. My mind stops; my tongue is silent, and my hand grows numb for you. I wonder and am astonished at how you are unable to exert yourself a little.

Oh, my child, if you could only see my pain and the tears that I shed for you! How much I worry until I hear that you have risen and slapped the adversary! For it is not you who are doing these things, but the evil one, the rebellious devil—may God destroy him!

So take courage, my child, and rise from your fall. Stand up. Get angry with the tempter, knowing that he is the one that contrived all this trickery. Don't let him get away with it; fight him.

When he brings that face to your memory, take a cane and strike your thighs hard, so that the carnal desire withers away. You will weep from the pain, but your nous will be cleansed from that memory. Thus the filthy images disappear and the deception of the *fantasy** leaves. My child, you should fear this temptation greatly because it defiles the soul. This unclean demon needs beating without mercy.

Here, all my young monks have a cane under their pillow. As soon as a carnal thought comes, they let him have it! Thus the desire withers and the soul flourishes. So there is no other remedy other than prayer, fasting, and the cane! Then the nous is cleansed; the soul becomes contrite; the heart is softened, and you are given boldness in prayer.

Don't despair. These things happen to everyone. It is a war of the tempter that will pass. Since you fought him in the beginning, he wants to pay off his debts now that your zeal has cooled. But once again rise, repent, and weep.

Don't you remember that brother who would tell the demons, "This cell is a forge. You hammer once, then you get hammered?" So fight strongly against the passion, and shortly, with God's help, you will be delivered.

However, you must realize the cause of this temptation. This happened to you because you allowed thoughts to remain within you against the elder and the brotherhood. The devil, being the malicious expert that he is, brings you hatred towards the elder and the brethren in order to sever the bond of love. He brings aversion toward all those who are virtuous to make them stop praying, because the prayers of many bind him and render him powerless. He looks for a way and an excuse to isolate those who are persuaded by his thoughts, so that he can separate them from the assembly of the fathers. And then he conquers them and has them under his control.

Therefore, understand that all these things are artifices and ruses of the evil one. For this reason, don't listen to what he whispers in your thoughts. See to it that he doesn't keep you from doing your *prayer rule*,* because then you will be lost for good. May he not rejoice in his expectations. I am waiting for you to gladden me with that slap you will give him in the face.

Now I shall make all the brethren here pray so that you receive strength from above. Even though I never cease praying for you, now a joint effort will be made. As for you, do not be negligent from now on and do not despair. Accept also this small prayer-rope, say the prayer, and receive strength. Love the elder and the brethren, and do not be embittered towards them unjustly. Truly, love is more powerful than all the enemy's skill and strength.

No matter what may have happened, don't think of it as anything, since you are not the one responsible. You did not bother them, and they did not bother you, but the tempter did, who fights and stirs up all of us—for this is his job. Today you were tempted, tomorrow someone else, and the next day another person, since the tempter will always exist in this life.

Yet, I repeat: listen to my voice; don't despair! We will go to paradise together. And if I don't place you inside, then I do not want to sit in there either. From my words know the abundance of my love in Christ Jesus our Lord.

Twenty-first Letter

A sin, whether small or great, is blotted out through true repentance.

ou wrote asking if your sin is forgiven. The Holy Fathers mean something else, though. Every sin a person commits is forgiven when he repents; however, the memory of it remains with him until his last breath. When he becomes a little slothful, when he is a little careless, the devil depicts it to him while awake or asleep in order to defile his thoughts and make him guilty of an old sin—or even just to make his mind wander.

Don't you see how the Prophet David cried out when Nathan reproached him because of Bathsheba, "I have sinned against the Lord!"?[1] And the prophet Nathan told him, "The Lord hath put away thy sin."[2] So, he was forgiven immediately, yet he was punished throughout his life: first of all, the child that Bathsheba had, died. Then his son sinned against his sister Tamar. Afterwards, his son Absalom pursued him—and he went through all of this after he had been forgiven. Do you see that even though the sin is forgiven, the penance remains in proportion to the fault?

---

[1] 2 Kings 12:13
[2] Ibid

Take a look at St. Theodora of Alexandria, who lived in disguise as a monk. She sinned, fled, repented, and became a saint. However, she hadn't received a penance for her adultery. When she was slandered and banished and had to raise someone else's child, only she knew why she was really being slandered.

But even the great Ephraim the Syrian—didn't they put him in prison because he had supposedly stolen a calf, even though he was a saint? "True," the Lord said to him, "you didn't steal this time, but when you were a child, didn't you let one loose, and the wild animals devoured it?" So then, even though a person's sin is forgiven, the memory of the sin and its effects remain.

Now as for you, since you have been negligent recently, God allowed the tempter to rise up against you so that you would wake up. Therefore, arise and shout, "Son of David, I want to receive my sight!"[3] And behold, the Light-giving Jesus is present, dawning the light of repentance and divine knowledge upon you.

So I am not distressed because of things past, my child, but I rejoice for the things to come. For the lesser is blessed by the greater,[4] and a sin, whether small or great, is blotted out through true repentance. Therefore, do not look at things which are behind, but reach forth unto those which are ahead.[5]

I am very delighted, my child, that you are seeking to learn. This is an excellent indication: when someone seeks to learn, he will most certainly progress. It is impossible for him not to. But even if he does not accomplish anything, he believes that there are others who do struggle. Moreover, by blaming himself, he is humbled and asks God to send His mercy to strengthen him. Thus, he reaches the measure of those who have achieved virtue.

---

[3] Mt. 9:27

[4] Heb. 7:7

[5] cf. Phil. 3:13

ℑwenty-second ℒetter

So, you don't want to suffer?
Then don't expect to ascend.

ove of my soul! Why are you despondent? Why do you despair? Why are you so weary? Is this how easily you give up the fight? Behold how God let the demons sift you as wheat[1] a little, so that you see where you are; so that your pride is revealed; so that your heart is humbled; so that you learn that you are human and "know thyself"; so that you become compassionate towards sinners and not judge them at all.

How will you get to know the weakness of human nature if the crows don't wake you up? If our sweet Jesus doesn't withdraw His grace, how will you learn the art of all arts and science of all sciences? Now you are learning the trade. Now you are reaping benfits. It is now, and not when grace is present, that you show you love Christ. What possible virtue can you show when grace is present? Then, it is grace that cries out for itself with groans which cannot be uttered:[2] "Abba, Father!"[3] Grace cries out to the Giver of grace, "Who shall separate me from Thy love, my Jesus?"[4] It is grace that says these things—the indwelling strength

---

[1] cf. Lk. 22:31

[2] cf. Rom. 8:26

[3] Gal. 4:6

[4] cf. Rom. 8:35

through our mouth—not the flesh; just as a demon curses and blasphemes through a possessed person's mouth.

Without grace, the flesh cannot do anything. Without grace, the flesh denies Jesus. The cock crows; Peter remembers. He weeps bitterly[5] and cries out, "I have sinned!" But still, he hides in the upper chamber.[6] He fears the Jews. His heart beats as a mouse's does when it hears the cats outside. "Even if I must die with Thee, I will not deny Thee,"[7] he says when Christ is present. But when Christ leaves, he denies him thrice.

So do you see? Do you understand what a great mystery is hidden behind these words? Christ intercedes for us in the Holy Spirit.[8] For this reason, when He comes we become orators; fishermen become teachers; harlots become chaste; thieves stop stealing, and everyone repents. And who worked all this? The only One Who knows. The good Helmsman. Our sweet Jesus. The only Love.

When can someone understand human suffering? When he also suffers. When he goes through the same, he learns and understands the other person's suffering. Otherwise, he is callous and is not grieved, unless he happens to have a good nature. But all natural attributes merit neither honor nor dishonor; achievements and falls depend on our own free will.

So then, how shall we learn this science of all knowledge if the tempter does not sift us like wheat? Since, when grace leaves, not only you and I, but even the holy apostles would not have been apostles! How can pottery hold water if it has not been baked in the fire? This is how God wants to make us— like a wrestler in the theater, or like a ball they kick around.

He raises you to the heavens. He shows you what the eye of a passionate man has not seen nor the ear of a man with

---

[5] cf. Mt. 26:75
[6] cf. Jn. 20:19
[7] cf. Mt. 26:35
[8] cf. Rom. 8:26

materialistic cares heard.[9] Then without your being at all at fault, He turns the page and throws you into the infernal depths. And He rejoices to see you wrestling like an athlete against all the demonic battalions. Don't take my word for it, but take Paul for example. After he ascended to the third heaven and saw and heard unspeakable words,[10] he still cried out, "There was given to me a thorn in the flesh!"[11]

This is what the Lord Who is mighty in strength does, until He establishes a person: He makes him ascend and experience theoria, descend and suffer, teaching him to regard both the one and the other as something commonplace, without either transformation effecting him. "Both of these," he says, "are for me."

So, you don't want to suffer? Then don't expect to ascend. Whoever does not endure sufferings should not expect grace from Him. He removed grace from you so that you may become wise. But it will come again. It does not abandon you. This is a law of God. But it will leave again. Yet once more will it come. As long as you don't stop seeking it, it will keep coming and going until it renders you perfect.

It is a fact that when a passionate person attempts to teach another passionate person, grace immediately withdraws from the one who teaches, and then he falls into the same faults and passions as the other person. For before "praxis," he has not been given this duty.

However, it is not as if this is the entire reason why God left you. Grace would have left necessarily during this period, even if this were not the reason. Don't you remember what I told you in the beginning, "After four years, I want to hear you say the things you are saying now." Look through my first letters and you will see it. It is an inviolable law of God that after three or four—and occasionally five—years,

---

[9] cf. 1 Cor. 2:9

[10] cf. 2 Cor. 12:4

[11] 2 Cor. 12:7

grace withdraws in order to train a person. And if he so desires, it will make him wise.

So do not grieve; it is a common cup. Read the life of St. Andrew the Fool for Christ to see what he said when Christ gave him the bitter portion. This holds for all of us, according to each one's measure.

So then, bear the chain of your Christ. Close your mouth tightly and don't let a single word escape. Give yourself courage, saying: "Why are you sad, my soul, and why are you disheartened? Nothing bad happened to you. Christ has left for a little while, but He will come back again. He delays a little to teach you patience and humility. The saints endured so much; are you unable to withstand this dispensation of grace?" You should say such things to your soul and not be fainthearted. For this is what gives joy to the temptations: when they see that you grieve and lose heart.

When grace comes and goes, and comes and goes again, you learn the art of warfare. Then vacillation makes no impression on you, but you rejoice and say, "Test me, my dear Christ, and try me like silver in a furnace." Then your roots grow deep like the trees whose roots go deeper the more the wind blows. God is my witness that it was during my greatest temptations that I found the greatest consolation.

So be brave and strong in the Lord. Endure the temptations and grace will come again.

𝔗wenty-third 𝔏etter

The cane is the remedy for every passion.

race always precedes a temptation, as if to notify you saying, "Prepare yourself and lock your doors."

When you see comfort in your heart, illumination in your nous, and theoria, prepare yourself at once. Don't say, "I have been given rest," but load your weapons—tears, fasting, vigil, and prayer—and set sentries on your senses to guard your nous. Ask yourself, "I wonder, from where will the battle begin? From the demons? From men? Or from my own nature?" Don't get drowsy before the battle trumpet sounds, and during the battle, your struggle and victory will show.

It is when grace is acting within you that you should be afraid. Conversely, when you see temptations and afflictions oppressing you from all sides, you should rejoice. Don't grieve, don't grumble, don't be despondent. Give courage to yourself, for joy and comfort will come. "Be brave, my soul," you should say, "This is only a temptation, a trial, an affliction. Afterwards, you will have peace and joy and grace for many days. Thank You, my dear Christ," you should say, "for in mine affliction Thou hast made room for me,[1] and with

---

[1] Ps. 4:1

chastisement hast Thou chastened me,"[2] and "Thou didst bring my soul out into a place of refreshment."[3]

But the cane is the remedy for every passion. Demons fear it and shudder when they see a man punishing himself like a martyr for the love of Christ.[†] Once in a while, when the passions rise up against the soul and want to "hurl the rider"[4] (the nous, that is), when each passion raises its head, give the battle cry, "Quiet, be still![5] Or else I'll put the cane to work!"

For example, the thought comes and distresses you in church, "Why should your brother chant again instead of you, since this is contrary to the proper order?" You should tell it, "It is better for my brother to be happy than for me." The thought persists, "But why, since this is just and correct?" You tell it, "Devil, leave me alone!" and keep your mind on the *Jesus prayer.* * The tempter revolts, ready to burst, "But no, why???" "All right," tell him, "wait a second and I'll tell you why!" Then at once leave the church on a pretext, and hurry to your cell. Grab a cane there and say with anger, "Here's your 'why,' devil! This is it. This is the justice you sought from me, so take it!" Next, after you wound him in your body, lodge a complaint about him to Christ as the cause of your pain. The devil flees shuddering, Christ comes, fills you with comfort, and alleviates the passion, and thus you learn the art of how to win.

Does sleep overcome you? Strike your laxity. Does anger agitate you? Crush your egotism. Do resentment and envy embitter you? The same. You don't like the food? Likewise. Does the warfare of the flesh rise up? Arise like a strong man and fight

---

[†] The elder is not advocating some kind of masochism here, but advises counteracting sinful pleasure–whether it be due to thoughts of anger, pride, or carnal thoughts–with physical pain. Similar techniques were used by Sts. Benedict, Martinios, Epiphanios, Archbishop of Constantinople, Nephon, Bishop of Constantiana, and many other saints.

[2] Ps. 117:18

[3] Ps. 65:12

[4] cf. Ex. 15:1

[5] Mk. 4:39

your enemies. And in general, whenever your body and your thoughts seek "justice" and "why," the answer is the cane.

"Either I shall live one hour as Thou dost want, my dear Christ, or may I not exist in this life." If you weep and mourn while praying like this, the mercy of the Lord will come. Your passions will subside and you will be at peace with yourself, with God, and with all of creation. The body will fall along with all its arrogance, and then it no longer needs beating, since it has learned to be subject to the spirit.

As for me, I broke many canes on my thighs before subjugating my body. I stood like a torturer over myself. My whole body trembled when it saw that I was about to lay hold of a cane. The demons fled, the passions were pacified, comfort came, and my soul rejoiced. For it is a law of God: whatever causes sensual pleasure is cured by pain.

Enough about this. If you want more, read lives of saints. Read and see how many hardships the saints used against their "old man"[6]; how much they afflicted themselves voluntarily and involuntarily, until the flower of purity—that fragrance of sanctity—blossomed within them. This is why the relics of these holy martyrs and monks are fragrant and exude myrrh.

St. Mark   the Ascetic

---

[6] cf. Rom 6:6

Twenty-fourth Letter

That night God showed me Satan's wickedness.

on't be surprised, my child; that is how a monk is. The life of a monk is a continuous martyrdom. Our sweet Jesus reveals Himself through afflictions. And as soon as you seek Him, He will send temptations. His love is found within sufferings. He shows you a little honey, while underneath He has hidden a whole warehouse full of bitterness. The honey of grace precedes the bitterness of temptations.

When He wants to send you sufferings, He warns you by sending you the corresponding amount of grace like a messenger. As if to say, "Get ready! Watch out where the enemy will attack and strike you." And thus your struggle and fight begin.

Be careful not to be frightened. Don't be surprised when cannonballs start falling, but stand valiantly as a soldier of Christ, as a practiced combatant, as a brave warrior. For this present life here is a battlefield. Repose will be in that life there. Here is exile; there is our true homeland.

Haven't I told you this story before? For eight years in the beginning, I had a frightful war with the demons. Every night was a fierce battle, and every day was full of evil thoughts and passions. They would come with swords, axes, hatchets, and shovels.

"Everybody on him!" they shouted. It was a martyrdom.

"Hasten, my dear Panagia!" I shouted, and I grabbed one of them. I let him have it and then beat up the others; but I broke my hands on the walls trying to do so.

By chance an acquaintance of ours came from the world to see us. That night I put him in my small hut to sleep. When the demons came for me as usual, they started beating him, and he started screaming! The man was horrified—he almost lost his mind. I came running at once.

"What's wrong?" I asked him.

"The demons nearly strangled me!" he said. "They almost beat me to death!"

"Don't be afraid," I told him. "That was intended for me, but tonight they thrashed you by mistake! But don't be alarmed." I told him also other cheerful things to calm him down, but it was impossible. He could stay no longer in that place of martyrdom. He was terrified and kept looking right and left, begging to leave. So in the middle of the night I led him to St. Anne's and came back. We were at St. Basil's then.

So after eight years like this, with all the beatings that I gave my body every day because of the warfare of the flesh, with all the fasting, from all the vigils, and all the other struggles, I became a corpse. I fell ill and lost hope of ever subduing the demons and the passions.

Then one night, as I was sitting, the door opened. I was praying noetically with my head bent down and did not look up. I thought to myself that it must be Father Arsenios. Then I felt a hand under me stimulating me carnally. I looked and saw the demon of fornication, that mangy wretch. I pounced

upon him like a dog—that is how much rage I had for him—
and grabbed him. His hairs felt like those of a pig. Then he
disappeared, and the whole place was filled with a horrible
stench. And that very moment, the warfare of the flesh left
along with him. Thenceforth, I was like an infant with much
dispassion.

That night, God showed me Satan's wickedness. I was in
a lofty, beautiful place, and below it was an open area with
the sea beside it. The demons had set thousands of traps. The
monks were passing through and falling; the traps caught
some by the head, some by the foot, others by the hand,
by the clothes—wherever each monk could be caught.
Meanwhile the dragon of the abyss had his head stuck out of
the sea—with fire coming out of his mouth, eyes, and nose—
and rejoiced with exultation at the falls of the monks. But as
I watched I cursed him. "O abysmal dragon!" I said. "This is
why you deceive and ensnare us!" Then I came to myself
with both joy and sorrow: with joy, because I saw the traps of
the devil; with sorrow, because of our falls and the danger
that threatens us all our life.

Thenceforth, I had great peace and prayer. But the devil
does not stop. He turned people against me. The reason why
I am writing these things to you is so that you and the rest of
the brethren have patience.

It takes a struggle in this life if you want to win; it's no
joke! It is with the unclean spirits that you are fighting, which
do not throw sweets and marshmallows, but sharp bullets that
kill the soul, not the body. Nevertheless, do not be distressed.
Do not be frightened. You have help. I am supporting you.
Truly I saw you last night in my sleep. We were ascending
towards Christ together. So then, arise and run behind me.
Just be careful now that you have seen the traps of the evil

one; woe to him whom they catch—it is not easy to escape from their claws.

Of course, the devil by himself cannot—no matter how much he wants to—condemn us to hell, if we do not cooperate in his wickedness. Yet neither does God want to save us all by Himself, unless we also collaborate with His grace for our salvation. God always helps, He always comes in time, but He wants us to work, too, to do what we can.

Therefore, don't say that you didn't make any progress, and ask why you didn't make any progress, and other such things, because progress does not depend only on man, no matter how much he wants it and how hard he labors for it. The power of God, His blessed grace, does everything, when it receives our contribution. It is grace that raises those who have stumbled and sets aright the fallen.[1] With all our heart we should ask this God and Savior of ours to come and heal the paralytic, raise Lazarus, dead for four days, give eyes to the blind, and feed the hungry.

Christ
blessing
the five
loaves

and the
two fish

---

[1] Ps. 145:8

Twenty-fifth Letter

The senses cease, and the one praying is caught up into theoria.

 y child, what you tasted while praying that night is due to the action of grace. Ask the Lord to give it to you again whenever He wills.

I know a well-known brother who encountered many temptations one day, and he passed that entire day with tears without eating at all. As the sun was setting, he was sitting on a rock and looking at the Church of the Transfiguration on the peak of Mount Athos. With tears and pain he was imploring God, saying:

"O Lord, as Thou wast transfigured to Thy disciples, transfigure Thyself also in my soul! Stop the passions and bring peace to my heart! Grant prayer to him who prayeth and restrain my unrestrained nous!"

While he was saying such things with pain, a subtle breeze full of fragrance came from the church, filling his soul—as he told me—with joy, illumination, and divine love; and from within, the prayer began to flow ceaselessly from his heart like honey.

So he got up and went inside the place where he was staying, for it was already night. Then he bent his head upon his chest and began eating the sweetness that gushed forth from the prayer that he had been given. Immediately he was caught up into theoria and was totally beside himself. He wasn't confined by walls and rocks; he was beyond all volition—without body and with a deep tranquillity, in extraordinary light, and unlimited breadth. His nous contemplated only this thought: "May I never return to the body, but remain here forever." This was the first theoria that brother saw, who then returned to himself and continued struggling for his salvation.

I sat down and came to my senses a little. As I thought of the things to come, I tied up the severed string. Then taking hold of my lyre, I extracted honey out of the thorns of my experience I gathered like flowers in the desert. So come and accept hospitality in my shade, and I shall gather a fragrant syrup from the thorns for you. Whenever afflictions come upon you, ruminate those things I have mentioned to you, and my words will seem sweeter than honey.

Now then, both methods of prayer are good. Although the second method—with words—is unsafe, it is more fruitful. I use both methods every evening. First with words, and then when I get tired and don't find any fruit, I enclose my nous in my heart.

I knew a certain brother when he was young, about twenty-eight or thirty years old. He would lower his nous into his heart for six hours; he would not allow it to leave from there from nine o'clock in the evening until three o'clock in the morning (he had a clock that struck the hours). He would get soaked with sweat. Afterwards, he would arise to fulfill the rest of his obligations.

So in short: for a man to obtain freedom, his flesh must rot[1] and he must not take death into consideration.

---

[1] cf. 2 Cor. 5:16 and Gal. 5:24

Prayer that is done with words is also done noetically, silently, and is called petition or entreaty. So he who begins his supplicatory prayer should begin like this:

"Invisible, incomprehensible God: Father, Son, and Holy Spirit, the only strength and help of every soul, the only one who is good and loveth mankind, my life, joy, and peace. . .," and he should continue for a while with this kind of improvised prayer. If grace becomes active, at once the door is opened and his prayer reaches the gate of heaven and ascends like a pillar or flame of fire. At this moment the change occurs. But if grace does not help and the nous is scattered, then he confines it cyclically in his heart. Then he calms down as if in a nest, and his nous does not wander—as if his heart is a place of confinement for the nous. Whereas when the change occurs, it happens during an entreaty. Then grace overflows and one is filled with illumination and infinite joy. And since he who has been seized is unable to bear the fire of love, his senses cease, and he is caught up into theoria. Up until this point, man acts with his own will. Beyond this, he is no longer in control, nor does he recognize himself. For he has now been united with the fire and has been entirely transformed—a god by grace.

This is the divine meeting during which the walls retract and he breathes another air, the air of the intellect, free and full of the fragrance of paradise. Later, the cloud of grace withdraws little by little once more, and this man of clay hardens like wax and returns to himself as if he has emerged from a bath: clean, light, shining, very delightful, sweet, soft as cotton, and full of wisdom and knowledge.

But he who wants such things must at every moment be walking towards death.

Twenty-sixth Letter

My sister in the Lord, most pious Abbess.

y sister in the Lord, most pious Abbess. I pray for your health which is precious for your synodia.

Blessed Eldress, today I received your letter. Since, according to your letter, you believe you will be benefited, I shall put my own will aside, praying that every word I say will be for the benefit and salvation of your soul.

So then, open your ears and receive my words.

When we came to the Holy Mountain, my sister, we did not lock ourselves up in a house, as most people usually do. But we searched, we shouted, we wept. There was not a single hill or crevice that we passed over in search of an unerring guide to hear words of life—not idle and vain talk. There was not a single hermit elder from whom we did not receive at least one drop of benefit.

One who was ninety years old told us that he had stayed on the top of a mountain for fifteen years. Lightning would strike and rend his clothes; yet he had extreme patience. Another one told us that he had given *antidoron** to holy ascetics who were naked and invisible. Another one would give them communion while serving liturgy at midnight. Another one was Russian and had spent years on the peak. Every ten years another hermit would come to meet him. While we were there with him, he told us that he was expecting him, and we would see him, too. But it seems that he died in the wilderness. All of them were fragrant like holy relics.

As I heard all this, the fire kindled within me even more. So I kept asking what they ate, how they prayed, what they had seen, what they thought, what they saw as they died. As their soul departed, one of them saw the Panagia, another saw angels. These things happen even today. Right before their death they saw visions, so that God would take them peacefully. Hearing such things, I would eagerly run when they were about to die in order to see and hear what they would say. From these saints I received my prayer schedule and "typikon" as to how I should conduct my life. They are the ones who taught me. I say nothing of my own.

I also know the house of the elder whom you mentioned, the tinsmith, the baker who fished, Father Neophytos, who made pectoral crosses, as well as many others. But I was looking to find where there was life, where I could benefit my soul. For the treasures will return to God's storehouse, and then hunger will strike; the word of God will no longer be heard. The lamps are going out, and we are walking in tangible darkness. Rarely do you hear anything about how to be saved. Only gossip and criticism. Everyone wants to teach the others. Seldom does someone give his life as proof of the Gospel—as a continuation of the life of the Fathers. All that is left is a great fear of temptations and inordinate boasting.

But that's enough about those around us, my blessed Eldress. They speak according to how they live. That is how they see, that is how they speak. They are all right.

When someone loses his way—since he has gone astray and does not know another path—he wants everyone to walk as he does. If someone tells him that there is another path, a shortcut, he will say, "You are deluded! There is no other path," because he does not know of it. That is why he is right. He says and judges only things he can see and consider from his own viewpoint.

Now that we have confined ourselves in order to practice hesychia, since that is how we were taught to live from the beginning, everyone is against me—or rather, the tempter incites them since he does not like to see someone caring for his salvation in our days. So may the Lord do away with him, and may the brethren be shown mercy for everything they say and judge. I leave everything to God and learn to endure without grumbling the temptations that come.

But let's talk about "the prayer" you inquired about. I think, my good Eldress, that you have been greatly wronged. You are not suited for so many cares, but for hesychia. So, if you want to listen to me, I consider it good to be moderate and combine the two: praxis and hesychia. For without hesychia, grace does not remain; and without grace, man is nothing.

Therefore, beg the elder to give you a separate little cell so that you may have stillness there. Receive people and talk until noon. Afterwards, once you eat, sleep until evening. And don't let them disturb you until the next morning, even if the monastery catches on fire. And once you wake up—if it is still daylight or the sun is setting—read by yourself or do your prayer rule, and when it gets dark, have a cup of coffee and begin your vigil; begin to pray. The goal is to activate grace; to make it active. And when grace acts, this is everything.

I begin first with the Compline and the Salutations. And

when I finish, I begin praying to Christ and to our Panagia with words as they come to my mind: "My sweetest Jesus, the light of my soul, the only love, the only joy, the only peace. . ." And I say a lot and with heartfelt pain. Then I turn to the Panagia. Our dear, sweet Mother shows so much love. May you always have her name on your lips.

And once your nous is calmed and your soul is sweetened, sit down and say the prayer noetically, as you wrote, until drowsiness approaches. Then chant very softly with sweetness and praise Christ the Master and His All-immaculate Mother. Say slowly and clearly, "O joyous light," "Which god is as great as our God," "Holy God," and as many others as you know. Then chant to the Queen of all, "Rejoice, O Queen," "In thee, O full of grace," "It is truly meet," "In the Red Sea," and others. And if drowsiness persists, also chant, "Thy fatherly embrace," "I wanted to blot out with tears," "Who tossed at storm and taking refuge," "I am a sheep," and whatever else you remember.

Say these with compunction while sitting on your bed, awaiting the mercy and compassion of God. And thus, if grace does not act while praying with your own words, it will act through the prayer; and if not, it will act through the chanting.

Never neglect reading from the Fathers. You will benefit greatly because the saints set an example for you. You see your faults and failings as if in a mirror and correct your life. Reading is like light in the darkness. In this way, you will benefit the sisters more than by tiring yourself all day long.

Afterwards, get up. If you want, go to church. Otherwise, if you remain by yourself, do the service with the prayer-rope and relax. In this manner, not only will you maintain your health, but also you will benefit your soul, and you will be a guiding light for the sisters. Or else, as you grow older amidst the noise, you will completely lose your prayer, for you are accustomed to stillness.

So then, my true sister, since you have experienced both living in stillness and living with many, you know the benefit of each. Therefore, combine the two and reap the benefits. See to it that you spend as much time as you can in stillness so that you depart from this life rested.

Twenty-seventh Letter

I am struggling for God.
I don't care what people say.

 ou said that your elder wants to make a pilgrimage to the Holy Mountain. He will do a good and holy thing. But he should not take into consideration that he knows me or that I even exist, for I live in absolute silence, with a program different from the usual. My gate is usually locked, except at certain hours; thus it would be difficult for him to meet me.

With the help of the brethren, I am able to help him with whatever he wants. By no means, however, shall I alter my schedule—by opening the door, talking, losing my prayer and hesychia—unless there is a need at a time I decide, because my hours are limited. I have to leave out part of my vigil and suffer a spiritual loss in order to talk with the brethren for an hour or two.

I am writing this in order to explain myself before I am misunderstood. I am accustomed to doing everything in this manner: to say and do everything clearly, as in a mirror; so that I am not misunderstood by anyone, whether in word, deed, or thought.

For many have come from various places without asking
beforehand to learn the schedule we have. And because I
didn't invite them in, they were scandalized. Even here, all
my neighbors are against me because I won't open my gate
to them. But I don't shut out the fathers to scandalize them.
Rather, now that I have so many years of experience, I see
that I do not benefit from these acts of "love," but only ruin
my soul. Therefore, I closed everyone out once and for all
and have found hesychia. Now I don't open to anyone, nor do
I have an extra room for a visitor. And if someone comes
from far away, he must come when the fathers are working,
in the morning. If necessary, he will stay in the room of my
priest, because every Saturday, Sunday, and feast day we
have a Liturgy. We have a priest who comes and celebrates
the Divine Liturgy, and we receive communion.

So behold, I have explained this to avoid scandal. I am
struggling for God; I don't care what people say, even if they
revile me, even if they mock me, even if they slander me, even
if they dishonor my name, even if all of creation busies itself
with speaking against me.

I have seen and experienced in many ways that if the grace
of God does not enlighten a person, no matter how much you
speak to him, you cannot help him. For a moment he will listen, but then the next minute he is recaptivated by his old
ways. If, however, grace acts at once through your words, a
change occurs at that time with the help of his good intentions. And from that moment his life changes tremendously.
However, this happens only to those whose hearing and conscience have not hardened. As for those who hear yet remain
disobedient in their evil wills, even if you speak with them
night and day, even if you pour out the wisdom of the Fathers
into their ears, even if you work miracles before their eyes,

even if you turn the flow of the Nile upon them, they will not receive even one drop of benefit. They only want to come, talk, and waste their time because of their laziness. This is why I lock my gate, and at least I benefit from the Jesus prayer and hesychia. For God always hears the Jesus prayer above all other things, whereas He always abhors idle talk, even if it seems spiritual. According to the Fathers, idle talk is mainly passing one's time with words, without applying them.

So when inexperienced people say such things, don't listen to them. Whoever has not tried it must do so, and through experience he will learn and find whatever he lacks. Experience cannot be bought. It is each person's possession, and it becomes his according to the toil and blood that he himself gives to obtain it.

Believe me, my sisters, there is much toil in the monastic way of life. I have never ceased crying out day and night, seeking the Lord's mercy. And I almost despair, as if I have never done anything, as if I have not yet "made a start." But by beginning anew each day, I am found to be a liar and sinner. But you should imitate the wise virgins and keep vigil, crying out mournfully, calling upon divine mercy, for the end has come for us. Perhaps the peace has ended, so we, too, are with the dead. Therefore, exert yourselves.

I have said enough for the time being. I shall write to all of you again in another letter, if these things bear fruit and you are eager. Now I am sad only for the young nun's mother who grumbles and says bad things, as you wrote me. Many mothers, unfortunately, have lost their children by grumbling, because they did not dedicate them to Christ with all their soul. The children are saved, by the grace of Christ; the mothers, however, remain far from them.

But you should have patience; pay no attention to what they say. Time, by the grace of God, will heal them. And in time, she will repent. Then she will feel sorry for everything she says and does now. But for the time being, forbearance, unadulterated love, and utter silence are needed. Whatever they say, your words should be few. When you do speak, pray noetically, so that your words will be vested with power from above.

As for you, blessed Eldress, combine everything together with much discernment and forbearance.

The Ship of the Church

Ꝺwenty-eighth Ꝺetter

To a nun about to receive the
holy and angelic schema.

I received your letter, lamb of my Jesus, and as I proceeded to read it, I attained my heart's desire. And at once, I leapt for joy as if beside myself. I bent my knees and stretched out my hands. What can I tell you! My tongue spoke. My lips whispered constantly, while my mind theologized unceasingly, and my eyes shed tears continuously.

"I thank Thee," I said, "O sweet breeze, life of my soul, light of my nous, consolation of my heart, my sweet Jesus. I thank Thee, my sweetest love, my most-desirable Jesus, for Thou didst not overlook my humble supplications, but didst hearken unto my voice and didst have mercy upon my little child."

Behold, in two days, after the past trial, she will receive the holy schema. A new person is born. The old one dies. Her name changes. She wears a wedding garment. Her sins are forgiven. She takes her vows before the angels. She is written in the heavens.

Henceforth, she no longer has parents and relatives in the world. She abandons worldly things and ponders heavenly things. She is united with the things above; she reflects upon them. No longer does she have self-will or self-complacency or authority over her own body. She renounces everything and clings to the words of the eldress until her final breath.

She no longer asks at all what her neighbor is doing, but lives continuously in hesychia. Henceforth she works noetically. She constantly has tears in her eyes, a tongue flowing honey, speech in moderation, a chaste body, a clear nous without fantasies, undistracted prayer, constant peace, perfect obedience, burning love towards Christ the Savior that continuously burns without going out—without ever going out; so that upon merely hearing the name of Christ, immediately the soul leaps, the lips are sweetened, and one's entire noetic part is aroused. For it is customary of love—and also a divine gift—for the heart to leap when it hears a beloved name; whether physical or spiritual, love's sweetness springs forth from the same heart.

When grace flashes the light of the Spirit's divine radiance, the entire person becomes delirious, and as the divine David, he leaps and dances[1] noetically before the divine icon, as David did before the symbolic ark.

So daughter of my Jesus, now you see why right after reading your letter and praying for you, I wrote back to you full of joy and exultation. And on Sunday—because now it is Friday morning—at the time when you will be taking your vows and receiving the schema of the angels, I, too, will be noetically present to chant along, "Thy fatherly embrace." And throughout the whole vigil, I shall be praying for you and for all the sisters.

As soon as you receive my letter, write to me your true, heavenly name, so that we may erase the old one for good and put the new one in its place. And see to it that henceforth your life is angelic, for from now on you have been ranked among the choirs of the angels to praise and glorify God with your body and spirit.

---

[1] cf. 2 Kings 6:16

Twenty-ninth Letter

Blessed is God Who raises mortals still in the body to the way of life of the bodiless angels.

od overcomes the order of nature wherever He wills. Likewise, he who wants to bear the Cross of Christ overcomes his own nature. Truly great is the power and grace of the holy and angelic Monastic Schema.

Rejoice and delight, my beloved child, together with the entire holy synodia, or should I say the entire spiritual fragrance. Rejoice, wise virgins in the Lord, for you have been blessed to live such an angelic way of life upon the earth. Blessed is God Who maketh His angels spirits;[1] blessed is God Who raises mortals still in the body to the way of life of the bodiless angels.

I pray, my children, and entreat from the depths of my heart that the divine sweet-scented grace, like a subtle breeze, like a myrrh-laden divine breath of wind, may continuously blow amongst your holy souls, making them fragrant and sanctifying your ascetical bodies.

But I earnestly entreat you: take care of your souls. May not one of you resemble our foremother Eve, but may all of you imitate the Theotokos Mariam, the Virgin Mary. She said,

---

[1] cf. Ps. 103:5

"Behold the handmaid of the Lord!"[2] and became the Mother of God and the Lady of the angels. Her fruit, our sweet Jesus, through obedience ascended the Cross and descended into Hades to heal the great wound of disobedience. Therefore, understand from this the power of this mystery.

The monastic schema is a cross, in place of the Cross that Christ bore to save us. Consequently, we who have worn the holy schema have clothed ourselves with obedience. And by attending to obedience, we walk in the likeness of Christ.

I shall tell you this as well: the burden of obedience is considered to be an epitome of the rest of the virtues, just as the Cross is of the Lord's Passion. And just as the thief entered paradise through the cross, we, too, enter the kingdom through obedience as through a cross. Thus, it is obvious that the disobedient are outside the kingdom.

So then, blessed is the way: compel yourselves. Be attentive and pray, so that you do not enter into temptation. Whoever does not have humility, whoever does not do what he is told, becomes a slave of the demons. Then his end becomes a grief and disgrace before men.

I have written things in short, so that you acquire a godly fear and not disobey the eldress. For you are not dealing with her, but with God, Who requires obedience for the soul's salvation.

As for the schema you mentioned, an angel revealed it to the divine Pachomios.

First of all, in the beginning of Christianity, all women who chose virginity—as you do now—were tried for three years, and afterwards, a crown was prepared for them with fragrant flowers. Then the bishop read prayers over them—as now with the schema—as brides of Christ. And when they died, the crowns were placed with them in their grave.

---

[2] Lk. 1:38

But to get to the point, today the schema is a Mystery like the crowns of a wedding. You wear the schema instead of the crowns. You marry Christ and promise virginity until the end of your life. In mortal weddings, they wear crowns and promise fidelity to each other until the end of their lives. Can they give those crowns to be used in another wedding afterwards? No, but once they die, they throw them in the grave. So, how can you give your crown for someone else to be crowned, or just give it away? How can you give your schema to someone else to become a nun? This is not right. But since you didn't know, it is forgiven. It should not happen again, though.

Let's discuss another issue now.

You wrote saying that you pester me a lot with your questions. But I tell you that since you entered this holy and blessed monastery, you will become blessed if you have patience and perfect obedience until the end. Therefore, crush your arrogance, your egotism, your pride under the yoke of Christ, and I shall always be beside you. Ever since you dedicated yourself to the monastery, I have followed your progress. I partake in the sorrows and joys of your sisters. Since I take care of so many others and do not cease praying and writing, won't I take care of you, my true sisters? Especially since my elder gave me this diakonema with his blessing.

It is enough for me that you have faith and love towards me as towards a spiritual brother of yours, so that you benefit spiritually. You will never see my face. I shall not harm you with my words. With all my soul I shall see to it that I help you. If you are unable to accomplish something in your spiritual struggles, I shall lower my demands. I shall stay as high as you can reach so that you can reach me.

But you, too, should pray for me, because many seek my help, and I bear the temptation of everyone I help. May the Lord be glorified for everything.

If at times you hear cold words against me, don't believe them, but ask me with brotherly love, "This is what they told us; this is what we heard." And I, with all sincerity, with the fear of God, shall tell you the truth with God as my witness. I shall never lie to you.

I beg you to be careful lest you are persuaded by that monk's way of thinking that you wrote about; I know very well that it is not in accordance with God. And don't tell his mother and sister what I shall tell you now, so that you don't grieve them.

Once, years ago, I saw that there were two roads that the Fathers had mapped out: the cenobitic and the ascetical. And I saw that brother was following neither the one nor the other road, but said, "I will go here!" Then he went downhill through a thicket that descended to the sea. And there was someone beside him who said to me, "Do you see him? The road he took will take him to the depths!"

At the same time, I also saw that I was at St. Basil's, up in the skete. I saw a dreadful fire burning the entire skete. So I said with grief, "Who lit this fire which will burn down the entire skete?" Then someone told me, "So-and-so lit it, trying to support his way of thinking!" This is why I am telling you that his way of thinking is not in accordance with God, but a trap of the enemy from the right.

I do not seek anything material from you; I do not need your material things, so you can't say that I love you for my own profit. Rather, I tell you these things for the sake of your souls because I sincerely love them. I love everyone. I am so agreeable that even though there are so many different ways of thinking, each person who talks with me thinks that I am on his side. I do not drive anyone to despair, even if I know that he is deluded. Since I realize that he will not listen even if I speak, why should I vex him and grieve myself as well?

I beseech you not to say these things to anyone, just in case he hears about it and sins more instead of being benefited. People around him will say as much as their tongue allows. Then who will have the sin, when we become the cause for them to backbite and gossip about us? Whatever they say about me does not bother me at all—even if they praise me! But for them it is a great sin that weighs down their conscience. Therefore, be careful lest we become the cause for another person's evil. If we are unable to bring him back from delusion, at least we can guard ourselves so that we ourselves are not deluded.

Enough, then, about spiritual counsel. I beseech you to pray with love for the brethren to repent. There is hope that one day they will get well and enter paradise with healthy souls, so that the demons, who tempt everyone in many ways, may be foiled.

ꟓhirtieth Ꝇetter

Without it being the Lord's will,
we neither get sick nor die.

he fear of the Lord is the beginning of wisdom,"[1] says the wise Solomon, and the Fathers agree. And I say to you, "Blessed and thrice-blessed is the man that feareth the Lord."[2]

From this divine fear, faith in God is born. Then a person believes wholeheartedly that since he has completely dedicated himself to God, God in turn assumes all solicitude for him. And besides food and clothing—which, again, God incites him to care for—he has no other cares. But with utter simplicity, he follows the will of the Lord and submits himself to it.

So when this faith takes root, that kind of knowledge is completely abolished which gives rise to doubt about everything, decreases faith, and many times eliminates it (for it has nature on its side, since we were brought up with it). But once faith is victorious after many trials, it turns and gives birth to spiritual knowledge, or rather it is given as a gift, which does not oppose faith, but flies with its wings and explores the depths of mysteries. And these two: faith and knowledge, knowledge and faith, are thenceforth inseparable sisters.

---

[1] Prov. 1:7
[2] cf. Ps. 111:1

So then, let us who are dedicated to God examine now whether we have this faith or, on the contrary, we are dominated by human knowledge.[3] If you leave everything to God, behold that you have acquired faith, and certainly, without a doubt, you will have Him as your helper. So even if you are tried a million times and Satan tempts you in order to dull your faith, choose death a million times and do not comply with human knowledge. And in this manner the door of mysteries will open. Then you will marvel that although you were formerly bound with the chains of human knowledge, now you fly above the earth with divine wings and breathe another air of freedom, which the others lack.

Conversely, if you see that human knowledge reigns in you, and if at the slightest danger you lose your head and despair, know that you still lack faith. Therefore, you do not yet have all your hope in God, and do not yet trust that He is able to save you from every evil. Take care to correct yourself here, as we have said, so that you are not deprived of such a great good.

And now, listen to this story: Once, someone from Switzerland who was a monk for many years came to us because he had three terrible, incurable diseases. He had spent a fortune on medicines, for he was a rich man. Someone had recommended that he come to me and tell me his thoughts; I felt very sorry for him. So I told him that he would get well immediately, if he would only believe that God is able to cure him. Anyway, if I were to write the whole story of what I went through to convince him, I would have to write four pages, because neither would he leave, nor did he want to believe, until finally God intervened and he distinctly heard a voice saying, "Why don't you listen so that you may get well?"

---

[3] vid. 1 Cor. 3:18-20

And in this way he was delivered. I demanded that he eat the opposite of what he was told (he was saying that he would die if he did so) and leave everything to God, laying knowledge aside and following faith; that he eat once a day instead of ten times, as he had been doing. Merely three days were enough for God to test him. I was praying ardently for him. Then at night, I saw in my sleep two fearsome vultures which had grabbed him to devour him, and a snake which had wrapped itself tightly around his neck. He was calling me with wild cries to save him. So then I wrestled with all of them, killed them, and then I woke up.

Then he came to me and said, "I have become entirely well, as I was when I was born!" Indeed, his flesh was renewed as if he were a small child. He had medicines and two cases of syringes. I told him to throw them all down the cliff onto the rocks, which he did. Thenceforth he lived healthily, eating once a day.

So do you see what faith accomplishes? Don't think that I did it. No, I am not at such a spiritual state. It is faith that has the power to do such things.

Listen to another story. Once a nun wrote to me that she was ill and would die if she didn't have an operation. I wrote to her saying exactly the opposite. She wrote back saying that the doctor told her that she would die in so many days if she didn't have an operation. I repeated my request, "Have faith; leave it all to God; prefer death." Later she sent me her response saying that the illness went away.

Do you see? I have experienced this thousands of times. When you put death before you and await it at every moment, it flees far away from you. When you fear death, it constantly pursues you. I buried three people with tuberculosis, nourishing the hope that I would also catch it. After I undressed the corpse, I wore his clothes, but death fled away from me to those who fear it. I have been ill my whole life. I have never had any treatment. I obstinately eat the wrong foods. But death is nowhere in sight.[†]

I write these things to you because you love perfection. The people in the world do not sin by living in accordance with human knowledge, since they do not seek another way.

What I am trying to say with all this is that without the will of the Lord, we neither get sick nor die. Therefore, flee far away from us, O lack of faith.

First of all, once we recognize God as the Creator of every good thing, as our Father, Provider, and Protector, we must believe in Him with all our heart and soul. We must have our hope only in Him, and when we perceive his manifold benefactions, we shall love Him. And when we love God with all our heart as the Creator, then we shall also love our neighbor as ourselves, knowing that we are all brothers—by nature, in Adam; and by grace, in Christ. And therefore a spiritual person should not regard affinity of the flesh, since he has dedicated himself to God, but spiritual affinity. For the flesh, male and female, is for reproduction which we have renounced and ascended higher. Therefore, as spiritual people that we are, we must perceive things spiritually. As for the soul, there is no such thing as a male or female soul, nor a young or old soul; only the grace of Christ over all.

Therefore, I entreat you to set your mind free to behold what a great mystery is hidden in the words I am telling you. Do not confine it to the law, since we are under grace. Let it taste innocent love. Let it fly to the theoria of the only God, our good Father.

Since we are all brothers, the breath of God, the divine inbreathing, and since our life-giving Father is in our midst,

---

[†] Obviously the Elder is not recommending such behavior, but is showing that nothing can happen to us without God allowing it. (see also Mt. 10:29)

all our actions, movements, and thoughts are clearly judged under His eye. And before you even move or think something good or bad, at once the breath, the soul as the inbreathing of God, stirs God. He knows beforehand what you will do, and only afterwards do you make a movement of your soul or body.

Now pay attention to what the prophet says: "I beheld the Lord ever before me."[4] I wonder, are the eyes of your soul always open, or do you think that since you don't see God beside you, He doesn't see you either? Or do you think that you can do something secretly from Him, since your nous is limited? However, He does see you, He is saddened but He overlooks; He reproaches your lack of faith and the darkness of your nous.

Don't you know that Jesus becomes for each person a remedy for every need? That is, He becomes food for the hungry, water for the thirsty, health for the sick, clothing for the naked, a voice for the chanters, assurance for those praying, and everything unto salvation for everyone.

My child, believe that for everything that we may be suffering, Christ is an excellent Physician of both the soul and the body. Just have complete self-denial, perfect faith, and devotion to Him without hesitation.

Since our sweet Jesus is so good, compassionate, and kind, why should you despair? We seek one small thing from Him, and He gives us so much. We ask for one beam of light, and He gives us Himself as all Light, Truth, and Love. So humble yourself and rest all your hope in Him.

Believe me, for I tell the truth: Ever since I became a monk, every time I got sick, I absolutely never took care of myself; nor did I let anyone care for my physical health, but I placed all my hope in the unmercenary Physician.[†]

---

[4] Ps. 15:8

[†] The Elder later modified his opinion of health care, as is evident in his Forty-ninth Letter.

I was tested so much in the beginning, that my whole back and all the way down got full of boils the size of lemons. I became like wood, unable to bend over. But I kept fighting with the illness, without at all changing my undershirt or any other piece of clothing. Then I loaded a sack on my back and went around all of the Holy Mountain, until all those boils ruptured and the pus ran all the way down to my feet. And I never changed, as I was saying, but kept fighting and suffering terribly. And my undershirt and clothes became a finger thick from the fluids that ran. A finger could fit in the holes of the wounds. Yet nothing bad happened to me. And to this day, with great joy I welcome whatever illness befalls me, because it might bring upon me the eternal sleep: to be found with the Lord Jesus. But the time has not yet come. In any case, it will come shortly.

Death, which is awesome and dreadful for most people, is a repose for me, something sweet that will relieve me from the afflictions of the world as soon as it comes. And I await it any time now. It is truly awesome; but then again, it is also a great struggle for one to bear all the burdens of the world today, when everyone demands that his neighbor fulfills all the commandments, while ignoring them himself.

This is how our times are. For this reason, patience is required until we breathe our last standing upright. Therefore be brave, and may your soul be strengthened for whatever is to come.

Because of these things and everything else, I have become a corpse. I beg God to take me so that I may rest. I ask your love to pray hard for me. For I have many souls that seek my help.

And believe me: for every single soul that receives my help, I experience the warfare that it has.

Once again I write these things to give you courage so that you do not fear illnesses, even if they make us suffer for life.

Since God is continuously present, why do you worry? For in Him we live and move.[5] We are carried in His arms. We breathe God; we are vested with God; we touch God; we consume God in the Mystery. Wherever you turn, wherever you look, God is everywhere: in the heavens, on the earth, in the abysses, in the trees, within the rocks, in your nous, in your heart. So can't He see that you are suffering, that you are going through tribulations? Tell Him your grievances and you will see consolation, you will see healing which will heal not only the body, but even more so the passions of your soul.

You wrote that you still partake of your "old man."[6] And I tell you that you don't even have the slightest semblance of the new Adam yet; you are all old. When the new Adam begins to be formed in you, I alone shall write to you about the shapes of the formation of the new man, if I am alive.

---

[5] Acts 17:28
[6] cf. Rom. 6:6

Thirty-first Letter

Henceforth the world has died to you, and you have died to the world.

aughter of my Jesus, my beloved child, I hope that you are well, together with the most holy eldress and the entire holy synodia. I received your letter and saw what you wrote. I am glad that you are healthy, but I am not glad about everything you wrote.

That zeal you mentioned is not due to grace. God does not seek from you now this kind of confession of faith you mentioned. Your own lifestyle right there where you live is a million times superior. For if you endure the daily ascesis, every time you coerce your soul to bear a cold word, a derision, a reproach, you become a confessor. Every time you have patience, you receive a crown, and it is considered by God to be a daily martyrdom for you. My witness is the truth at hand. All those things you wrote me are an artifice of the evil one to disband the monasteries so they won't bother him!

But seriously! If salvation were out there in the world for us, then why did we leave everything? Why did we renounce it with frightful oaths when we put on the holy schema? Read the promises you gave then and see if they agree with the things you wrote.

Didn't you promise, my child, that you would deny the world and all things of the world? Didn't you say that henceforth you would blot out the "old man"[1] so that God, too, would blot out your previous life? When the priest asked you, didn't you say that you would remain in the monastery until your last breath? So where are those words now? Or perhaps since your mind is turbid with thoughts, you don't remember them, and you think that Christ has forgotten them too? But angels wrote down every word you said that hour, and you will be accountable on Judgment Day.

So then, imitate those holy souls around you who bear the yoke of Christ and endure the confinement within the monastery. Behold, the fruit is within you.

The bee produces honey in the darkness, so that no one sees her. If you bring her out into the light, you destroy her. If you put her in a glass jar, she coats it and darkens it. Behold an example for our monastic life.

Don't you see how the eldress and the rest of the sisters made progress? Look at me also, the least of monks, who has enclosed himself in a tomb and does not care to learn if the others are alive or how they live.[†] I see my soul dead, and I moan over it. I suffer, worrying about nine souls that obstruct my path, for I bear responsibility for their souls and am in pain. In bygone days, monks were strengthened because they had much grace and good examples in abundance.

But as for you, you have everything there you need to become good. Emulate them and be at peace. Emulate their virtue and this is enough for you. And if you want to surpass them, the way is to become a zero. For this is the height of virtue and spiritual ascent: to descend to zero. It is not to grow

[1] cf. Rom 6:6

[†] This statement does not suggest an absence of Christian love, but it is an expression of the ideal of monastic renunciation. (See also Mt. 10:34-37 and *The Ladder*, Step 3:16.)

wings, to fly, to leave the monastery; but to become dirt for them to trample upon. For out of nothing you became dust. Behold your origin. Don't forget from where you were taken. You are clay; don't be haughty. You are mud; you deserve to be used as plaster for walls in the outhouse. Don't hate, don't grumble, don't backbite the other clay. For all of us are fit for plaster.

If you bear this truth, it will be well with you. If you knew this purpose of yours, even if the monastery were full of snakes, you would say, "It is better that I be eaten by snakes than to exit the door of My Repentance.† My mother is now the Panagia, and my second mother is the blessed eldress. As siblings I have the saints and the sisters of the monastery."

The monastery is an earthly paradise, and all of you ought to become rational flowers giving off a spiritual fragrance. If you exert yourselves you will be saved eternally. You will become sweet-smelling myrrh, fragrant incense— and what is more precious and more acceptable before the Holy Trinity?

Well, my daughter, henceforth the world has died to you, and you have died to the world.[2] Do not desire to become a pillar of salt like the wife of Lot who turned back.[3] Do not make pretexts with excuses in sins,[4] or you will suffer what the monks went through at the monastery of St. Sergios, as St. Nilos has written. I don't know if you have read it. Anyway, it is not the time for me to write about it now.

You wrote about the mother who is grieving to death. However, I didn't understand very clearly what you wrote. Who gave the promise: the mother for her daughter to

---

† "My Repentance" is what a monk calls the monastery where he was tonsured and vowed to complete the remaining time of his life in "peace and repentance."

[2] cf. Gal. 6:14

[3] vid. Gen. 19:26

[4] Ps. 140:4

become a nun, or the daughter for herself? Anyway, whatever the case, she should not be sad. She is not accountable to God since He, as Lord of life and death, took her daughter so soon and suddenly. The Lord would seek an account if the daughter lived and did not fulfill the promise she had given. Now Christ the Crown-giver will reward the good intentions. Nevertheless, they should do a *Forty-day Liturgy** for the name of the girl, and give as much as they can to charity.

Likewise, the mother of the hieromonk should not despair. Yes, it was wrong for her son to leave his place of Repentance without a blessing and to be in the world now, but the prayers and tears of a mother have great power before the Lord. Instead of grieving, she should pray. And in time, God will enlighten him.

God's actions are not like those of us men. With all patience, He gradually works out the salvation of all those who want to be saved. I believe that here, too, He will not let the sighs and tears of the mother be in vain. Only he who has seen and known the knowledge and grace of God knows how far the thoughts of men are from the way God judges the world. If He Who loves man only receives into His hands man's repentance, He knows how to arrange everything else most wisely for salvation.

As for Abba Isaac whom you quoted, he does not only say that God will put him who struggles together with those who have reached perfection, if he exerts himself yet fails to reach perfection because he was overtaken by death; but he also says that He will put his relics along with the martyrs' if he falls in the battle and dies.

As for the father who thanks his child for the light he is sent with the lamp of the monastic schema; that is the truth. The parents are blessed by their children, if they are saved.

And the luminous life of the children becomes a lamp for the parents—they are given grace. The grace of monastics benefits up to seven generations of their family, and many are saved through us, if our life is pleasing to the Lord. Therefore, we must struggle until death with patience and obedience.

So then, have perfect faith in the blessed eldress and endure afflictions without grumbling, so that you may be counted worthy of the good things of the Lord, and so that others may be saved because of you, when you become as Christ the Judge of the contest wants.

One time, I saw the priest who baptized all of us back in our village. He was a holy man. He lived in virginity and gave many alms. In my sleep he said to me, "When I was alive I thought that only Liturgies free souls from Hades. But now that I have died, I indeed see that the prayers you say also pull out condemned souls." Therefore, do not cease praying for departed souls, for the merciful God looks for a reason and an opportunity to save a soul.

Thirty-second Letter

Faintheartedness is the mother of impatience.

 ehold once again I, your humble father, come to arouse your eagerness with my words.

Arise, my child, from the sleep of your indolence. Listen to me and sleep no longer. Awaken and shake off the drowsiness of your despondency. Take up your weapons once again and stand bravely against your enemies. Fight patiently. Do not turn your back. Fight face to face. It is better to fall in the battle victoriously than to be defeated.

O wonder of wonders! People in the world struggle all night long to catch two little fish. Then they eat them or sell them and continue on their way. They do not hope for anything else from them. And their life ends after being tormented with this job all their life.

But we wretches are pitiful because of our great ignorance, since Christ feeds us for free and rewards us a hundredfold. We work one day and He pays us for a hundred; that we may eternally rejoice and exult in His kingdom; that we may be with our Panagia as her true children, in the likeness of the holy angels in extraordinary light and inexpressible joy! But since we senseless ones do not see the visible gain—those few little fish or anything else transitory—we lose our patience.

If we had been born slaves, we would get beatings and slaps every day. But now we don't even bear a cold word from a weak brother. O foolish and uncircumcised in heart! At a small temptation, we are quick to deny Him. We prefer eternal separation from Christ and eternal union with Satan, rather than humbly enduring a momentary trial!

Now what are these words, O slothful and beloved soul, which you say in times of faintheartedness, other than foolishness? When you say, "I will find a way to kill myself and end my life!" O blindness and tangible darkness! Will you kill yourself, or will you unite yourself eternally with the devil? Will you end your life, or will you descend forever into Hades? And do you not fear, O cowardly soul, eternal damnation and separation from our sweetest Jesus, the Life and the Light?

Oh, how much Christ the Master is saddened, how much the Bridegroom of souls is embittered when, at the slightest temptation, we put a crown of thorns upon His head! As soon as we call Him our Bridegroom during our *tonsure,** at once we demand a divorce! Isn't this the gall of denial mixed with the bitter vinegar of impatience? Let us be cautious, my child, because in this way we greatly grieve our sweetest Jesus and unexpectedly gladden the malicious devil.

Oh! Who will give me fountains of tears and inconsolable grief to weep day and night for my fainthearted brethren!

I pray, my child, that you will walk aright from now on and be very careful that no similar temptation befalls you or another sister. Be careful, children of Christ, for these things happen to everyone. Do not be hardened, but have perfect obedience and love towards the blessed eldress so that her prayers may protect you in times of temptation.

Wherever there is hardness and pride, there also are disobedience and scandals. Wherever there is obedience and humility, God rests. The Holy Fathers say, "Pride goeth before a fall, and humility before grace." Whereas faintheartedness is the mother of impatience. Have you seen a man, and especially a monk, without patience? He is a lamp without oil whose light will soon go out.

From faintheartedness are born many offspring: grumbling, disobedience, depravity, complaining, blasphemy, despair, and other such things. Pride and hardness are true sisters from which millions of offspring are born, which all together lead to the soul's destruction. But humility and perfect obedience abolish all of them with one blow.

So my child, attend to blessed obedience. Submit yourself completely, because now that the enemy has learned that you are easily defeated, he will go for a while and then return. Don't let him find you off guard and knock you down. Get ready. When he comes, make him understand that you have as a guardian both the power of Christ and the prayers of all, here and there.

Do not grow accustomed to falling easily, because with every fall the fortress walls of your soul crumble, and thenceforth it is easier for the enemy to enter, until he renders the one defeated completely captive.

Do you remember what I wrote you when you first went to the monastery? I said, "After four years, I want to hear you say the things you are saying now." And, "As you see the sisters now, so should you still see them then." If you look through my first letters, you will find these words written there.

So now once again I tell you: be careful. Be careful, because it is still the beginning and you can still make a good start. But if you do not compel yourself now, there will come a time when you will not be able to do what you are presently neglecting, even if you want to. You put in your mite, and God will put in His million talents.

Throw yourself down. Become dirt for them to step on. Become like Abbacyrus.[1] Crush your heart and weep with pain of soul, so that God may pity you. I also weep every day, but Christ seeks your tears as well.

So wake up and shake off the faintheartedness. Knock your enemy down once, so that you learn to defeat him with the Lord's strength. Victory is patience, victory is humility, victory is obedience.

In addition, know this: the tempter is accustomed to fighting combatants artfully. After he fights them in all different ways and cannot defeat them, he brings lifelong illnesses upon them. And many times the entire body aches, and the whole person becomes one big wound, and a constant "ouch!" However, the end and repose are then at hand.

---

[1] vid. *The Ladder of Divine Ascent* 4:29

ᘔhirty-third ᘔetter

***I cannot describe to you how much our
Panagia likes chastity and purity.***

 y child, I have seen all that you wrote
about, and I have gone through them
time and again. I also wrote a book
about these changes, so that in case
someone experiences them he will not
despair. But do not remain idle as you
are now. It takes forcefulness; it takes
a struggle; it takes extreme humility and perfect obedience. So
don't just stand there, but cry out, "My dear Christ! My dear
Panagia!" Do not become enervated and do not accept
thoughts from the devil. Cry out to Christ continuously. Do not
let the tempter have time to create the thought in your nous.
Before he has time to do so, you should destroy it with the
prayer. When you allow the filth that the enemy throws in you
to remain inside you, well, in a little while he will bury you
in it. Afterwards, what a struggle it takes to be cleansed!
Therefore, exert yourself. It takes toil and pain; it is no joke!
Your heart will drip blood. Bitterness and venom will you
drink, and thus you will receive freedom and taste sweetness.

Do not underestimate the struggle. You must keep crying
out like a lunatic, "Save me, my dear Jesus! All-holy

Theotokos, help me!" Your tongue should run like a motor,[†]
"Lord Jesus Christ, have mercy on me! Lord Jesus Christ,
have mercy on me! Lord Jesus Christ, have mercy on me!"
And when you get tired, a consolation will come to you that
you have never tasted before. However, if you remain idle and
negligent as you are now, you will not be cured unto the ages.

A man who sits at home cannot simultaneously be travelling to Constantinople, and a monk who neglects the prayer
does not become worthy of the heavenly Jerusalem.

So arise! Put in your mite so that the grace of God puts in
a thousand talents. Show your good intentions. Turn your face
away from the enemy. Why do you let the demons commit
adultery with your soul?

Where is your humility when you feel and say that everyone wrongs you and that only you are good? Humility is,
when the other person is at fault, for us to do a metanoia to
him saying, "Forgive me, my brother, I am sorry!" before he
has time to seek forgiveness. This should not seem difficult
and burdensome to you. It is nothing in comparison to what
Christ the Master did for us. Before the angels He stooped
down and did a metanoia from heaven to earth; "He bowed
the heavens and came down"[1] —God to men! Whereas you
turn the world upside–down so that you don't say one
"sorry"! So then, where is your humility? When you humble
yourself, everyone will seem saintly to you; when you are
proud, everyone will seem bothersome and bad.

What is more filthy than pride and what is more malodor-
ous than the foul demons? Yet you tolerate them, and they
defile you. You let them enter easily, and they ruin your
fences, but let's see how they will leave! You can easily accept
obscene and unclean thoughts, but let's see how you will be
cleansed afterwards! There is nothing God hates more than

[†] The Elder always stressed the importance of saying the prayer out loud as
an aid to keep the mind from wandering.

[1] Ps. 17:9

the illicit sensual filth of the body. When a person commits adultery with obscene thoughts, he thoroughly reeks like a dead dog. Whereas when a person struggles to keep his body pure and his nous chaste from filthy thoughts, his life and his prayer ascend like fragrant incense to the heavens.

I have seen in practice what I am telling you. There is no sacrifice to God more fragrant than chastity of the body which is obtained with a bloody and dreadful struggle. I have much to say about this blessed chastity, the fruit of which I have tasted and eaten. But neither you nor your sisters are able to bear now what I would say. Only one thing shall I tell you now: when such people change, even their clothes give off a fragrance that spreads throughout the entire house as if a refreshing vial of myrrh had been opened. This is a sign from God of blessed chastity and their most holy virginity.

Therefore, force yourselves to purify your soul and body. Do not accept filthy thoughts at all, and you will see what I am telling you, and then you will certainly be persuaded by my words. Test everything I have written to you so far, and you will find in practice that I am telling the truth from experience.

Wherever there is obedience, humility, and struggling, the demons can never take a person captive. Hardness, disobedience, and pride give birth to despondency and negligence. Then all the demons come and turn the soul of that person into a dunghill and a stable. And they do not relent until they make him responsible for new and old sins, and totally captive.

So exert yourself, my child, along with all the other sisters. For if you are negligent, you will of necessity undergo bad and awful things. But if you exert yourselves, you will save yourselves eternally. You will become fragrant incense and precious myrrh. You will truly become a rational sacrifice, pleasing to the Lord.

I cannot describe to you how much our Panagia likes chastity and purity. Since she is the only pure Virgin, she wants and loves everyone to be like that. As soon as we cry out to her she rushes to our help. You don't even finish saying, "All-holy Theotokos, help me!" and at once, like lightning, she shines through the nous and fills the heart with illumination. She draws the nous to prayer and the heart to Love. Many times the entire night passes in tears and sweet cries, singing praises to her and especially to Him Whom she carries.

So exert yourselves, be silent, pray, be obedient, and humble yourselves so that you find every good thing. You have the blessed eldress who is a fragrance of Christ. Don't sadden her, don't talk back, keep silence and the prayer, and let her have her peace. For after she dies and you lose her and are left as pelicans in the wilderness,[2] then her worth will be evident, but it will be too late for you then.

In conclusion, I beseech you once more, my little child: exert yourself and lose no time. Don't just tire me by making me write, but arise and trample upon your enemies. Become dirt for people to step on, and be obedient for the life of your soul.

---

[2] cf. Ps. 101:7

ᗠhirty-fourth ᖾetter

My child, these changes happen to all of us.

Athos

fter a long time, at last I received your letter today, my child. During this period I was rather sad because recently you were not well, and I had scolded you a little. This is why I felt sorrow and pain in my poor heart. Anyway, I rejoiced a little today, hearing that you came to your senses somewhat and have begun to repair your little boat so that you may sail towards the calm and quiet harbor of dispassion.

Truly, my child, great is the struggle against the passions, but by the grace of God, everything can be accomplished. With His help, the impossible become possible. My child, these changes happen to all of us, but it takes patience and perseverance in the struggle. All these abnormalities—the agitation, the hatred, the aversion, the fierce movements of the passions—are all from Satan. They all must be repelled with force, with pain, with affliction, right from the start, before they enter and seize the provisions and cut off the water from the outside and starve the soul from the heavenly dew. Do you see? When you *consent** to the thoughts that the evil one sows, then your boldness in prayer is immediately cut off.

Behold how he has cut off your water supply from the outside, as well as the provisions for your soul, and now in a few days you will starve to death. Whereas in the beginning, you can repulse them with a little bit of rebuttal. But you are negligent and sluggish and pay close attention to what the demons say. Once they enter, they will drag us captive.

Be careful and don't trust yourself even if you think they have left. The prayers of your elders drive them away temporarily, but they will come back again. Grace restrains them so that the soul takes courage, but once more they will return.

However, in times of peace don't be negligent, but pray, correct yourself, prepare yourself for war. Give yourself courage. Be patient. Have perfect obedience. In this manner, you will certainly be delivered from them some day. But it requires a great struggle and much caution.

For every step forward that a monk takes, he must shed many tears, drops of blood, and spend much time. Then the devil comes, the primeval evil, gets a crowbar under him and turns everything upside-down, if grace and the prayers of others do not act in time. And then, back to square one again—bloodshed once again.

Therefore, it takes patience. Don't be despondent. Don't be fainthearted. Be patient so that grace may protect you. You have many supporting you. Every step of yours towards cheerfulness cheers me as well. Your resurrection resurrects my soul, too.

From myself and from my own torments, I am quite familiar with the temptations of the eldress. She suffers and endures greatly, bearing your burdens every day because of her responsibility before God. She tastes bitterness every day with excessive pain, and she only rejoices when all of you walk along the good path.

Now you see that grace has come again. Be careful, because it will leave again. And when it leaves, be brave, patient, and perfectly obedient. It will return again. I told you that it would come at Nativity. It came but did not remain because it did not find zeal in you. Now it has come, but again it will leave in order to cleanse you from the passions. This will happen until you become the way the Lord wants you to be, so that His grace may find a place and a way to stay. So exert yourself in the struggle. Don't get lazy, and don't let time pass, for you will not recover the time that you waste idly every day. You will have to give an account for all the days and hours and moments of your life. Man is not meant only to run, but he should also count the miles on the road. On the other hand, he should not remain behind out of negligence, either.

In addition, learn this: with love towards Christ and the Panagia, you obtain more watchfulness and theoria than with other struggles. Everything else is also good, when done properly, but love surpasses them all. So when you venerate her icon, kiss it fervently with tears as if she were alive. "My dear Mother," cry out, "My Panagia, save me for I am lost if you leave me! O Lord my God, have mercy on me, through the intercessions of Thine All-immaculate Mother and of all Thy saints!"

And when you say such things and see so much love that you want to keep kissing the icon, this is a sign that she is returning the kiss. I am unable to kiss the icon of the Panagia just once and then part from her. But when I approach her, she attracts me like a magnet. And I have to be alone, because I want to keep kissing her for hours. A certain living breath fills my soul, and I overflow with a grace that does let me leave. Love, *eros** of God, burning fire! As soon as you enter the church, it overtakes you— when it is a miracle-working icon—and it gives off such a fragrant waft that you remain in ecstasy for hours without being in yourself, but in a fragrant paradise.

Our Panagia gives so much grace to those who keep their body pure. For it seems to me that she loves purity dearly. This is why I fought against the flesh more than any other passion. And I was given the gift of purity: the gift of not differentiating between women and men. The passion is not roused within me at all. By the Lord's grace, I received the gift of purity, in full knowledge of what I was receiving.

I write these things to you, my child, and to your sisters so that you exert yourselves and imitate me. Otherwise, there would be no reason to reveal my spiritual state, nor do I want you to praise me. But since I, as your true brother in Christ, have all of you within my soul, I wish to help you as much as I can. Let each one of you try it out. If you exert yourselves, you will see how much our Panagia loves us.

One evening as I was kissing her icon, I became tired. So I sat down in a stall and dozed off a little. Then she came to me in bodily form—not as an image—and was tenderly kissing me. I was filled with ineffable joy and fragrance. And that heavenly Infant caressed my entire face while I kissed His plump little hands as if He were real. And you would think that it was not a dream, but a perception of some other life, unknown and unexperienced by those who do not know such things.

ᘘhirty-fifth ᘚetter

*The prayer stops, the bodily members cease
to move, and only the nous is in
theoria within an extraordinary light.*

y beloved little child and all the sisters in Christ according to rank, rejoice and be healthy in the Lord.

I begin once more to speak into ears which desire and seek to hear. "Ask," says our sweet Jesus, "and it shall be given you; seek, and ye shall find; knock, and it shall be opened unto you."[1] I honor your good intentions; I praise your zeal; I appreciate your love, and I emulate you.

So, listen to me once more.

First of all, the method of beginning your prayer that you mention, my child, is very good. With such thoughts you are able to keep your mind from wandering—by thinking that the prayers of the elder and the eldress ascend like a pillar of fire and that they converse noetically with God. When the nous thinks and believes such things, it stops for a moment, the prayer is sweetened, and tears start to trickle. Then that grace which is found in beginners, which you mentioned, approaches and like a mother teaches her young how to walk. When

---

[1] Mt. 7:7

she goes away and leaves them, they seek her. They cry, shout, and look for her. After a little while she comes back, only to withdraw once more. Again they cry and shout; again she returns. Until she rears us, there is no way for her to stay with us because our passions prevent her.

The passions are a hard material. Ural mountains! Thousands of feet high! Grace is like the sun. The sun rises, but the shadow of the mountains does not allow it to warm the entire noetic man. As soon as a beam finds him, he is immediately set on fire with joy. The rest of his soul, though, is still beneath the shadow of the passions, and the demons are able to act as soon as grace retracts. Many times they obstruct it as clouds obstruct the sun's light, for the shadow of the passions raises steam that obscures the little beam of light just dawning. This steam is the thoughts of despair you wrote about. Cowardice, fear, impudence, profanities, and other such things wither the soul and deprive it of its boldness towards God.

Every thought that brings despair and heavy sorrow is from the devil. It is the steam of the passions, and you must expel it at once with hope in God, with confession to the eldress, and with the prayers of those older than you, by thinking that they are praying and entreating God for you.

A small sorrow mixed with joy, tears, and consolation in the soul is from the grace of God. Throughout our life, it guides us towards repentance whenever we err. A sin drives away boldness towards God, but repentance brings it back at once. Grace does not bring despair, but it continually brings to repentance a person who has fallen. On the other hand, the words of the demons bring despair at once; they blight him like hail falling upon delicate little leaves that have just sprouted.

Now pay attention to this little lesson of "praxis":

When you see grace acting and your soul rejoicing and tears

falling effortlessly (because of the mercies that God has given you), if you are praying, be still. If you are standing, don't move. If you are sitting, remain seated. If you are saying the prayer, keep saying it without any childish thoughts, and accept the "rain" of the Spirit for as long as it comes upon you. For even if it comes while you are working, if you get up to pray, it stops. It wants you to remain wherever it found you, so that you do not become its master. It wants to teach you never to trust in yourself, as long as you are in this life.

The rainfall of grace of a single day provides enough water for the things planted in the soul for the entire period that grace leaves.

The grace of the priesthood is one thing, the grace of the great schema is another, the grace of the Mysteries is different, and the action of grace in ascesis is also different. They all spring from the same source, but each one differs from the other in eminence and glory. The grace of repentance, which acts in those who struggle, is a *patristic** inheritance. It is a divine transaction and exchange in which we give dust and receive heaven. We exchange matter for the Spirit. Every drop of sweat, every pain, every ascesis for God is an exchange: a loss of blood, and an influx of the Spirit.[†] The magnitude of this grace depends on how much a person can contain, in proportion to how much his own vessel can hold. This grace of praxis is also called purifying grace.

Now then, "illumination" follows "praxis." Illuminating grace is the second stage. That is, once a struggler has been trained well with the grace of praxis and has fallen and risen countless times, he is given the enlightenment of knowledge and clarity of the nous, which perceives the truth. He sees things as they are, without artifices and methods and human syllogisms. Everything stands naturally in its true state.

[†] This (and similar passages) must be understood metaphorically, as Abba Longinos says in *The Sayings of the Desert Fathers*: "Give blood and receive the Spirit."

However, many trials and painful changes are encountered before arriving at this point. But here he finds peace in his thoughts and rest from the temptations.

Illumination is followed by interruptions in the prayer and frequent theorias, rapture of the nous, cessation of the senses, stillness, profound silence of the bodily members, and union of God and man into one. This is the divine exchange in which, if one endures temptations and does not stop struggling along the way, one exchanges the material for the immaterial....

Therefore, run behind the heavenly Bridegroom, deers of my Jesus.[2] Smell the noetic myrrh. Make your life—your soul and body—fragrant with chastity and virginity. I do not know of anything else that pleases our sweet Jesus and His All-pure Mother more than chastity and virginity. Whoever desires to enjoy their great love should see to it that he makes his soul and body pure and chaste. Thus will he receive every heavenly good.

Now, let me explain what the phrase "interruption of the prayer" means, when grace abounds in a person.

The grace of "praxis" is likened to the radiance of the stars; whereas the grace of illumination is like the full moon; but the perfecting grace of theoria is like the midday sun traversing over the horizon; for the Fathers have divided the spiritual life into three categories.

So when grace abounds in a person and he knows all that we have written, he attains great simplicity; his nous expands and has great capacity. Just as you tasted that drop of grace when much joy and exultation came upon you, it comes again in the same manner when the nous remains in prayer. But much more comes, like a subtle breeze, like a mighty gust[3] of fragrant wind. It overflows throughout the body, and the

---

[2] cf. Song of Solomon 1:4

[3] cf. Acts 2:2

prayer stops; the bodily members cease to move, and only the nous is in theoria within an extraordinary light. A union of God and man occurs. Man is unable to distinguish himself. It is just like iron: before it is thrown into the fire it is called iron, but once it ignites and becomes red-hot, it is one with the fire. It is also like wax which melts when it approaches fire; it cannot remain in its natural state.

Only when the theoria has passed does he return to his former state. Whereas during theoria, he is not functioning in this world. He is totally united with God. He thinks that he has neither a body nor a hut. He is entirely rapt. Without a body he ascends to heaven! Truly great is this mystery, for one sees things that a human tongue cannot express.

When this theoria has passed, he has such a deep humility that he cries like a small child, wondering why the Lord gives him such blessings, since he himself does nothing. He then obtains so much awareness of who he is that if you were to ask him, he would say that he considers himself destitute and unworthy to exist in this life. And the more he thinks like this, the more he is given.

"It is enough!" he cries out to God, and grace abounds even more. He becomes the son of the King. And if you were to ask:

"Whose are these things you are wearing?"

"My Lord's," he answers.

"And the bread and food you eat?"

"My Lord's."

"The money you carry?"

"My Lord's."

"What do you have of your own?"

"Nothing.

"I am dirt, I am mud, I am dust.

"If you lift me up, I stand.

"If you throw me down, I fall.

"If you take me up, I fly.

"If you toss me, I hit myself on the ground.

"My nature is nothing."

He never has enough of saying this. And what is this "nothing"? It is what existed before God created the heaven and the earth: nothing. This is the beginning of our existence. We come from clay; this is the raw material we are made of. And our power? It is the divine inbreathing, the breath of God.

So receive, O God, Lover of good desires and Creator of every good thing, receive the divine inbreathing which You breathed into our face, giving us thus a living spirit, and we shall decompose into clay once more.

Therefore, what hast thou, O proud man, that thou didst not receive? Now if thou hast received it, why dost thou glory as if thou hadst not received it?[4] Acknowledge, lowly soul, your Benefactor and be careful not to usurp things belonging to others—things of God—as your own accomplishments. Realize, wretched soul, your existence, be aware of your ancestry. Don't forget that you are a foreigner here and that everything is foreign! Now, if God the sweet Benefactor gave you something, render it with a clear conscience, "Thine own of Thine own."

If you have ascended to the heavens and seen the natures of the angels and heard the voices of the divine Powers, if you theologize and teach, if you have defeated the wiles of the demons, if you write and speak and do things, all are a gift of God.

So say to your Lord, "Receive, O my sweet zephyr, my Jesus, 'Thine own of Thine own'!" And then—oh, then!—my soul! What things you will see when the treasures of God

---

[4] cf. 1 Cor. 4:7

open and He says to you, "Receive everything, my son, for you proved to be a faithful and good ruler"![5]

---

[5] cf. Mt. 25:21

Thirty-sixth Letter

Circular prayer within the heart has no danger of delusion.

ay the God and Lord of all Who dwells in the heavens, Who gives us breath and life and everything, and constantly cares for our salvation, send forth into your holy souls the comforting Spirit; may He enlighten your nous as He enlightened the Disciples of our Savior; may He shine the light of His divine radiance upon your entire spiritual and noetic being; may your whole heart burn with divine eros as did Cleopas's, and may it leap for joy learning of the conception of the new Adam, and the utter destruction of the old Adam along with all his passions. Then, in this manner, tears will continuously flow every moment like a fountain streaming forth sweetness. Amen.

Today, my little child, I received your letter and saw what you wrote, and I shall answer your questions. The method of noetic prayer is as your holy eldress tells you. *Circular* prayer* within the heart has no danger of delusion ever. The other method or methods are dangerous, because a fantasy can easily approach them, and then delusion enters the nous.

O how dreadful is the delusion of the nous! And how imperceptible! Let me write a little about it for your information. I was very daring with these things and examined every kind of prayer. I tried out everything, because when grace approaches a person, his nous—that "shameless bird" as Abba Isaac calls it—seeks to penetrate everywhere, to try out everything. It begins with the creation of Adam and ends up plunging into depths and soaring to such heights that if God did not set any boundaries, it would not return.

So, this method of prayer of the heart is a method belonging to "praxis" which we employ to keep the nous in the heart. And when grace overflows, it raptures the nous into theoria, and the heart burns with divine eros and is all afire with love. Then the nous is completely united with God. It is transformed and melts like wax before the fire or like iron assimilated with fire. Iron's nature does not change, but as long as it is in the fire, it is one with it. But when the flame withdraws, it returns to its natural hardness.

This is called theoria. Then tranquillity reigns in the nous and the entire body is calm. At this point, a person can pray both with words and with improvised prayers and ascend to theoria, without enclosing his nous in his heart.

For we pray noetically so that grace may come. When grace is present, the nous does not wander. And when the nous stands still, it employs all the kinds of prayer; it tries out everything.

So then, the method of prayer which they are using is not delusion; however, it can easily turn into delusion because their nous is simple. It has not been purified, so it accepts fantasies instead of theorias.

Take, for example, a spring by the seashore that wells up clean water. Suddenly a storm breaks out, the sea rises, and our little spring is polluted with sea water. No matter how clever you are, you will not be able to separate the sea water from the spring's water. The same thing happens with the nous.

Now pay attention to what I shall say: the demons are spirits. Therefore, they are akin to and can be assimilated with our spirit, the nous. The nous is the purveyor of the soul, for it brings every appearance and perception of a noetic movement to the heart, which in turn filters it and gives it to the intellect. Therefore, the nous can be deceived just as the spring was polluted in the example. That is, the unclean spirit stealthily pollutes the nous, which in turn, as usual, gives whatever it has to the heart. If the heart is not pure, it gives the murk to the mind, and then the soul is darkened and blackened, constantly accepting fantasies henceforth instead of theorias. In this manner, all the delusions arose and all the heresies occurred.

But when a man is filled with grace, is always cautious, and never becomes overconfident or trusts in himself, but rather has constant fear throughout his life, then when the evil one approaches, he notices some anomaly—a certain disparity occurs. And then his nous, heart, intellect, and all the strength of his soul, seek the One Who can save him. He seeks Him Who brought everything to existence out of nothingness and scrutinizes everything; Him Who is able to divide the waters from the waters.[1] And when you fervently call upon Him with copious tears, the deception is revealed, and you learn how to avoid delusion. Once you have experienced such things many times, you become a "practiced" man. Then you endlessly glorify and thank God Who opens our nous to recognize the traps and wiles of the evil one so that we may escape them.

---

[1] cf. Gen. 1:6

Truly I tell you that I have entered into all the lairs of the enemy, and after a harsh combat one-on-one, I emerged victorious by the grace of the Lord. And now, if anyone is ill, I am able by the grace of God to free him from his sickness of thoughts and from his illness of delusion, as long as he obeys me. For when someone gripped by delusion obeys someone else, it is possible for him to be delivered from it, and for the evil one to lose control of him. This is why the devil advises and persuades him not to believe anyone anymore and never to obey anyone, but henceforth to accept only his own thoughts and trust only in his own discernment. Lurking within this haughty attitude is that huge ego, the Luciferian pride of the heretics and of all who are deluded and do not want to return to the truth. So may our Christ, Who is the true Light, enlighten and guide the steps of each person who wants to approach Him.

As for all of you, if you love noetic prayer, mourn and weep while seeking Jesus. He will reveal Himself as burning love which consumes all the passions. Then you will become like someone deeply in love whose heart leaps and whose eyes shed tears as soon as he thinks of the person he loves. This is the kind of divine eros and the fire of love that must burn in your heart, so that as soon as you hear or say, "My Lord Jesus Christ, sweet love! My dearly sweet Mother, All-holy Virgin!" tears should run.

All the saints wrote many praises to our Panagia. But I, the poor one, have found no words more elegant or sweet to describe her, than to cry out to her at every moment: "My dear Mother! My dear, sweet Mother! When my soul departs may it come into thy hands, and through them may it be given to its Creator, thine Only-begotten Son. We desire nothing else, our dear, sweet Mother, except to give up our soul amidst that flaming love, at a time when the divine eros is afire; when our soul is on fire and the nous stops and breathes a fragrant zephyr in a gentle breeze and is covered by the cloud;[2] where the senses cease, and our Beloved, Eros, Love, and Life, our eternally sweet Jesus reigns."

Therefore, little children of the heavenly Father and heirs of His kingdom, run, hasten, weep, rejoice, shed tears of love. Sink your nous in Him Who sank His body into the earth to save us. Our sweet Jesus descended so that we may ascend. He died and rose in order to raise us. Rejoice and leap for joy, for we have been blessed to become His children, to enjoy His eternal blessings, and to rejoice together even here in His infinite love.

As a brilliant light shining to those in darkness do we behold the holy Virgin

---

[2] cf. Ex. 20:21

Thirty-seventh Letter

***Out of my love for you and for the benefit of your
souls, I am going to sketch out my life for you.***

gain and again I write to my
beloved daughter as well as to the
entire sisterhood in Christ. I pray
for you full of tears, with pure and
full love in Christ.

Well, you wrote that you have
many temptations. But it is through
them, my child, that the purification
of our soul takes place. Amongst
sorrows and temptations, grace is found as well. There you
will find our sweetest Jesus. It is suitable for you to show that
you love Christ now, when you endure afflictions. Grace will
come once more, and again it will leave. Just don't stop seeking it with tears.

You have before your eyes the eldress and the entire holy
synodia. You have your elder who enters into the sanctuary
behind the veil, and when the divine cloud descends, he
beseeches God. And you have last of all me as well, who,
when the Bridegroom visits, tells Him everything and fervently entreats Him on behalf of you and all the sisters. Many
times He cries out to me, "In your patience possess ye your

souls.[1] Not in impatience. Everything will happen, I hear everything, but all in good time!"

Therefore, my beloved mothers and sisters in the Lord, listen to me once again; hearken unto my words; incline your ears unto parables. Out of my love for you and for the benefit of your souls, I am going to sketch out my life for you, so that you obtain strength and patience; for without patience, it is impossible for a person to triumph. A monk without patience is a lamp without oil.

I am writing with tiny handwriting to save paper, because I do not have any. The paper I do have smells from the pesticide for bedbugs and fleas. A doctor who corresponds with me sent it to me. Please forgive me.

So in a few words I shall tell you briefly:

When I was in the world, I secretly had harsh struggles full of blood. I ate only once every two days and only after 3:00 p.m. The mountains and caves of Penteli knew me as a pelican[2] hungering, crying, seeking salvation. I was testing myself to see if I was able to endure the toils and become a monk on the Holy Mountain. So once I had practiced well enough for a few years, I begged the Lord to forgive me for eating every other day, and I promised that when I would go to the Holy Mountain, I would eat once every eight days, as is written in the lives of the saints.

So when I arrived at the Holy Mountain, I diligently searched but did not find anyone who ate less than once a day. It makes me feel dizzy just to tell you of the tears and the pain in my soul, the cries that could rend mountains; weeping day and night because I did not find the Holy Mountain as the saints describe it.

All the caves of Athos received me as their guest; step by step, like the deer that seek refreshing water to quench their

---

[1] Lk. 21:19
[2] cf. Ps. 101:7

thirst, I sought to find a spiritual father to teach me heavenly theoria and praxis. Finally, after arduously searching for two years and shedding enough tears to fill a baptismal font, I decided to stay with a simple, good, and guileless little elder together with another brother. Well, my elder gave me his blessing to struggle as much as I could and to confess to whichever spiritual father I felt comfortable with. So I practiced perfect obedience.

Before I stayed with my elder, I used to go and sit every afternoon for two or three hours in the wilderness—where only wild beasts are—and cry inconsolably until the dirt became mud from my tears. I would say the prayer orally. I did not know how to say it with my nous, but I kept begging our Panagia and the Lord to grant me the grace to say the prayer noetically, as the saints write in the *Philokalia*. For when I read it, I understood that something existed out there that I did not possess.

Then one day I had many temptations. That whole day I cried out with even more pain. Then in the evening at sunset, hungry and exhausted from crying as I was, I collapsed. Withered and wounded, I was looking at the church of the Transfiguration on the summit, beseeching the Lord. Then it seemed to me that "a mighty gust"[3] of wind came from there which filled my soul with an ineffable fragrance. Immediately, my heart began like a clock to say the prayer noetically. So I got up, full of grace and infinite joy, and went inside the cave. There I bent my chin upon my chest and began to say the prayer noetically. As soon as I said the prayer a few times, I was at once raptured to theoria. Even though I was inside the cave and the door was closed, I found myself outside in heaven, in a wondrous place with profound silence and serenity of soul—perfect repose. I was thinking

---

[3] cf. Acts 2:2

only the following: "My dear God, may I not return anymore to the world, to that wounded life, but please may I remain here." Afterwards, once the Lord had consoled me with as much repose as He wanted, I came to myself once again and found myself inside the cave.

From then on, the prayer did not cease being said noetically within me. Afterwards, when I went to stay with my elder, I began great struggles—always with his blessing.

One night as I was praying, I came to theoria once again and my nous was raptured up to a plain. I beheld monks there lined up for battle according to rank. A tall general approached me and said, "Do you want to enter and fight in the front line?" And I answered that I greatly desire to duel with the Ethiopians on the other side, who were screaming and breathing fire like wild dogs, and whose mere sight aroused fear. Even so, I was not afraid, because I had so much fury that I could have ripped them apart with my teeth. It is true, though, that even as a layman I had a very brave soul. So then the general separated me from the lines where there was a multitude of fathers. After we passed three or four lines in the regiment, he brought me to the front line where there were one or maybe two monks face to face with the ferocious demons. The demons were ready to rush against us, but I was also breathing fire and fury against them. He left me there and added, "I shall not hinder, but shall help whoever desires to fight bravely against them." Then I came to myself once more and reflected, "I wonder, what kind of war is this going to be?"

From then on fierce battles began, in which the demons did not let me have peace day or night. Fierce battles! Not even an hour of peace. But I also raged against them.

I would sit for six hours in prayer and would not allow my nous to leave my heart. The sweat flowed from my body as if from a faucet. I beat myself relentlessly. Pain and tears. Extreme fasting and all-night vigils. Then I finally collapsed.

For eight whole years, every night was a martyrdom. The demons would flee shouting, "He burned us! He burned us!" One night, my neighboring brother happened to visit, and he also heard them and asked who those people shouting were.

However, on the last day, when Christ was about to drive them away, I was already pondering in despair, "Since my body has broken down as if completely dead and since my passions are active as if I were perfectly healthy, the demons have won. Surely they have burned and defeated me, instead of my beating them." Finally, as I was sitting there wounded, despairing, and virtually dead, I perceived that the door opened and someone entered. I did not turn to see who it was, though, but kept saying the prayer. Suddenly I felt that beneath me someone was stimulating me towards sensual pleasure. I turned and saw the scurvy demon whose wounded head stunk! Then like a wild beast I dashed to grab him. However, as soon as I grabbed him—he had hairs like a pig—he disappeared. He left the sensation of his hairs on my fingers and the smell of his stench in my nose. At last, from that moment on, the war ended; all the turmoil ceased. Peace came to my soul, and I was completely freed from the filthy passions of the flesh.

Finally, I went into ecstasy again that night, and I saw a spacious place that was separated by a sea. In this spacious place, traps were strewn everywhere, but they were hidden so that they would not show. I was in a place very high up, and I saw everything as if in a theater. All the monks had to pass through this area. And in the sea was an enraged dragon, a horrifying demon, whose eyes emitted flames. He would stick out his head to see if the monks were getting caught in the traps. As they passed by without fear or caution, one was caught by the neck, another by the waist, another one by the foot, another by the hand. And seeing this, the demon laughed with delight and exultation. But I was greatly distressed and cried, "Oh! Evil demon! The things you do to us, and how you deceive us!" Then I came to myself once again and was inside my little hut.

My rule was to eat a little bread and food once a day in moderation. And even if it was *Pascha** or the day before Lent, we had food only once a day. Furthermore, the entire year we kept vigil all night long.

Elder Arsenios and I received this rule from a holy elder who practiced watchfulness, Father Daniel. There were also many other holy men at that time. He was one of them; he was both a priest and a profound hesychast. He would not let anyone attend his Liturgy. It lasted three and a half or four hours, because he could not say the petitions due to his tears; the ground would turn to mud. That is why he took so long. He was a celebrant for more than fifty years. He never even considered omitting the Divine Liturgy for even a day. During Lent, he did Presanctified Liturgies every day. Finally, he fell asleep in the Lord without ever getting sick in his life.

Another one was Russian. He had ceaseless tears night and day. He lived completely in rapture and was filled with theoria. He surpassed many saints of old. He said, "When you see God, you have nothing to say; you only cry for joy." He also had foreknowledge, for he would know who was coming.

So we received this rule of vigil and fasting from Father Daniel. As I said, he would not accept anyone, but since I was very good at searching out things to learn—or by God's dispensation, since I ardently begged him—he consented and received me. Every time I came, he told me a few words full of grace. I would walk all night to go there alone and see that truly divine spectacle and hear one or two words.

Both of these elders were total recluses. There were also many others. Each one had his own gifts, and all of them were holy, like lilies perfuming the wilderness.

Once I was walking at night under a full moon. I was going to the elder to tell him my thoughts and receive communion. After arriving, I stood a short distance away on top of a rock so that I would not disturb their noetic vigil. It must have been ten o'clock at night. As I was sitting and saying the prayer noetically, I heard the sweet voice of a bird singing, and my nous was raptured by the voice. I followed it to see where that bird was, carefully looking here and there. As I was searching, I entered a beautiful meadow and proceeded on a road as white as snow, with diamond and crystalline walls. Inside the walls were all kinds of golden-hued flowers. So my nous forgot about the bird and was entirely captivated beholding that paradise. As I went farther, I saw a tall, splendid palace, amazing both nous and intellect. In the door stood our Panagia carrying our sweetest Jesus as an infant in her arms. She was all white as snow and glittered. And I approached and kissed her with infinite love. And she embraced me like an infant and said something to me. I cannot forget the love she showed to me as a true Mother. Then without fear or shyness I went up to her, just as I would approach her icon, and did what a small and innocent child would do when he sees his sweet mother. I still do not know how I left her side, for my nous had been entirely engulfed from above. I departed from there on another road and came back to the meadow where there was a beautiful mansion. There they gave me something as a blessing and told me, "Here is the bosom of Abraham; it is customary for us to give a blessing to anyone who passes by here." So I passed by there as well and came to myself, and I was leaning against the rock once again.

After this, I abandoned the purpose for which I had gone, and went down full of joy to venerate the icon of the Panagia in the cave of St. Athanasios the Athonite, because I had great reverence for her. I had stayed there six months in the beginning out of love for her and used to light her oil-lamp. Night and day I meditated on her. So while I was wholly captive that night by divine love, I went down to thank her. And as soon as I went inside and venerated her—I was standing across from her icon and was thanking her—so much fragrance, like a refreshing breath of air, emanated from her sweet mouth that it filled my soul and I remained speechless in a second ecstasy for a long time. And when the chapel's caretaker came up to attend to the oil-lamps, I fled as if I were delirious, just in case he perceived something and started asking me questions.

Similarly, another time I was keeping vigil by myself in my tiny little hut—for Elder Arsenios and I kept vigil every night by ourselves with the prayer and tears—and I came to theoria again. My cell was filled with light as if it were daytime. And three little children, no more than ten years of age, appeared in the middle—with the same stature, the same countenance, the same garb, the same face, the same beauty. I marveled at the sight of them and was entirely enraptured. They were right next to each other, and all together the three of them blessed me, as a priest blesses, while melodically chanting, "As many of you as have been baptized into Christ have put on Christ.[4] Alleluia!" Then they walked up to me and went backwards again without turning around, and then once more they walked up to me while chanting. I wondered, "How did children so small learn to chant and bless so beautifully?" It did not cross my mind that on the Holy Mountain there are no

---

[4] Gal. 3:27

Elder Joseph as a young monk. (circa 1928)

The Huts of Elder Joseph at St. Basil's Skete.

The Elder's cell at St. Basil's

Above: The Chapel of St. John the Forerunner at Small St. Anne's Skete, photographed from the mud hut on the next page.

Left to right: Father Haralambos, Elder Joseph, Father Ephraim. (1959)

The mud hut at Small St. Anne's Skete where the elder lived with his synodia. Photographed from chapel on opposite page.

The Synodia of Elder Joseph. Left to right: Fr. Athanasios (the elder's brother), Fr. Ephraim (later abbot of Philotheou), [...] Fr. Theophylactos, and Fr. Haralambos (later

The Elder with his Synodia in 1959 at New Skete at his last Pascha. Left to right: Fr. Athanasios, Fr. Theophylactos, Fr. Ephraim, Elder Joseph, Fr. Arsenios, Fr. Haralambos. (1959)

The tomb of Elder Joseph.

such children so small and beautiful. Then, just as they had
come, they left to go bless others. I was amazed, and days
passed for the joy to wane, for it to fade from my memory.
However, such things can never be forgotten.

Another time I was very grieved. (And let this be known:
God neither consoles a soul nor does He reveal such things
without dangers and terrible temptations—only when there
is a need, not just simply by chance.) In my immeasurable
sorrow, as at other times, Jesus appeared full of light on the
Cross, bent His head, and reminded me, saying, "Behold
how much I suffered for you!" And all my afflictions dis-
persed like smoke.

What can we say about the great love that the Lord shows
us to save us! But we forget everything at the slightest temptation, yet it is in temptations and afflictions that Christ is
found. Worries and cares about how to make a living cannot
be called afflictions. I mean afflictions for Christ: to be per-
secuted; to suffer in order to save someone else; to struggle
for the love of Christ and to be opposed by temptations; to
suffer misfortunes until death for Christ; to endure insults
and derision unjustly; to be despised by everyone as if deluded. Then the Lord justly consoles and gladdens the soul.

My whole life was a martyrdom. For the most part, I suffer for the others: wanting to save them while they do not listen; crying and praying while they sneer and are overcome by
the tempter. One time when I was in deep sorrow and great
pain, I came to theoria. As I was walking, I found myself in
a plain where the ground was as white as snow. I was completely astonished and wondered, "How did I get to such a
beautiful landscape?" I was looking for a way out, lest someone come and scold me because I had entered without permission. And as I was looking curiously right and left to find

an exit, I saw a basement door and entered there. It was a temple of our Most Holy Theotokos. Some beautiful youths were sitting there dressed with splendid garments and had a red cross on their chests and on their foreheads. One of them, who wore a brighter garment and looked like a general, arose from his throne and said to me,

"Come. We are waiting for you." Then he urged me to sit down.

"Forgive me," I said, "I am unworthy to sit there, but it is enough for me to stand here at your feet." He smiled, left me, and went in front of the *iconostasis** to the icon of the Panagia and said,

"Lady and Mistress of all, Queen of the angels, Immaculate Virgin Theotokos! Show thy grace to this thy servant who suffers so much for thy love, so that he be not engulfed by sorrow." And suddenly, so much brilliance came out from her divine icon and the Panagia looked so beautiful, in full length, that from the extreme beauty—a million times brighter than the sun—I fell down at her feet unable to gaze at her and cried out in tears,

"Forgive me, my dear Mother, because out of ignorance I sadden you!" And crying thus in reality, I came to myself soaked in tears and full of joy.

But now I am only recounting the consolations. I must also recount what those extremely unbearable afflictions were, and those deadly bitter temptations. Every consolation of this kind was preceded by a deadly affliction. Strangulation of the soul and attacks of infernal darkness....

ᗝhirty-eighth ᒪetter

My beloved Mother and all my brothers, relatives, and friends.

y beloved Mother and all my brothers, relatives, and friends: rejoice in the Lord, all of you.

I am quite healthy through the prayers of our parents and grandparents. I rejoice and thank God Who counted me worthy to receive such a great and heavenly gift: to wear the great and angelic schema and to be called a monk, though I am unworthy of such a gift.

May our merciful, compassionate, and good Father be glorified, Who did not loathe me, but had mercy on me like the prodigal son.[1] He singled me out of the world and brought me to the Holy Mountain, to such an earthly paradise.

I yearned and my soul was aflame to hear about your spiritual and bodily health. But the commandment of the Lord that says, "He that loveth father or mother more than me is not worthy of me,"[2] forces me to forget not only parents, brothers, relatives, but even my very own body. All my soul's eros and love yearns to be turned henceforth towards God. Upon Him does it want to gaze and behold, to pray, to seek, to receive the appropriate medicines for

---

[1] vid. Lk. 15:11-32
[2] Mt. 10:37

the cleansing of the heart and the development of the spiritual man.

But now, seeing the tremendous calamity that has befallen the world, and fearing lest the danger of impiety reaches you as well, and fearing that I am wasting the constant vigils that I do for you, I was compelled to resort to the maxim: "Necessity overrides law." And I said, "May I transgress one commandment, so that I might win my beloved ones."

My desire, the burning of my heart, the divine eros that continuously kindles my emotions is how to save souls; how rational sacrifices can be offered to our sweetest Jesus.

My only desire is to see all of my relatives—mother, brothers, their children—all become children of God, a sacred sacrifice pleasing to the Holy God. Oh! But the passions, the wrong diagnosis, the darkening of the soul, do not allow the nous to rise even slightly towards heaven and thus perceive what is profitable for the soul's salvation. But I am not complaining, since the rest of the world is much worse.

I say to myself, "All these brethren of mine in comparison to the others are like angels of God. May the Lord be glorified, since divine love unites all of you, and Christ is in your midst. And wherever Christ is, there are also all the blessings of eternal life and of this present life. For He, the only Truth, said, "Seek ye first my kingdom, and all transient things shall I give unto you in addition."[3] And furthermore He said, "What is a man profited, if he shall gain the whole world, yet remain outside of paradise?"[4]

Now who, awaiting such blessings would not disregard all the world's mockeries, slanders, and insults, all the injustices and crimes of evil men, as well as all the temptations and afflictions from the merciless demons, in order to become worthy of that heavenly joy?

---

[3] cf. Mt. 6:33
[4] cf. Mt. 16:26

Ah, and who could be beside me to hear my prayers, the sighs of my heart, to see the tears that I shed for my brothers? All night long I pray and cry out, "Either save Thy servants, O Lord, or erase me as well from the Book of Life. I do not want paradise without them!"

If for the whole world I pour out all the might of my soul and heart before the Lord of all, how much more so for you?

So listen to me, the lowly and least of monks, and do not disregard me as someone ignorant and uneducated. But open the eyes of your soul and see what exists beyond this life. Men of the world love the world because they have not yet discovered its bitterness. They are still blind in soul and do not see what is hiding behind this fleeting joy. The noetic light has not yet come to them, the day of salvation has not yet dawned upon them.

But you, who have seen and heard so much, must realize that the pleasure from temporal things passes away like a shadow. The time of our life passes, elapses, and does not come back. The time of this present life is a time for harvesting, and each person gathers spiritual food—as pure as possible—and stores it up for the other life.

It is not the clever, the noble, the polished speakers, or the rich who win, but whoever is insulted and forbears, whoever is wronged and forgives, whoever is slandered and endures, whoever becomes a sponge and mops up whatever they might say to him. Such a person is cleansed and polished even more. He reaches great heights. He delights in the theoria of mysteries. And finally, it is he who is already inside paradise, while still in this life.

And when that hour of death comes, as soon as these eyes close, the inner eyes of the soul will open. And as he contemplates the things there, suddenly he finds himself in those things he longs for, without at all realizing how. He passes from darkness to light, from affliction to rest, from the storm to a calm harbor, from war to continuous peace.

Therefore, my good and beloved brothers, whoever is wronged in this life and wants to seek justice, let him know that it is this: to bear the burdens of his brother, of his neighbor, until his final breath, and to be patient in all the sorrows of this present life. Because every affliction that befalls us, whether from men, from the demons, or from our very own nature, always has enclosed within it the corresponding profit. And whoever passes through it with patience receives the payment: its pledge here and its fulfillment there.

So patience is necessary, like salt in food. For there is no other road for us to gain, get rich, and reign. This is the road that our Christ traced out. And all we who love Him ought to follow Him for the sake of His love. Even though the wormwood is bitter to us, it nevertheless cleanses the blood and makes our body healthy. Without temptations, pure souls are not known, virtue does not show, patience is not discernible. Without temptations, it is impossible for the soul to become healthy. They are the cleansing fire which makes the soul pure and bright.

I forgot to write to you a sweet little story. Once while I was kneeling—I had become tired while praying—I saw something wondrous: a fiery youth had two beautiful small girls beside him. One of them was our Maria and the other was Virginia—the two little ones who had died. The young man said to them, "This is your brother. Do you recognize him?" Maria was older. "I recognize him," she said, "but many years have passed since then." The other one said, "I did not see him when I was alive." Then he said to them, "Embrace him and then we shall leave." And the two little ones kissed me like sweet-smelling flowers and left. Then I came to myself with eyes full of tears, recalling the joy which takes place in the heavens when sinners repent and when the righteous enter paradise.

Thirty-ninth Letter

My beloved sister, rejoice in the Lord.

y beloved sister, rejoice in the Lord. Today I received your letter full of love and piety. I threw up my hands with a fervent soul and ardent love, and I entreated the Lord with hidden shouts of my humble heart.

"Hearken," I said, "O sweet love, Jesus my Savior, the Light above all light, begotten of the beginningless Father; the knowledge and truth, my hope and solace, my strength and might, my love and illumination; hearken and send the light of Thy divine consolation to my sister, and break the bars and bolts of her darkened and distressed soul; and with the bright light of Thy radiance comfort her heart, that her sorrows and the successive waves of temptations lessen. Yes, my sweet Christ, the Light that illumines reins[†] and heart, soul and body, tendons and bones, nous and intellect, and the entire composition of our being; hearken unto me as I pray for my afflicted and suffering sister."

These and many other things—tokens of my affection towards you—do I cry out to my Master. For I remember and am not unaware of your many and countless sufferings since

---

[†] Literally "kidneys" in Greek. The kidneys were considered to be the seat of affections.

childhood. Because of them I love you exceedingly, and amongst all of my beloved, I give the most love to you, for the first-fruits of my love belong to you.

I only ask that you do this for me as repayment for my immense love towards you: be a little more patient. And I trust that Jesus, Who has already shown so much love to us, will fulfill all of your requests even more. You will find not only peace and quiet in your soul, but also everything that is beneficial to our wretched souls will the Lord grant you. Just keep seeking with tears that the Lord's holy will be done—in the way He knows best—and not yours.

As soon as you realize that you have sinned against the Lord, add no more wounds to your bruises. But if as a human you fall again, don't get despondent, don't despair. For how will the loving Lord, Who told Peter to forgive seventy times seven in a day, not forgive us?

Let your husband do as he wishes. Tell him that you gave those things to charity. Don't give to others the alms you were planning on giving them. Don't do another benefaction to someone else. This one is enough. Give up your own will so that you may find peace of soul. For the will of man is a bronze wall that blocks illumination and peace from God.

Take as an example our sweet Jesus, Who was obedient to His beginningless Father unto death on a cross. He gave His body over to scourges, His cheeks to slaps, and He did not turn His face away from spitting. Do you see, my sister, how much love the compassionate Lord showed to us? So let us give up our will as well; let us forgive those who wrong us. Then with boldness we shall say, "Forgive us our debts, as we forgive our debtors."[1]

For we are all human, born of dust, and we have all sinned. We are clay, we are ignorant. Clay robs clay. Clay insults clay.

---

[1] Mt. 6:12

Clay slanders clay. Clay is haughty against clay. Clay gets rich with clay. Clay rules over clay. Clay beats clay. Clay imprisons clay. And in general: clay considers itself wiser, stronger, richer, nobler, and more honorable than clay; amassing wealth in his stupidity and ignorance of his own existence. He does not care about whence and where he is, how he was born, what his purpose is, where he will end up, what is to come after this.

So since forgetfulness and ignorance have devoured all of this self-knowledge, and a chaos of insensibility has resulted, all of us who remain unrepentant suffer here as well as in the other life. Therefore, anyone who can see better and is slightly less darkened in the nous must forgive and sympathize with his neighbor, his brother of like soul and passions.

In the beginning, God did not make man to be like this, to suffer and grieve, but He made him equal to the angels; only slightly did he differ from the angels. He made Paradise in Eden and placed him there to rule as a king with free choice and free will. He bound him with only one commandment, so that it would show that he is governed by Someone superior. But since he was deceived by the devil and took delight in the thought of receiving equality with God, he was expelled from paradise to this exile here and fell into afflictions. Banished by God, he was doomed to reap thorns and thistles all the days of his life.

Now, what else are these thorns and thistles but the successive misfortunes and daily afflictions caused by temptations, by perverse men, and even by our toilsome nature itself, which has acquired bad habits and tendencies as second nature? We suffer more painful temptations from it than from the other enemies. And if the mercy of God does not reach us in time, we are in danger of perishing. When will all of this end? When, as He says, "Out of dust wast thou taken, and unto dust shalt thou return."[2] So this is the end of the pains and afflictions that the loving Lord has set.

So, my dear sister, what are you searching for? What road can we find that does not bring forth thorns and thistles? What other path is there that is not included in God's banishment? Show me the kings who just recently had music playing for them, and at whom the whole world trembled. Where has all of this gone? The thorns choked them. Where are those who were rulers just a moment ago, who were eaten alive by swarms of bees? Behold the thistles.

So then, who was able to disentangle himself from the thorns? No one—only death can do that. Come, therefore, and let us cry out Solomon's verse together, "Vanity of vanities; all is vanity!"[3] Blessed is he who endures until the end, disregarding everything, who through forbearance decreases the thorns and thistles and allows earthly loss for the sake of heavenly riches.

For this reason, my beloved sister, soul of my soul, set aside your "rights" and "wills" for the sake of my immense love towards you. Unite the good pair of patience and forbearance. Pray that the Lord will protect me as well, because I perceive that your beloved, sisterly, spiritual prayers greatly help me. And when you find time, do a Forty-day Liturgy, too, to lighten my spiritual burdens.

You wrote for me to order an icon, but you forgot to write which saint and what size. Write, and I shall tell them to make one.

Just now, this very moment, I received the little basket and opened it and found the measurements of the holy icons. So be at peace. It's just that they will be a little slow in finishing.

I also received your sisterly gifts. Not just simple gifts, but gifts of love, gifts from a sister who has been fighting the good fight since childhood. And because of these small gifts, she receives in return from the munificent God comfort and delight in His heavenly kingdom.

Oh! In the little basket I saw foods from the days of our youth, the fruits of our homeland, and I remembered our childhood and said:

"O vain world! How miserable you were, are, and will be until the end! And how blessed for the blessed ones is that eternal and unending delight!" O my sister! If you taste only a small amount of grace from these heavenly things, you will become like iron in patience.

You wrote that you are agitated and are making plans as though for building. You speak the truth. But these are the things this world has. But take heart. Whoever has learned how to build, will learn some day to take no account of the world. Perhaps the Lord will find us while we are building and take us where there is no longer any place for the plans of men. And then we shall have a house forever.

So take heart; I am building with you and for you, and no one can destroy it. Only see to it that you send me a drachma or two to buy nails for the doors and windows! Take heart and have patience. I thank you very much for everything, and I pray for you with all my soul. Give my humble prayers to all our brothers. I kiss Mother's feet. I embrace your benign husband and your children, and I wish them to become good children.

As for your questions, the son whose mother asked you cannot be commemorated by the Church because he committed suicide. If she wants, she can only give to charity for him. The Lord is great and the depth of His charity is infinite. If she wants, she should send alms especially to the ascetics, who pray day and night and whose prayers the Lord hears. As you mentioned, she knows many monks. She should give them alms to distribute amongst themselves, or to nuns. Nothing else can be done for him.

As for the girl who says she has taken an oath, that oath does not count because it is contrary to God. So she has to tell everything to her spiritual father....

Fortieth Letter

**God always helps. He always comes in time,
but patience is necessary.**

ome, my good and beloved sister. Come and I shall comfort your sorrow once again. Come and we shall bless God with the sweet voice of our heart, intoned through our mouth, and resonating in our nous, saying, "Bless the Lord, O my soul, and let all that is within me bless His holy name."[1]

Do you see how much the Lord loves us? Do you see how fortunate we ungrateful ones are for everything that His goodness gives us every day? But the time of the real harvest still awaits us: that blessed moment when we shall leave everything here and depart to the other homeland—the true one—the blessed life, the certain joy, so that each one of us receives the portion that the munificent, sweetest Jesus will give him.

O joy! O gratitude! O love of the heavenly Father! He cleanses us from all defilement, honors us, enriches us, bestowing His riches! There, my golden sister, there are no crafty people to wrong us. Envy and jealousy will have disappeared. There are no passions there whatsoever; those who have them have remained on the other side of the bridge. For a great gulf is fixed between here and there.[2]

---

[1] Ps. 102:1
[2] cf. Lk. 16:26

But, O sweet love of Christ, what good didst Thou see in us that Thou didst lead us along Thy divine path?

So rejoice and exult, my beloved sister. Thank and glorify God, and behold, the time draws near. The time will soon come for us to hear the blessed voice, "Come unto me."[3] And as soon as these bodily eyes close, the noetic eyes of the soul will open. Then as if from sleep we shall wake up into the other life. Then you will see parents, brothers, relatives. Then you will see angels, saints, and the blessed Mother of all, the pure Virgin Theotokos, whom we all call upon at every moment and to whom, after God, we owe everything. Then, whom shall we speak with first, who will kiss us first, whom shall we kiss? With all purity, with all modesty, with all holiness. So who, expecting such blessings, would not endure every sorrow here of this present life?

Therefore, my good beloved sister, make a review of your life. Examine in what manner you have passed your life. Recall the innumerable benefactions of our Savior Jesus Christ and His sweetest Mother, and be patient in the temptations that come.

God always helps. He always comes in time, but patience is necessary. He hears us immediately when we cry out to Him, but not in accordance with our own way of thinking.

You think that your voice did not immediately reach the saints, our Panagia, and Christ. On the contrary, even before you cried out, the saints rushed to your aid, knowing that you would call upon them and seek their God-given protection. However, since you do not see beyond what is apparent and do not know how God governs the world, you want your request to be fulfilled like lightning. But this is not how things are. The Lord wants patience. He wants you to show your faith. You cannot just pray like a parrot. It is necessary also to

---

[3] Mt. 11:28

work towards whatever one prays for, and then to learn to wait. You see that what you longed for in the past has finally happened. However, you were harmed because you didn't have the patience to wait, in which case you would have gained both the one and the other: both the temporal and the eternal.

Now you become angry and fainthearted and grieved, thinking that the heavenly Father is slow in answering. But I tell you that this will also happen as you desire—it will definitely happen—but first it takes prayer with all your soul, and then you must wait. And when you have forgotten your request and have ceased asking for it, it will come to you as a reward for your patience and endurance. When you reach the verge of despair while praying and seeking, then the fulfillment of your request is near. Christ wants to heal some hidden passion within you, and this is why He delays in granting your request. If you obtain it sooner, when you demand it, your passion remains uncured within you. If you wait, you obtain your request and the cure of the passion. And then you rejoice exceedingly and give warm thanks to God Who arranges all things in wisdom and does everything for our benefit.

So then, there is no point in losing heart, getting upset, complaining. You must close your mouth. Let no one perceive that you are disturbed. Don't fume with anger, as if to work it out of your system, but rather be calm. Burn the devil through patience and forbearance.

The Lord, Who destroys all who speak lies, is my witness that I have greatly benefited by the advice I am giving you. The temptations I had were strong enough to make you think that your soul would depart due to the pain, as if from a flaming furnace. Nevertheless, once the trial is over, so much consolation comes that you feel as if you were in paradise without a body. Then Christ loves you, our Panagia loves you, the saints praise you, and the angels admire you.

Do you see how many good things temptations and afflictions cause? So if you too want to see, to taste the love of Christ, endure whatever comes upon you—not whatever you like, but whatever the Lord wants to test you with. What we suffer voluntarily is absolutely nothing in comparison with the trials the Lord sends us against our will. The hostile devil fights us bone against bone and blood against blood, as much as God allows. He fights so much, that one melts and flows like wax before the fire.[4] But when the trial passes, you are totally filled with joy. You are encompassed with extraordinary light and see mysteries which the human tongue is unable to utter. And henceforth you thirst for more temptations, when they will come again, since you have already learned how salutary they are.

This is truly the road, my sister, and the one writing to you bears witness to the truth out of his own experience. So be brave and strong in the Lord, enduring whatever comes to you, expecting, along with the pain, the peace and grace of God. Be strong and give courage to your soul, considering that the lame and the maimed do not enter into these good things. Christ allows temptations so that we may be purified of our predispositions. Temptations are like soap and a mallet which hits us and whitens us. All the clothes that are firm are useful for the Bridegroom. But those which do not endure the mallet are torn and thrown out in the trash.

Therefore, let us exert ourselves a little bit here, for the time draws near. Keep the letters I send you, so that you will have them when afflictions trouble you, because it seems to me that I shall soon leave you. The more that time passes, the

---

[4] Ps. 67:2

more seriously ill I become. I am like a paralytic now.

Postscript:

I don't have time to write to you about the miracle that the Lord showed me to correct a mistake I was making out of ignorance, as you know. So, do you see the great goodness of our Lord? Do you see that He even works miracles when His divine providence deems it suitable? Many times a person is deluded out of ignorance or because others mislead him. But when he has an upright soul and good intentions, the Lord does not abandon him, but will bring him enlightenment in various ways. This makes me feel like dirt, ash, and a worm of the earth.

Most truly, great is the mercy of the Lord. The Psalmist is right in saying, "Not according to our sins hath He dealt with us, nor according to our iniquities hath He rewarded us."[5]

So then, why shouldn't you thank God? Why should you grumble? If I were to write to you the temptations I undergo, you would not be able to bear it. Nevertheless, the grace of Christ and our Panagia dispels them all. Have patience, for the Theotokos, the Queen and Lady of all, does not abandon us. She prays for us.

---

[5] Ps. 102:9

Forty-first Letter

**The springtime is at hand—the winter of
sorrows is dissolving little by little.**

 y dear sister, I received and joyfully read
your very pious letter which filled my
soul with happiness. I can mentally see
the abundance of your heart blooming
and bearing witness to the birth of the
new man, the spiritual infant.

So, be stouthearted and strong in temptations, and embrace patience as a great guardian. Again and
again may your might be strengthened in sorrows, for soon
we shall depart from here.

The springtime is at hand. The winter of sorrows is dissolving little by little. Soon we shall dwell in the nests which
we built by enduring continual temptations and sorrows. Then
there will be no one to quarrel with us, no one to envy us, no
one to injure us and take vengeance on us; all these things will
remain here in this world. We shall tear away from our toilsome body full of suffering with which we are clothed here—
which does not want to carry out the commandments of
God—and we shall leave it in the mother earth which gave us
birth. Then, as high-flying eagles in the open sky, we shall
occupy the holy mansions.

After the resurrection we shall receive this earthen vessel—our body—once again. But then, it will no longer be heavy and burdensome, sensual, and sluggish, but entirely changed by the fiery gleam of our Sweetest Jesus; it will shine rays brighter than the sun, enlightening even the ether.

The sufferings here are small in comparison to the future compensation. "Therefore," tell your soul, "have patience." And as for those things you wrote to me, we all had them when we used to consider the vanity of the world to be something great. But now that we have come to full knowledge and have perceived the lie, God looks no longer at the past, but at the present. All those things are blotted out with one straightforward confession. It is enough for us to proceed now according to the commandments of the Lord in accordance with our strength.

You asked me to send a letter to our friends. But since there is nothing to build upon, no willingness of soul, how can I work? They must seek to learn, and then I shall speak. Otherwise, we shall be aimlessly beating the air.[1] One person wants to correspond, but he doesn't ask about his soul, his sins, his mistakes—how to fix them. He only says, "What's new!" Another one writes about the weather. The others don't ask at all. Besides, even the Lord does not tell us to speak without being asked, but rather He says, "Give to him that asketh of thee."[2] He does not say, "To him that does not ask." There are thousands of souls that seek our advice, and God demands that we give it. Those who do not seek it are benefited more by prayer. Let us pray for them to come to their senses, and then they, too, will seek advice. Then we, too, with joy and love will easily give to them from what God has given to us.

---

[1] cf. 1 Cor. 9:26
[2] Mt. 5:42

As for the wine you sent, the priest was afraid that it might have water in it, and didn't use it, so I drank it to your health. And I remembered days of old and meditated at night with my heart and said:

"Vanity of vanities, and all is vain!"[3]

Everything was a dream and disappeared. They were bubbles that burst, a spider's web that was torn.

"All human things are vanity, everything that does not exist after death."

Alas! We are in exile and we do not want to realize it. We do not want to see from what heights we have fallen. But with our own evil will, we cover our ears and shut our eyes, blinding ourselves willingly so that we might not see the truth. Woe to us, for we consider the darkness here to be light, and for a paltry pleasure that this world offers, we avoid the light there as if it were darkness. We avoid it because of the small sorrow that the body encounters, and lose the repose there. Woe to our wretchedness! For God calls out to us to become His children, but we become sons of darkness. We exchange eternity for a little bit of honey. For the small pleasure of luxury or glory, we deny and fall away from the glory of the kingdom of God. So blessed is he who sees this deception and abstains from the fleeting pleasures of this world, and aspires to the enjoyment that awaits us.

And you, my good and beloved sister, who have chosen God from your youth, struggle to brighten the garment of the bridal-chamber. Entreat the Lord day and night to forgive you all things of the past, to give you strength from above to keep His divine commandments. And when He receives you in repentance, may he count your soul together with the righteous. Then, we shall enjoy each other up there insatiably unto all the ages.

---

[3] Eccl. 1:2

Forty-second Letter

This, my sister, is the art of arts and the science of sciences.

owadays, my sister, things are not the way they were in the days of old which you have in mind. The condition of most people today is limited to an external formality. Beyond this, there is no concern or care for the inner soul, which is really everything. This is where the material unites with the Immaterial; man with God, as much as our earthly nature can hold. This union is the most beautiful thing and very good. But we all avoid it; we all turn our backs, because it takes a struggle. The human mind greatly shudders even to hear about the struggle needed.

In this struggle God must help, for without Him nothing can be achieved. The human will must struggle and the body must shed blood, because the skin of the inner man has to be shed. The "old man"[1] has to melt like wax. And just as rust falls off iron when it enters the fire, a similar thing happens to man, too.

Grace comes gradually, and as soon as it approaches a person, he melts like wax. And at that moment he does not

---

[1] cf. Rom. 6:6

recognize himself; he is wholly a many-eyed, very clear nous. During this supernatural activity, he cannot distinguish himself, because he is completely united with God. Then the rust falls off. The seal is removed. The "old man" dies. The primeval blood is removed. The whole man is renewed. The person does not undergo a bodily change, but his natural talents and gifts are enlightened, strengthened, and renewed by grace. And the Adam of old, who was formed in the image of God, is vitalized. Since we are evil, prodigal, and perverted by having inherited the sin of Adam, we are in the image of the evil one now. This is how he has rendered us: of blood and phlegm.

However, before these changes take place, many things are necessary. It takes extreme fasting so that the primeval blood leaves and the phlegm—that filth—is cleansed. The predispositions that one has grown accustomed to since childhood must be obliterated. Fasting must also be coupled with perpetual vigils. Not once or twice, but constantly so that the slothful and fat nous is made thin. Furthermore, it must be accompanied by ceaseless prayer—with the nous, lips, and heart.

Just as man dies when he stops breathing, so, too, does the soul die without continuous and endless prayer. It dies because that living flesh which is beginning to be conceived by the perpetuity of the prayer falls asleep, and the passions are rejuvenated. For the enemy does not sleep, but fights continuously. And just as an infant which is conceived in its mother's womb suffocates and dies if it ceases to breathe, the same thing happens with spiritual conception if the noetic work ceases.

All this is fine, but the struggle does not end here. We have many struggles. You have to fight with multitudinous spirits, the greatest one being the spirit of fornication. It raises its sail as high as the heavens, and sinks it as low as the abysses. You fast, keep vigil, cry out, weep, are in pain; it, however, with the help of Satan, does not stop fighting for even a moment, but continuously provokes—fire proceeding from fire, seed of Esau, son of Babylon. You cry out seeking Christ. You beat yourself, weep, and are in pain. And this lasts not for one day or year, but for eight or ten years, until God sees your patience—until you reach despair—and then the Lord takes away the evil and eliminates the passion. This happens with all the passions, but the others are not completely eliminated like this one, nor do they have such strength, because they are outsiders. Whereas the conjugal passion is natural, and a person has to struggle to change his nature. Yet he cannot change his nature, but God changes it. As the Lawgiver, He can break the boundaries and alter nature as He wills.

But if I were to write about the temptations and passions one by one, I would have to write a book. For in addition to all those that fight man and that he fights against as long as he lives, there are also all those which God permits to test us. Since the latter occur without our own will, they cause much toil and are difficult to fight.

Do you know what it is like not to bother people, while they irritate you? Not to rob them, while they rob you? To bless, while they curse you? To show them mercy, while they treat you unjustly? To praise them, while they criticize you? For them to come to censure you for no reason and constantly call you deluded all your life, while knowing that it is not as they say? To see the temptation that provokes them, yet to repent and weep as if you were guilty of being such a person?

These are the strongest temptations, because while you are being fought by them you are also fighting with yourself to convince yourself that this is how it is, as people are saying, even though it is not so. You see that you are totally right, yet convince yourself that you are wrong.

This, my sister, is the art of arts and the science of sciences: to flog yourself until you are persuaded to call the light darkness and the darkness light, so that every right leaves, so that all arrogance is obliterated, so that you become a fool with complete understanding, so that you see everyone, without anyone seeing you at all. For he who becomes spiritual examines everyone, yet he himself is examined by no one.[2] He sees everything. He has his eyes fixed above, and no one sees him.

Virtue does not have a bell that rings to rouse your curiosity, to make you turn and see him. It is an immaterial gift of God. Why is it called grace? Because it cannot be seen, contained, visualized, or colored. A gift of God. An inexpressible, incomprehensible, and most rich miracle.

This is why, when the Lord walked down the road, He looked like the rest of the people, even though He is the True God. "He eats and drinks," they said. He was called a deceiver and possessed. And today, if someone speaks about grace, about purification of the inner man, he is considered deluded. "He's deluded!" you will immediately hear. The idea of taking care of the inside of the cup, as the Lord tells us,[3] has been completely removed from people's minds.

So this in brief is one drop of the sea and was written to you, my sister, only because you wrote that you see the monks' faults and don't respect them. But I don't want you to write such things, because you are a member similar to them, and you are not entirely free from blame.

You, too, must go through fire and water[4] and thus your merit will show—at what value you have been appraised by the Lord, not by men. Men do not know how to value things.

---

[2] cf. 1 Cor. 2:15
[3] cf. Mt. 10:26
[4] cf. Ps. 65:12

The Judge must appraise us—He Who sets the contest, arranges the match, gives the strength, subdues the adversaries, crowns the athletes, and awards glory. This is neither easy to learn with words, if you do not enter the furnace of trials, nor easy to understand, if you have not experienced it.

So then, humble your thoughts, and don't think that it is easy to undergo and learn such things.

Forty-third Letter

***Truly, I know a brother who fell into ecstasy
while sitting under a full moon.***

y the good-will of God, my golden sis-
ter, behold I am speaking with you
again through ink and paper. I have
been back on the Holy Mountain for
more than fifteen days now. Before
leaving Thessaloniki, I wrote you a letter. Likewise, I sent you the holy icons
and a basket full of goodies. However,
I forgot what I had put in–I think it was tea and hazel-nuts, a
blessing for the children. You will receive them from Sister
Veronica at the monastery of Meletia. Anyway, by now they
must have brought them to you.

When I was in Thessaloniki, since I was in a rush to return,
I didn't write for you to come because you were slow in writing and it might have taken you some time to get there. That
is why I broke my promise. But another time, if God wills,
you will see me and I shall see you, however the Lord provides.

Now, I only ask that you have patience in temptations.

Don't worry about the money for the holy icons. Whenever
you get it, you can send it together with the money for the

other icon of the Three Hierarchs. It's being done now; it's almost finished. And please, if that lady is poor, don't ask her for more money, because she might not have any. I shall take care of things here, as the Lord wills. I just want her to send the name of her deceased parents to be commemorated.

If another woman wants icons, let her write to me and send the money, and I shall order them. It is no trouble for me, and in this way I help the ascetics. And they in turn help me out, too. Here there is no profit, but we fulfill the commandment of love, as the Lord says, "Love one another."[1] Besides, a monk ought to sacrifice himself day and night for the glory and love of God.

We here, my sister, don't sleep at all at night. Every night we have a vigil. We pray for the whole world all night. Only in the morning and midday do we rest a little after we eat. This is our rule: half the day we work, and the rest of the time we rest in silence and are content. Ascetical life! Wilderness! Angelic life, full of grace! If only you were here to see us! Oh, if only it were possible for you to see us!

Here, my sister, it is an earthly paradise. And if from the beginning one lays hold of a demanding, lofty lifestyle, he becomes a saint. Otherwise, if he takes a path which is a little bit wide, later he will go downhill. Sometimes he may even become worse than worldly people.

The devil fights very much against the monks. He wants to get revenge on Christ. He says, "Behold your soldiers, Nazarene! You promise them an eternal kingdom and they deny you! For a little pleasure of the palate, they follow me!" This is how the devil boasts.

This is why one who wants to become a monk must have great self-denial, and must say that he will not live in this life any longer. He must crucify himself, enduring every tempta-

[1] Jn. 13:34

tion that comes: hunger, thirst, nakedness, injustice, abuse, and every kind of affliction. But if he does not take these things into consideration, but comes in order to relax, it would be better for him not to come, but to live in the world as a good Christian, whether a man or a woman.

For a monk, there are times when grace is present and it helps him. Then he is in paradise and lives like a bodiless angel. But when grace leaves to test him, then he tastes the poisonous waters of Hades at every moment. Darkness and grief overcome the soul. But again, light and consolation come–and then unbearable pain again. But the married person walks on a moderate path: neither greatly uphill nor severely downhill. So, may God help each one with the burden which he is able to bear.

For there is a great burden in the monastic way of life, and the struggle is enormous, and he who approaches it needs great vigilance and continuous constraint of nature. And until death he must not become overconfident and lose his watchfulness, otherwise he immediately falls and is ruined, because the bloodthirsty and crafty demons vigilantly wait for an appropriate time. So, may God enlighten and protect us.

All we monastics leave the world and all things of the world for one purpose: so that we be counted worthy of the incorruptible and eternal good things. Whoever forgets this purpose shows that he does not understand why he chose this hard path of monastic life. Our struggle is to disregard not only the pleasant things, but also all the sad things of the present life, every day transporting our life to the heavens. Let us love with all our soul and heart our Lord Jesus Christ and His sweetest Mother, because of all their love for us. After we pass the storm of this life, we shall be inseparable from them.

So let us always look ahead to the indescribable glory and that ineffable beauty which have been prepared for those who have struggled and endured.

Truly, I know a brother, and I am not lying, who fell into ecstasy while sitting under a full moon, in the depths of the wilderness. Perfect silence. No person or hut was there. While he was keeping vigil and praying, he heard the sweet voice of a bird which attracted all his mind and took away from him all perception. He followed it, to see where such a sweet voice was coming from. And he was looking here and there as if beside himself—yet not with feet and eyes, but seeing and walking in ecstasy—and he proceeded and saw a brilliant light, full of fragrance and grace. He left the bird's warbling and was lifted, or rather captured into theoria of the abundant light. And walking as St. Andrew the Fool for Christ, he entered a road as white as snow. On both sides the walls were set with diamonds. Everything there was impossible to describe. He looked inside, and there was an exquisite paradise, decorated with all kinds of flowers. Everything was covered with gold, such that no human tongue could describe it. He stared and wondered at it all like a crazy man. And as he proceeded, he saw in the middle a huge palace, as white as snow and as tall as heaven. In the door stood our Lady Theotokos, the Queen of the angels, our only relief, the indescribable fragrance and comfort of every Christian soul, carrying the snow-white Infant in her arms, Who shone brighter than a thousand suns. As that brother drew near, he fell down like a son before his mother, all ablaze with divine eros. Then she embraced him as a true child and kissed him. O eros of the love of God! O love of the Mother towards a son! She embraced him like her own child. She filled him with ineffable fragrance. And that truthful brother told me that all the years of his life, whenever he recalls this divine vision, he feels fragrance and sweetness in his soul. That indescribable, sweetest Infant caressed his face with His plump little hand, and he was informed by the Mother regarding a mystery which he had been fervently praying about for many days. Furthermore, the Son told him, "To enjoy such grace, you must struggle and suffer all your life."

Then he left again the same way he entered, without wanting to. The farther he withdrew, the more clearly he heard the voice of the bird again which had captivated him in the beginning. Looking up, he saw a large bird with millions of colors which covered the entire paradise with its wings. There were thrones all around and little birds were sitting uniformly making that ineffable melody, and everyone there was enjoying himself. After seeing all this, that brother came to himself again, and was in the same place he was before he saw these things.

So, hearing such things, we endure every sorrow and affliction for the multitude of good things which have been prepared for us. For things that seem beautiful here are darkness and hell in comparison with those things.

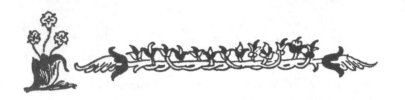

Forty-fourth Letter

Be careful, my good little daughter, for you have already grown up now and thoughts begin to change.

y beloved daughter, my good dove, my good little child; I hope, my child, that you are well in body and soul. A thought came to me a few days ago, and I said to myself, "How is it that my child is so late in writing to us? How did she neglect it? Perhaps my daughter is busy with her studies!"

Finally I received your letter and was glad to hear about your health, but grieved for the sins you commit all the time. For you are such a small girl, and yet you quarrel with everyone. I wonder, when you become a little bride of Christ the Master, when you put on the holy monastic schema, will you correct your unbecoming behavior, or will you still quarrel?

Anyway, let everything be forgiven now. Just be careful from now on, or else I shall give you a severe penance! Since you are a bride of the heavenly King, you should not do anything unbecoming, but should be the smallest, most modest, and most humble before everyone. You should weep with many tears in your eyes, entreating to be counted worthy of the joy of the wise virgins along with all the angels and saints.

Be careful, my good little daughter, for you have already grown up now and thoughts begin to change. The darts of the evil one have begun to fly near you. Guard your soul; guard your honor greatly. Christ and our Panagia want us to have caution and fear of God always and in everything.

Don't expect to find joy and rest in anything that grieves your soul and upsets divine grace. Joy is a gift of God to our soul. And if you dishonor it, it will not come back, unless you feel sorry and repent with much pain for every sin you committed. But what is the point of thoughtlessly chasing away the dove of grace, and then with regret and many sighs seeking it back again? Many people have chased joy away by foolishly dishonoring it, and then it never came back.

Therefore, be careful, my good little girl. Without your mother don't take a single step. Don't have many friends. Don't love ornaments. Don't seek perfumes. All these things are worldly pursuits, which are not only superfluous, but also sinful.

You should have the fear of God as a constant adornment, humility as a modest garment, the Queen of all as your mighty protection, the angel of your soul as a guardian and guide, the virginal fragrance of your soul and body as a scent of perfume. Yes, my child, do so and you will live now and unto the ages.

The death of your soul is walking beside you; it precedes your steps, it hovers around your heart, flies into your eyes, wrestles with your thoughts. Be careful with your life, guard your soul greatly!

Yes, my golden daughter, this is because the world has gone bad. Since the tempter sees your divine love and godly zeal, he places "an obstacle and a stumbling block"[1] in the road of life. Therefore, listen to my words and keep them, so that they guard you from the stumbling blocks.

---

[1] 1 Pet. 2:7

Read the divine books so that your nous may be enlightened by them and that your soul may be directed along a spiritual path. And this divine reading will become your heavenly dowry and eternal riches. In addition, make sure that you disobey neither your father nor your mother. Keep yourself from meeting with worldly people. Your young and innocent age has already passed.

Do not acquire the habit of talking a lot. Few words are better, whereas silence is spiritual wealth. If you become talkative, not only will you lose the "Jesus prayer" shortly, but also you will greatly tire your soul and without fail will harm many others. For "in a multitude of words thou shalt not escape sin."[2]

And henceforth, my daughter, see to it that you always be prudent, humble, obedient, silent, patient, abstinent, diligent, praying night and day without ceasing. Your mouth should not stop saying the prayer. Then you will see how much your nous will be enlightened, how your heart will pour forth joy and peace.

Do everything with discretion after receiving good advice. Love confession and receive communion frequently. Do not look at the world, so that God may look at you. And if you always keep virginity of body and soul, the All-holy Virgin will keep you from every evil, from manifold visible and invisible enemies.

And I pray, my humble daughter, that the will of the Lord will be fulfilled in you quickly. "May the Lord God grant thee according to thy heart."[3]

---

2 Prov. 10:19
3 cf. Ps. 19:4

Forty-fifth Letter

Greetings in the Lord, my dearly beloved son.

reetings in the Lord, my dearly beloved son, who is very good, but a little irascible; very wise, but a little stubborn; very kind, but a little jealous. I hope, my child, that I shall see you soon, as my soul desires.

I received your letter, but please, my child, write a little more clearly, because with all the scribbling, I couldn't read it. For, as you can see, my good child, I am uneducated. Only by saying the syllables out loud can I barely read the words—and only some, not all. Thus, I forget the beginning by the time I get to the end.

And why, my child, do you keep complaining that I don't write to you? I, the unfortunate one, don't even have time to respond to those who write to me. How much less to whoever doesn't write. Don't you know, my child, that your letter incites me to write?

Don't you know that as a monk, I also have many spiritual obligations that do not let me be idle for even a minute? For I am obliged to pray for all of you. So instead of writing a letter, I compensate for it with prayer.

As for homilies, you can find many people there to listen to, whereas prayer is extremely difficult to find in the world. But here where it is quiet, it is easier for us. Therefore, do not complain, because whatever I do, I do it with knowledge and the fear of God.

When you want a letter again, do not grow weary, but write, and then once more I shall be obedient to you. For the Lord says, "Give to him that asketh of thee,"[1] not to him who doesn't ask.

I pray with pain of soul and with many tears, my child, that the Lord guards you from every evil. Run quickly and escape like a deer jumping over the snares of the devil; treading upon asps and basilisks,[2] rejoice without ceasing with the joy of our sweetest Jesus and of His All-immaculate Mother.

If, God willing, you come some time after Pascha, we shall talk about wonderful spiritual things. We shall discuss many things then. Then you will see here in the wilderness our tiny, beautiful huts. You will truly rejoice. You will leap like a deer; you will dance like a lamb. You will see how the soul wakes up, how it is nursed like a baby, how it develops in knowledge with time, and how it grows, if it is well taken care of. Likewise, you will see how it becomes ugly, sick, entirely dead, and utterly lost.

So, dream with good hopes, await the spring to come, and have the summer ahead of you. Reflect upon what I am writing to you, and the time will pass by swiftly. Force yourself also in your spiritual obligations, so that the enemy does not find an opportunity to ensnare you.

In short, that is all, my son, with much love to you.

---

2 Mt. 5:42
3 cf. Ps. 90:13

ℑorty-sixth ℚetter

This world, my child, is so vain.

 rejoice that you are well, my child. I also see your mistake. Since you nearly blasphemed, now you will do twice as many metanoias every day for forty days, but you will start after Pentecost. And be careful henceforth, my child, not to acquire this kind of demonic habit.

Oh, my child, be careful because the world is very bad nowadays, and the devil sows evil thoughts to enfeeble the soul's eagerness. For this reason be as abstemious as you can, because overeating gives birth to evils and fantasies. In times of temptation, always take refuge in Christ and our Panagia. Call upon the saints for their help, and be careful. For once the devil beguiles you into committing a sin, you cannot become a priest.[†] It would be a shame to regret it all your life. Therefore be careful, be careful as much as you can.

Flee from evil thoughts as though from fire. Pay no attention to them so that they do not grow roots within you. Furthermore, do not despair, since God is great and forgives sinners. Only repent when you make a mistake, and force yourself not to commit the same sins again.

[†] One who has lost his virginity before marrying cannot be ordained, according to the Sixty-first Apostolic Canon and the Fathers of the Church.

Moreover, be careful with your fellow students. Do not talk superfluously and do not listen to improper things, because your soul's ears will be soiled. See to it that you are obedient, prudent, humble, virtuous, a friend of prayer and reading. Pray with tears; pray while you study. Let your mouth never stop saying, "Lord Jesus Christ, have mercy on me."

And get ready to become a good monk, when our holy God wills, pleasing to God and men. This world, my child, is so vain; full of every evil; a place of exile for Adam and subsequently for us as well. But blessed is he who has traded well during this exile and reached the haven of salvation, for he will eternally rejoice with the saints and reign together with Christ unto all the ages.

Forty-seventh Letter

But we here have chosen the heavenly philosophy . . .

y child, child of our sweetest Jesus, child of the Panagia and of the saints, what shall I say to you?

Where shall I find words to warm your soul? From where shall I draw water to give you to drink? Where shall I find bread to fill you? Woe to me! Woe to me the wretch, for I have been counted worthy to give birth in the Holy Spirit to such a son, such a good youth, of like mind and zeal!

When will I be made worthy to see you near me? When will I enjoy your pleasant company? When will I see you in the middle of our church prostrate and crying in front of the icon of our sweetest Jesus? I wonder, will I be worthy to see such things? I wonder, should I hope? I wonder, should I wait until I see you, and then say along with the divine Symeon, "Now lettest Thou Thy servant depart in peace"?[1]

Woe to me the wretch! Tears shut my eyes. My hand is paralyzed. My pen is dry. My heart throbs from emotion, hearing that you are about to become a wise man among the wise, a teacher among teachers, an orator among orators, a theologian among theologians, a preacher among preachers, a monk

---

[1] Lk. 2:29

among monks, a priest among priests, and a son of God among the sons of God.

Therefore, my beloved nestling, come fly to me. Behold, I open to you my fatherly bosom full of affection. Run as a deer, and I shall give you living water to drink. Come, my son, to our table, and I shall give you the bread of life.

Walk quickly. Lose no time. For death pursues us as an evil wayfarer, and the world is a liar. Life is full of Satan's snares, and brings a two-fold death upon us. The pleasure of the world passes away like a shadow. Everything is a dream, like bubbles they burst. All is vanity!

But we here have chosen the heavenly philosophy and sojourn in the depth of divine mysteries, making our nous clear. As much as possible we see to it that we grasp things unattainable for the hands, but attainable for the nous, having God as our helper, and holy, fiery angels speaking to us and showing us heavenly paths through a good conscience. Then in the end, when our soul departs and this lowly body of ours returns to the earth as if to the mother of all, then we shall depart as if returning to our true homeland, and we shall converse with angels as with brothers, giving one another a divine embrace, and continuously marveling at the heavenly choirs with amazement, until we come before our Master and Savior and thenceforth remain inseparable.

So come running, so that you do not fall away from these things. Arise and gird your loins like a man.

Come, and I shall be waiting for you. Perhaps after a few years I shall depart, and then I shall not be able to benefit you at all.

Forty-eighth Letter

Listen to my voice, my good son.

 isten to my voice, my good son. There is nothing more beautiful or sweeter than to love the Lord Jesus. There is nothing loftier than to philosophize about heavenly things and to behold the eternal blessings by looking at the present things as if in a mirror.

Truly, virginity is the loftiest thing. It turns man into an angel on earth; great is its glory in the heavens and great is its boldness. In the heavenly kingdom, the virgins will follow Jesus the slain Lamb,[1] they will behold His godly beauty, and they will delight in the luxuriousness of His extremely sweet love.

Blessed is he who was enlightened to choose beautiful virginity as a bride. With her beauty she will make him happy. Blessed is he who avoided the vain cares of married life and followed Christ, carrying His yoke since youth. He will undergo afflictions, but they will only adorn the unfading crown of most holy virginity even more.

Come, my child, and occupy yourself with divine philosophy. A new world will be created within you, a new spirit, another heaven, which are unknown to you because the people you have talked with till now have no idea about them.

---

[1] cf. Rev. 14:4

A monk is not like someone you meet who speaks words without fruit. A true monk is a product of the Holy Spirit. When through obedience and hesychia a monk's senses have been purified, his nous has been calmed, and his heart has been cleansed, he then receives grace and enlightenment of knowledge. He becomes all light, all nous, all lucid. He overflows with so much theology that even if three people were to start writing down what they were hearing, they could not keep up with the current of grace coming out in waves, spreading peace and utmost quiescence of passions throughout the body. The heart burns with divine love, and he cries out, "Hold back, my dear Jesus, the waves of Thy grace, for I am melting like wax." Truly he melts, unable to bear it. His nous is caught up into theoria. A mixing occurs; he is transformed and becomes one with God to the point that he cannot recognize or distinguish himself, just like iron in a furnace becomes one with the fire.

So you will taste all these things when you attach yourself to an experienced elder, a spiritual father, and struggle with noetic prayer. You also have me who will write to you often and reveal mysteries to you, of which you will not savor even a drop, if you stay in the world. Lay aside your endeavors and puffed-up words. The inner man is what divine grace wants you to unite with God, and then you will be useful to others as well.

Read, if you want, the *Ecclesiastical History* by Meletios of Athens, and see how many teachers—Origen and thousands of others—were at first great luminaries of the Church possessing extensive learning. But since they gave themselves over to the sea of knowledge before receiving in hesychia the purification of their senses and the peace and tranquillity of the Spirit, they sank in the ocean of the Holy Scriptures. They thought that their scholarly learning was sufficient. Thousands were lost and anathematized by the Councils, of which they had previously been champions. Read and you will see.

I know that you will remember my words, if you live, even if you do not listen to me now. But it will be late, for I shall no longer be in this life. No one loves you more than I do, nor does anyone dare to tell you the plain truth, if he sees it. From all those people you have met until now, you have heard only flattery, trickery, and the teachings of the eighth millennium–everything false and commonplace. Whereas you, as a tender little shoot, need spiritual wisdom and the plain truth. Your soul needs pure light, and your heart needs deep incisions to discharge the poison of pleasures and passions.

But don't tell to many others these things I am writing to you, because people of this age do not occupy themselves with such things. This is why if someone speaks to them about noetic work and prayer, they think that he is talking about some kind of heresy. This, unfortunately, is how the people of our evil age are. Whereas a true monk must occupy himself day and night with the contemplation of God, whether he is eating, sleeping, working, or walking. God is the one closest to us, with Whom we may speak continuously. For God is in your sight; God is in your nous, in your speech, in your breath, in your food–wherever you look, God is there. In Him we live and move;[2] He holds us in His bosom.

So cry out constantly, "My dear God, do You like this? My dear God, is that Your will?" Day and night, constantly speak to God with all the simplicity of a son towards his father. Then you feel the love of the Father and His divine protection. Then you love, since you are loved, and you are afraid lest you violate His divine will. You tremble lest you

---

[2] Acts 17:28

sadden your good Father, Who showed you so much love without any self-interest; it is for you that He died on the Cross.

You will not fix the Church or the world. Whereas you will be corrected, perfected, and enlightened so as to enlighten those who are willing. Only a war will fix the world, which probably has already come, or is coming at a gallop. Misfortune will bring many people to their senses, whereas the unrepentant will have no excuse.

Remember, my son, that although you were formed out of clay, you are the breath of God. Do not disregard your worth and do not be engrossed in material things. You are the breath of God; force yourself to become worthy of God's gift.

Rejoice and delight in the Lord. I, too, rejoice as I keep hesychia here with our God. I leap for joy and exult in my beloved hesychia, chanting my healthful and philosophical little hymn:

I found here a haven of stillness;
Be healthy, my soul and my body;
Swim, O my nous, in the sweetest tranquillity,
and ask not at all what your neighbor is doing.

"He that is able to receive it, let him receive it."[3]

---

[3] Mt. 19:12

Forty-ninth Letter

My life has passed with pain and illnesses.

y child, I hope you are well.

Just recently, I got somewhat better too. This is how my life has passed, with pain and illnesses. Now I have approached death once again for your sake. I said, "Let me die, only let my spiritual children live." And I didn't eat at all.

I was already exhausted, and now I eat almost nothing once again. You sent so many sweets, but I didn't even taste them. I didn't have any cheese–only boiled greens without bread. It was only a short time before I collapsed. They had to give me one hundred and twenty injections....

Three times they stayed up all night thinking that I would die. They called everyone to come by my side. I bid them farewell for the last time. They cried by my side day and night. Finally, I recovered once again. They sent me a special medicine, and it, after God, healed me. I hadn't eaten for forty days. When I took the medicine, I ate, slept, and got better. Glory to Thee, O God! I began to move somewhat and to write again.

As long as I live, my child, I shall pray for you, until you write that you are well. And if I die, you will remember that this old man got sick and died to save all of us.

Courage! It's not just you. There are many others. Many people have come to me, and with prayer and fasting they were healed. But now, the Lord doesn't hear me, so that I learn about medicines and doctors and be lenient with others.

I also read the letters of St. Nectarios, and I saw how much he, such a great saint, paid attention to the doctors and medicines! I am just a poor ascetic who has grown old in the wilderness, and I wanted to heal only through faith. But now I, too, am learning that both medicines and grace are necessary. So now I shall say like the saint, "See to it that you get well." Fix your nerves in any way you can, and you will find your prayer and peace again.

See to it that you help yourself as much as you can. Take control of your appetite: don't eat things that you know are harmful to your health: fried foods, salty foods, sauces, pork, meats, salted fish, alcoholic beverages in general. Avoid all these things, and it will be considered to be fasting in the eyes of the Lord.

And, my child, don't say in your thoughts, "Why is this?" and, "Why is that?" The Lord's judgments are an abyss. Glory to God because He loves us all. His love is manifest in our illnesses and our sorrows. "For my strength," He said, "is made perfect in weakness."[1]

This love of Christ has also made me grieve and suffer with you. But do not fear temptation. It is a trial. God allows as much as He thinks is best, and in the end, His goodness will prevail.

As for me, I eat one hundred grams of bread a day now and a little bit of food, and I keep vigil all night long. Satan comes from afar and howls, but does not approach. He goes to your brethren and threatens them with fantasies. They should not

---

[1] 2 Cor. 12:9

be afraid. In the beginning of my monastic life, the demons fought with me for eight years in every way, and I wouldn't sleep lying down—only standing up or sitting down a little.

So, don't be afraid. Only, prayer, faith, fervency, and tears. Only someone who commits a sin should fear the devil. Then the enemy can do him harm, because the Lord abandons him.

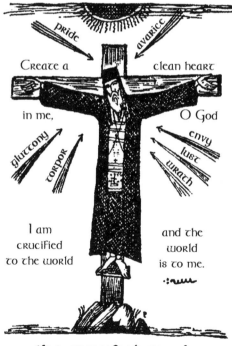

the crucified monk

Fiftieth Letter

Who knows, my child, the judgments of God?

ho knows, my child, the judgments of God? Everything is known to Him. He sees everything and nothing escapes His notice, but no one knows His will. The works of Satan are nothing next to the power of God. So when the Lord tests us as He knows best, we should show our patience and thankfulness.

Now then, my child, if His divine will is in accordance to our desire, certainly you will get well. But if He foresees something that we do not know—since as God He sees and judges differently from above—then you will not get well. Nevertheless, we do not lose our reward: it is stored up in His kingdom. So be patient and struggle.

Just recently, on the eve of St. Catherine's, I had a great struggle with Satan because of you. A visible fight. I was wondering if perhaps you had gotten well. He was furious, screaming. I stood at prayer all night for you and all day as well, so that God might show mercy. Finally he left and did not come back. So tell me how you are doing, how you are getting along. Is Satan troubling you? Have patience.

It is in this manner that you should pray: "I, my dear God, want You to make me well so that I may bless and glorify You. But on the other hand, if You know differently what is profitable for the salvation of my soul, may Your will be done."

The All-good God, my good child, does not do anything that is not for the benefit of our soul. Whether it be an illness or a temptation, whatever He lets happen to us, He does for our benefit. Many times we grumble, become indignant, and do many bad things. Whereas He, out of His great love, has only our soul's best interest in mind. For He knows that we are here temporarily and that everything will soon pass. When this exile of ours ends and the true eyes of our soul open, then we shall gratefully thank Him for everything.

So then, my good child, always have patience. I am informed that God gave you this trial because of your kindness. But whenever He wills, He can take it away.

When I saw your parents, I told them to go to their spiritual father; to confess everything which they have never yet confessed, to say everything clearly, to remember any sinful thing since childhood that they have forgotten. For without frank confession, neither are you helped, nor do they go to paradise. In confession, your father should tell about the oath he took, your mother should tell about the burden she carries since the first years of her marriage, and likewise, all your siblings should confess everything. Everyone in the house should make a general confession—to be cleansed, unburdened, and to become children of eternal life.

And you, my child, write to me about whatever happens to you, and do not be afraid of the tempter. Just say the prayer without ceasing. He, my dear child, is the tempter—the devil—and only the prayer burns him, and fasting severs his nerves; it unnerves him.

So, have infinite patience and thanksgiving; pray and fast intensely, and may God destroy him. I am praying for your health, for your happiness, as well as for your parents and siblings. Let them be careful; let them exert themselves; let them take care of their salvation.

The Treasure

Fifty-first Letter

***Blessed is he who remembers death day
and night and prepares himself to meet it.***

y beloved son, my child, son of Joseph:

I received your letter, my son, and remembered days past. I fell on my knees and wept bitterly. I said, "How vain and unsteady this world is!" This period of life does not remain in one state, but continually alters and changes things! Alas! How much man labors in vain! Today we are together; tomorrow we are separate. Today we are happy and rejoice; tomorrow we argue and are upset. Today we are alive and sing sweetly; tomorrow we shall die and the worms will eat us. O vain world! O deceived man!

Yesterday I had many sons, and I boasted in them. Today, I am left with only one inside a humble cave, and I sigh in my chest. And perhaps tomorrow they will be doing my requiem.

How truly vain this life is, my son! How deceptive and short!

Behold, another new year! Once again, wishes and hopes. But death is lurking somewhere, waiting for us, too. Some day or night will be the last one of our life. Wherefore, blessed is he who remembers his death day and night and prepares himself to meet it. For it has a habit of coming joyfully to those who wait for it, but it arrives unexpectedly, bitterly, and harshly for those who do not expect it.

Therefore, my son, you, too, should reflect on the falsehood, the illusion of this deceiving world, and with the help of God's grace, be careful never to sin. For this deceiving world pushes everyone to be by its side. And if it is able to catch them in its nets, it will have them as its own forever! For men deceive and are deceived. As mortals, they work on their mortal affairs. But you, day and night listen to the divine voice within you:

"Do not love the world, all the deceit of the world, for it passes by quickly along with all its pleasures. Only he who does the will of God remains unto the ages."

Remember every day, my son, that you have been called to live this life as a monk, and not as a layman. There are enough laymen in the world.

I rejoice when you rejoice. I am sad when you are sad, my good son. I suffer when you suffer. Do not grieve beyond measure for anything. Leave it all to God. He knows what is beneficial for the soul better than we do. With all the worries and thoughts, you are harming yourself more than you are helping yourself. The wrongdoings of the past are corrected only by good repentance and a change of life.

So rejoice in the Lord, and see to it that you spend the rest of your life in repentance.

Fifty-second Letter

Woe to me, the lowly wretch!
What account shall I give on Judgment Day?

ove of my soul, my son whom I begot through the Holy Spirit:

I received your letter, my beloved son. When I saw your news I wept bitterly. I raised my hands to our sweetest Christ and, with all my strength, I cried out with tender love:

"Open," I said, "O my sweet breeze, Jesus my Savior, open the showers of Thy Divine Spirit and pour the water of Thy comforting grace into the soul of my son. Console and heal his heart, sweetening it with the sweetness of Thy divine and inexpressible sweetness, of which no tongue can speak. Send forth, my light-giving Jesus, an illuminating beam of Thy divine knowledge, and shine in the soul of my son the light of Thy divine effulgence, so that he may rejoice and leap like a deer and forget his afflictions and everything in the world. Yes, my sweetest fragrance; yes, my most fragrant breath; yes, my beloved Christ; have pity on Thy creature and do not let him suffer beyond his strength."

Such things do I say to our Lord for you, my dearest son. I speak and pray sincerely, not just simply out of habit. I

stretch out my hands with pain of soul and soak the ground
with tears, saying:

"Grant Thy grace, my sweet breeze, Christ, my life; bestow
it upon Thy servant and deliver him from the enemies which
have encompassed him. Dispel everything and miraculously
transform it into tranquillity and peace, as Thine all-seeing
divine power is wont to do. For Thou art the succor and the
power, the mercy and the compassion, and to Thee do we send
up glory, now and unto the endless ages."

I, your humble father, say and do such things, my beloved
son, ever since I received the first letter in which you wrote us
about your afflictions. And behold, as I was anxious to hear
from you, the basket came to us with apples like those of St.
Euphrosynos. I searched out your note and hastily sought to
learn the news of your soul. But when I saw that your
sufferings were not over yet, I turned my intellect to prayer
once more. And when I eat the apples, my soul will
abundantly bless you and you will be blessed by the Father,
Son, and Holy Spirit, the one, holy, consubstantial, and
undivided Trinity, the only source of every good thing and of
every blessing.

You wrote to me that you are considering doing a holy
deed. Well, if you complete it favorably, thank God. But if
you are hindered for any reason whatsoever, do not be
distressed. You will do it another time, if it is the Lord's will.

Many things are hindered for a while, because their time has
not yet come, sometimes because men hinder them—for, as the
saints say, men are able to hinder the Lord's will for many
years—and sometimes because they are completely against the
Lord's will. There are innumerable examples in the lives of the
saints, which undoubtedly your Reverence reads, although you
already know a great deal through your personal experience.

Therefore, no matter how the sphere of our life full of suffering rotates, you must remain composed and bear like Atlas the adversities of your life, since, as you said, you have been called to be a shepherd of many sheep.

I, on the contrary, as has been shown, am only fit to guard the rocks, since I lack such a gift and am unworthy to preach.

Woe to me, the lowly wretch, if I do not contemplate such things and acknowledge the graces of my brethren. What account shall I give on Day? For after being tricked once and twice into preaching by flattery, I tried but failed completely. And now I still suffer the consequences.

Woe to me, the lowly old-timer! As I gather from the appearance of things, twice have I gone against the divine will out of ignorance. With what words shall I rebuke my wretched soul? In what way shall I implore my Lord? Or what work shall I do which will be pleasing to my God? Woe to me, the lowly one, for tears have dried up from my eyes! A thick night has overtaken me, and I become insensitive when I am praised by the fathers here. But may our sweet Jesus be merciful, through the prayers of our Holy Fathers.

I have digressed, my dear priest, and wandered off the subject, remembering days of old. Forgive me, your father. Nevertheless, lowly as I may be, I have begotten you through the Holy Spirit.

𝔉ifty-third 𝔔etter

Oh, my child! A person is never entirely bad.

I suffered, my good son, to make you a son of Joseph the sinner. Later, I painfully grieved because you left me. But recently I have felt much love for you again. I roam about calling, "My son! My son! Where are you? Where are you going, my child? Why, my child, did you leave your light burden of obedience, and choose the burden of Sisyphus?"[†]

Saying these things I remain silently sorrowful, leaving the rest to silence. But I remember your good service which I now lack, and I forget the bitter wormwood you gave me to drink by leaving.

You came, you passed by again, my son, and said that you would write. And truly I waited for you to write me a few words. But I said, "My beloved son has fooled me once more." Just a little while ago, our good Deacon brought me an envelope. And with utter joy I opened it to see what you wrote, but unfortunately instead of a letter, I found inside only a muzzle: the number "five-hundred." As if to say, "Shut up and eat!" Even this is good, my child, and I truly thank you very much. But it is nothing like a little letter from you!

[†] In Greek mythology, Sisyphus was punished in Hades by being condemned eternally to roll an enormous boulder up the slope of a mountain. Each time he was about to push it over the summit, it pushed him back to the bottom of the mountain.

O my child! A person is never entirely bad. Each person has his good and bad points. When you remember his good points, you pray for him, you are moved, your soul feels for him, and you entreat God for him. And as for his bad side, he is not to blame, but our enemy the devil is. Therefore, don't be sad, my child, and don't remember the past. For those things have passed. Worse things have come upon me, so that yours seems like a fragrance to me.

Since then, I pray and hurt more for you. So don't be sad. We are human and children of transgression, having as a cornerstone the sin of Adam and Eve. So the Lord is condescending towards us and forgives everything when we repent.

And don't forget the spiritual discussions we had at night when you came to my poor little hut, the joyful fasts, the feasts, the tranquillity and silence, the unceasing prayer, the compunctious fragrance of the lilies of the humble wilderness, our beloved old Arsenios who made you cake and lovingly teased you. Remember these things. Leave aside those other things regarding your departure because they will embitter you. You are going through enough now as it is.

I forgot to tell you that we have now built a separate little hut farther down. But it's not done yet. For the time being, I live next to it in a small cave. I made it because I would talk at night with Father Arsenios, and this would ruin my quiet. Now I have amazing stillness.

I am the most fortunate of men, because I live without worries, enjoying the honey of hesychia without any interruption. When grace withdraws, though, hesychia like another grace shelters me in its bosom. And the pains and sorrows of this evil and toilsome life seem smaller. For the sorrows and joys of this present life alternate until our last breath.

That is why Philip of Macedonia, as is described in history, when three notices full of joy and honor came to him at the same time, took off his ring—an expensive one—and threw it in the sea, so that with the loss of his ring, he would moderate his excessive joy. "Just in case," he said, "I am not able to endure the many sorrows that may simultaneously befall me."

Do you see, my son, that although they lacked grace, the truth of things made them wise enough to redeem the time[1] and live in moderation? But how much more we Christians who have been perfected and have tasted abundantly of the gifts of Christ, ought to live in a godly manner, redeeming the time and patiently enduring all the sorrows of this temporary life?

Yes, my child. For as long as we live, life has no rest. It is leavened with tribulations. Everything is mixed, and blessed is he who has the wisdom to profit from everything he encounters.

But things which seem awful to us are the things that bring greater profit to the soul, when we endure them without grumbling.

It is amazing, though, how all the temporary, all the vain things of this present life change and shift. And then, in a moment, the first shall become last and the last first.

---

[1] cf. Eph. 5:16

𝔉ifty-fourth 𝔔etter

*Living in the wilderness has its own struggles,
whereas living in the world has many other
different kinds of struggles.*

ou yourself know from experience that wherever we may be, my son, we need much patience. Living in the wilderness has its own struggles, whereas living in the world has many other different kinds of struggles. So be brave. And since you have chosen this burden, bear it with fear of God.

And believe me, my child, I shall forcibly gather my strength, weakened and deadened from the toils, to entreat God that you suffer no harm from the foolish plots of the enemies of our faith. However, if it is written from above that you will undergo some trial for the benefit of your soul, I shall beseech God to grant you patience and bravery of soul.

Do not fear. The Masons are devising many plans and want to do many things, but only if the Lord of all allows them to. Without His will, as He said, neither a hair nor a leaf falls.[1] He shall disperse their counsels.[2] For the time being, this is

---

[1] cf. Mt. 10:29-30
[2] cf. Ps. 32:10

sufficient for us. As for later, let God, Who keeps us alive, take care of it.

Your endeavors should begin with God and end with God, and do not fear the temptations that come. For, by the grace of Christ, they dissipate like smoke.

As for that temptation of yours that you mentioned, I think this is the truth: for that demon to trouble you, it seems that something good is happening that bothers him. But you also gain much when you are tempted. In addition to the reward for patience, you become practiced and learn about people. If a stone does not strike against another stone, no spark is produced. An untried man is completely worthless.

You learned much when you were here, and now you are learning much there. But be prudent from now on and walk with caution "understanding what the will of the Lord is, because the days are evil."[3] Learn to redeem the time[4] and the circumstances.

The temptation you have now will pass, but another one will come, because the enemy never rests. Didn't you see what he said to God when He asked him about Job?[5] It is the same for all of us. The temptation comes in accordance with one's stature. And you must endure in order to emerge victorious. Christ, Who sets the contest, allows temptations for this reason: so that we may gain victories against the enemy, be purged from passions, and be perfected.

So, struggle and be patient. Do not grow weary. Do not turn back. When you see that you are exhausted, make a trip here and rest. You will regain your strength and then return once again to struggle. The struggle lasts for life, and the tempter, wherever you are, wherever you go, is beside you.

You thought that by departing from here the pressure of the spiritual warfare would cease. But now you fully realize

---

[3] Eph. 5:16,17
[4] cf. Eph. 5:16
[5] vid. Job 1:6-12

that there is no such thing as a place without temptation. A person needs to win in the place where he is being fought, so as to bring sorrow and shame to the devil, and joy and glory to God.

The Awesome Protection

The Holy Mountain

Fifty-fifth Letter

**Teach them all noetic prayer,
to say "the prayer" without ceasing.**

y son, my blessed priest: may mercy, enlightenment, strength, peace, love, and the abundant grace of the Lord be upon your noble soul. May the Lord our God send you a good angel to direct your steps in the way of peace, according to His holy will.

My truly beloved son, who won my love with your noble feelings, may your fiery soul be graced with brilliant splendor. May the Holy Protection of our sweetest Queen, the pure Virgin and Theotokos, cover you like Moses, along with all of your children, as the divine Andrew the Fool for Christ saw in Constantinople.

May our sweet Jesus make your nous and heart shine with His holy seal, as well as every God-pleasing work of yours, so that the enemy will not find anything at all to plunder. At His Second Coming may he reward and bless and crown every single one of your good deeds done with love. May He enrich all your children through His rich endowment and heavenly grace, and may they become fragrant flowers of paradise, so that you will see them in that day and rejoice.

I, too, rejoice, seeing all of you as flowers with the sweet smell of good works—I who am empty of every good. This is my happiness and joy and wealth in my poverty, my great boast: that I am a father of a good son and grandfather of many children. Thus, through your spiritual works, the Father is glorified, the Son rejoices, and the Holy Spirit exults. My enormous gratitude for everything ascends to the seventh heaven, and my prayers above bear witness to this. Please, send me the names of those in your synodia so that I can pray for them at least once.

Teach them all to pray noetically, to say the prayer without ceasing:

"Lord Jesus Christ, have mercy on me."

In the beginning, with the lips and the nous; later, with the nous and the heart. And they will quickly find the path of life, the door of paradise, or rather, the prayer itself, when said with desire, will become like a paradise within them.

Prayer of the heart is not susceptible to delusion, unless one is passionate and already deluded. With prayer of the heart, as soon as the nous enters the heart, immediately its darkness is cleared and straightaway it becomes peaceful and calm. It rejoices, is sweetened, rests, and is cleansed. It rejoices and becomes like a small child free from passions. Bodily members which used to tempt him become peaceful and humble, just like the hand, the nose, and the rest of the members of the body.

Therefore, whoever wants to, let him taste this honey, and it will become a fountain of joy and happiness within him, unless one is cunning, hypocritical, envious, miserly, sensual, vainglorious, or in general passionate, and wants to say the prayer while voluntarily remaining with his passions—unrepentant, incorrigible. Such a person obviously disdains the action of the prayer and the mercy of the Lord. The prayer helps everyone, but each person must struggle in accordance with his own strength. God gives His grace according to one's intention. If anyone says the prayer without repenting, either the prayer will cease, or he will fall into delusion.

Women in particular make progress in the prayer more easily because of the self-denial and obedience they have to their spiritual guide. However, the faster they make progress, the more easily they fall into delusion, if they proceed thoughtlessly without caution.

It is not just a matter of saying the prayer, but it is also a matter of being attentive. You must be vigilant with your thoughts, masterfully controlling them. Otherwise, they will take control of you and in the end you will become the laughing-stock of the demons. I have never seen a soul make progress in the prayer without frank confession of secret thoughts.

My child, do you want to crush the head of the serpent? Openly reveal your thoughts in confession. The strength of the devil lies in cunning thoughts. Do you hold on to them? He remains hidden. Do you bring them to the light? He disappears. And then Christ rejoices, the prayer progresses, and the light of grace heals and brings peace to your nous and heart.

So, my priest, that lady you wrote about is a holy soul. But see to it that you explain to her the things I shall write here, so that she will be careful. For the enemy does not sleep; he hates man, and contrives everything to deceive him. Since she suffers such a martyrdom from her husband, God comforts her with those consolations and various visions. But she should not consider such things to be the main power of the soul, because the evil one intervenes and quickly changes things.

The main power of the prayer and the entire appetitive power of the soul lies in the cleansing of the heart by means of noetic prayer. What does the Lord say? "Blessed are the pure in heart, for they shall see God."[1] He does not say, "Blessed are those who see visions and revelations." So one should not rejoice in these things, even if they are from God. But one should rejoice when one sees that the nous has found the heart and remains inside it. Then the entire body is at peace, the soul is calmed, the heart leaps, the nous illuminates its powers, and tears run like a stream. The evil one is able to transform everything, but these things that we are talking about now, he cannot imitate. Nevertheless, when she sees something, she should not tell anyone about it, except her elder and spiritual father—no one else.

These things are happening now because she is suffering and has great simplicity and fear of God. But these things do not last until the end; the evil one changes them when he finds a way. Later, they lead to delusion. Therefore, much caution and humility are needed. She must think of herself as a worm of the earth, and accept as true only whatever her spiritual father tells her. Because if she starts accepting them, in a little while her thoughts will become sick, and she will end up accepting all demonic and silly things as true and sent from God.

What happens after that? A person becomes the mock of the demons. They fool him with writings and visions, with dreams and revelations, with symbols and numbers, with oracles and a heap of superstitions. May God protect her from this kind of change. Therefore, my priest, see to it that your Reverence always humbles her, lest her thoughts change and she becomes proud.

Now, as for that brother who prays, see to it that you guide him correctly with what we are saying now, that he correct his

---

[1] Mt. 5:8

spiritual ailment. Other monks here have suffered the same thing. That activity is not just grace. It is zeal, blood, strength, demons, passions, desire, pride, and love all mixed up together. Everything has to be put in place, and then all will be well.

First of all, he needs a strict fast to thin his blood, to humble his heart which is full of indecent sensuality. He must also undertake other struggles at night to help prayer. Then, he must be attentive to his nous, that it does not go below the heart, below the belly. He must not imagine various things, but must hold his nous at the pinnacle of his heart. He should not breathe rapidly, but say about five prayers or more with each breath. If he feels a stimulation of the flesh, he should hold his breath and stand up as long as he can. And if he feels a great deal of pleasure going to his heart, he must prevent it, he must not seek it but should detest it.

When grace comes, all the schemes of the evil one cease, for it abolishes them. It comes like a gentle breeze, like a subtle, fragrant zephyr which deadens the flesh and then raises the soul. It enlightens our nous. And in the end, when it comes, grace itself teaches a person.

Read my letter to your synodia so that they learn humility. For there are some who are running without a bridle, without moderation and discernment. This is how I see things from here and how I am informed.

Man is not meant only to run, but also to count the miles. Nor should he remain behind out of negligence. It seems to me that there are some who have become slothful. See to it that they don't neglect their duties, for each day incurs debts with its own account. So, let them make a new beginning. Let them compel themselves in the prayer. They must collect and hold their nous inside their heart, and say the prayer slowly. And we are praying that they will soon obtain the Lord's mercy.

Tell them first to bring the nous down into the heart with their breath. Next, the breath along with the prayer goes in and out, while the nous remains within. It must be held violently. It must not be allowed to leave. And once it stays there, then it is like two mad lovers who meet each other after many years. Love, joy, and heavenly delight. But there is a great deal of hard work and sweat in the beginning.

𝔉ifty-sixth 𝔔etter

*He Who made the ages, and existed before the ages,
and in profound silence created the heavenly Powers
of the holy angels.*

hrist is born to save everyone. Therefore, rejoice and exult with the angels and shepherds and all of creation, beloved children of Jesus.

First of all, like the Magi, I bring you the splendid news that our sweet Jesus is born, and all creation exults and is fragrant, for it sees its Creator held in the Virgin's arms. The angels rejoice together with it and chant melodically, "Glory to God in the highest, and on earth peace!"[1] For God, the Prince of peace, is born—He Who made the ages, and existed before the ages, and in profound silence created the heavenly Powers of the holy angels. He is held today in the arms of His sweetest Mother. He is fed with milk and warmed in her bosom in order to save us all.

Our sweet Jesus is born so that we may be reborn. He became man to save us and show us the way in which we must follow Him and imitate His deeds. He left us command-ments so that we would not wander onto roads leading no-

---

[1] Lk. 2:14

where and walk in darkness. Our sweet Jesus took on flesh so that we may eat it and enjoy the blessed affinity; that we may become brothers of our Christ and children of His All-immaculate Mother; and finally, that we may become in all respects imitators of the Lord and children of the heavenly Father by grace.

So let each one of us, both young and old, with every word we say, with every step we take, at every moment of night and day, examine if perhaps we do, say, or think something that is not pleasing to Christ. I wonder, are we always worthy when we approach to commune Christ? I wonder, do we walk in imitation of Him? I wonder, does our sweet Jesus remain within us? Does he find a place in our pure heart, or does He depart immediately?

A true Christian ought to examine all these things at every moment, especially one who wants to walk the strait and narrow way[2] of our Lord and reach perfection; just like you do, the beloved children of my good and kindly spiritual son, who suffered so much and lost his health so that you would find your spiritual happiness and health. Indeed, every shepherd of rational sheep ought to sacrifice himself for the flock,[3] imitating Christ the Master, Who came to give His soul as a ransom for many.[4]

So see to it that with much mutual love, with a pure conscience, with pain of soul, and with Christ's love, you have perfect obedience to him, so that Christ is pleased and so that this father of yours, who cares for all of you and seeks your benefit, does not grumble.

Give up your own will, for it is one's spiritual death. And let each one of you cover up each other's faults, so that Christ in turn will cover up yours. For if you seek justice from your brother, immediately you find yourself up against God, Who

---

[2] cf. Mt. 7:14

[3] cf. Jn. 10:11

[4] cf. Mt. 20:28

puts up with you the sinner. Now that He has awakened you with His grace, you don't want to put up with your weak brother. So where is your justice? And what if Christ takes His grace away from you and demands the ten thousand talents you owe?[5] What hast thou, ungrateful man, that thou didst not receive? Now if thou didst receive it, why dost thou glory every day as if thou hadst not received it?[6]

Say to yourself: "If you are standing, my soul, you do so only because grace is supporting you. And if your brother falls, he falls because grace is absent." Therefore, thank God and do not usurp foreign things as if they were yours, because then God takes His grace away and gives it to him, with the result that you fall and your neighbor rises. You will see your mistake then, but it will be too late.

So whoever amongst you seeks justice, let him know that it is this: to bear the burden of one's brother until one's last breath, and to have perfect obedience to one's guide. Only with love is a weak person edified. And when your spiritual father sees your concord and love, he has joy and gives joy. But when he sees complaining and quarreling, his health breaks down, and he meets an untimely death, leaving you orphans.

I pray with all my soul for all of you together,
my beloved grandchildren,
humble Fr. Joseph.

---

[5] cf. Mt. 18:24

[6] cf. 1 Cor. 4:7

Fifty-seventh Letter

The beautiful rocks theologize like voiceless theologians, as does all of nature.

y dear priest, I wrote and sent that short letter of mine before reading yours, because they were in a rush to make it to the post office in Daphni. Upon reading it, I was very moved to see that you remember the beautiful crags, which are so carefree and quiet.

As for me, after I sent you that long letter about the demons, my attitude towards you changed. Abundant love! Often your face revolved around in my mind. I mentally kissed you many times and wondered, "What could this mean?" I said to myself, "Either my good son is taking great care to comfort us, or something else happened to him." And now that I have seen your letter and the treats you arranged for us, I understood that this was it, and I marveled at the consoling and clairvoyant revelations of the All-wise God. How swiftly does He inform us when another person changes!—a spiritual bond, an invisible communication, an exchange of love, notification from God. There is nothing sweeter or more precious than to understand divine revelations.

So come, my dearly beloved son. Come now, even if for only one day, to talk about God and to theologize; to enjoy what you yearn for; to listen to the rough crags, those mystical and silent theologians, which expound deep thoughts and guide the heart and nous towards the Creator. After spring it is beautiful here—from Holy Pascha until the Panagia's day in August. The beautiful rocks theologize like voiceless theologians, as does all of nature—each creature with its own voice or its silence. If you bump your hand against a little plant, immediately it shouts very loudly with its natural fragrance, "Ouch! You didn't see me, but hit me!" And so on, everything has its own voice, so that when the wind blows, their movement creates a harmonious musical doxology to God. And what more shall we say about the creeping things and winged birds? When that saint sent his disciple to tell the frogs to be quiet so that they could read the Midnight Service, they answered him, "Be patient until we're done with Matins!"

So, my beloved son, this is what the wilderness has that you long for. Whenever you wish, come with one or two people of your synodia.

The truth is, these days I was expecting you to come and rest a little. In fact, I was going to tell you to stay in this cell of ours to have perfect silence. But since you didn't come, we shall wait for another time, in the summer.

For your therapy, stay here a little in the summer. Rest and quiet are very conducive to man's two-fold health. You see that during these bad times, you have been very useful to us. I need you to stay alive as long as I am also alive. But when I die, you can follow too if you want to, and we shall go together to the place where our sweet Jesus will give us repose with His eternal blessings, where we shall rejoice together continuously with our sweet and dear Mother, the sweetest fra-

grance of every breath of Christians; where we shall delight
with the angels and the saints.

I am not doing so well. I have this "hyperalbuminemia,"
and I am constantly all swollen up andfeel faint. Perhaps I
have just a few days left. I am begging God to take me so that
I can rest. I have become tired of this life. If I die, do not forget me in your Liturgy. And I shall pray for you much more
from there, if I find more quiet!

The Sweet-
kissing

Fifty-eighth Letter

As the priest was censing . . .

y blessed and beloved priest,

It has been a while since I last received a letter from you or from any of your spiritual children. May our Panagia protect you from every evil, from every machination of the enemy.

Now Great Lent is approaching to lighten our nous and body. So I pray that we may all pass through it with health, and that with the grace of our Holy God we may also reach Holy Pascha. But a greater struggle and more caution are needed during Lent.

In the previous letter I sent you, I did not explain completely the meaning I gave to the feeling of your spiritual and noetic presence. Therefore, I shall give you an explanation now:

Since your Reverence took care to comfort us with perfect love that time more than any other time, and since your mind was, as you wrote, in the crags of the wilderness, your face was constantly revolving around in my mind noetically with much joy and love.

It reminded me of that priest, or rather that saint, who saw a vision when the priest was censing. Some who were sitting in their stall he did not cense, while others who were away doing an obedience—their stall was empty—he did cense, because their mind was in church. Whereas the others, who were thinking worldly things, were not there.

Something similar once happened also to me with Theodora of blessed memory: her presence was so vivid that I even felt her breath beside me when she was alive, even though I was here on the Holy Mountain and she was in the world.

Fifty-ninth Letter

We shall use plagal of the first tone which is joyous.

y dear priest, I hope that this letter finds you in full health. We, by God's grace, are moderately well.

We received your letter and the photograph, which moved me deeply. It had been a long time since I had received a letter from you, and it was like hearing news from someone in the other life. That is how it seemed to me, also because you are so far away. I don't know how you ended up there, but may God not abandon you. May He remember the hard work you did as a beginner, the zeal of your youthful ascesis, and may He extend His mercy and compassion upon your repentance.

I never forgot even once, nor did I erase your name from the "list" for the liturgy, because you are my child. No matter what a child does, his father feels for him, even if he saddens him momentarily.

The reason why I kept silent and did not write is the following: since you forced me to have you released—although I didn't want to, since I wanted you to be an Athonite monk—finally, not to be disobedient, I did so, but without being responsible anymore, since you yourself had taken up the burden. And see how badly it turned out. Then within a month you asked me to have your name reinstated. You insisted at a time when it wasn't possible anymore, because thousands of lies would have been necessary. Therefore, since I was afraid of burdening my soul, I sadly chose silence to avoid the burden.

But now all these things have passed, and I always remember you, love you, feel for you. I haven't forgotten your kindness. Only when my soul will be harmed I don't agree, for God greatly surpasses human love. And even if you gave me all the good things in the world, if I realize that something is not according to the will of God, I would never do it unto the ages. Since day and night I seek to do God's will, how can I transgress it? So don't say that I don't love you, but say that God does not agree with your ideas.

You write about your sorrows. I am informed even without your letters that you are suffering very much. I see you fighting with beasts in the dark inside a labyrinth, not knowing what you are doing. And like another Ariadne, I am giving you the string to escape. I am opening the door for you, and with unadulterated fatherly love I am inviting you to return. Come, my child, come let us make peace, so you can come to your senses. Like a physician, I am able to cure your passion of agitation and grief, which now has laid a strong hold of you. Come and see that I shall change the tune. We shall chant plagal of the first tone which is joyous. I shall slay the fatted calf and we shall make merry. I am full of love and forgiveness. As a loving father, I shall receive you in my arms, like the son in the parable.[1] I shall kiss your mouth which may have said unseemly things, and it will be blessed henceforth to speak decently. Never again will it judge anyone. I have had my fill of such things, and no matter what I hear and no

---

[1] cf. Lk. 15:11-32

matter what they tell me, it doesn't bother me. Besides, we are human. You see things one way, and I see things another way—as long as we see in God. I, the lowly one, do not feel as if I have saddened or annoyed either you or anyone else by siding with the monasteries.[†]

Don't believe everything you hear. The truth is a precious thing and is not found in everyone's word. Each person speaks according to his own manner of living. Based on his way of life, fathom how true his words are. Understand what I am saying.

You know that I do not talk more than is necessary. Whatever I have to say, I tell it to you straight, because I love your soul more than I love anyone else, and I desire your salvation. Behold, by buying grapes for the wine, I did your service this year, too. I say to myself, "When my son comes, he will find the cup of my fatherly love and affection ready."

So farewell, my beloved son, and I entreat you: as long as you are far away, be careful! Be careful! Be careful! Don't let my priest go to waste! Don't forget why you became a monk.

Two days ago, a Walachian father died here at Lakoskete. He came back to life when they were about to bury him, and he said that he came out of hell where he was being punished because he used to get drunk while he was alive. "So," he told them, "be careful that you do not end up there too." Then right away he died again that very moment, and they laid him in the tomb.

Therefore, my son, my son Absalom,[††] listen to my fatherly voice, flee like a gazelle, and save yourself in the midst of snares, being careful not to be caught in the tentacles of sin. For, as you know, my soul truly loves you more than it loves all others, and with all my heart I am

---

[†] Elder Joseph was with the Old Calendar zealots of Mount Athos until they declared that the New Calendar Church is without grace.

[††] Absalom, a son of the Prophet David, killed his brother and then fled to escape the wrath of his father. But instead of being angry, his father mourned for his son and missed him. (vid. II Kings, ch. 13)

ardently entreating you on behalf of your immortal soul. Take care of it, so that you don't weep in vain in the hour of death.

I kiss you as my son and I pray for you as my beloved. I clothed you with the purple of repentance and put a ring on your finger. So see to it that you enter the bridal chamber; don't end up crying bitterly outside.

Your father and intercessor, sinful Joseph.

Sixtieth Letter

Well even now, see to it that you come back.

ay God be merciful to you, my blessed priest. I pray that you are well. I hope that my letter finds you in full health.

We received your letter, my son, and I was very moved, because it had been awhile since I heard from you. I had sent you another letter, but I am sad because it seems that you didn't receive it.

I became seriously ill from a pimple on my neck. I paid no attention to it and left it to God. But it nearly killed me because the entire left side of my body was infected, and death was imminent. I became delirious and could not recognize the fathers. Everyone was weeping and clamoring to call doctors. I felt sorry for them and let them do their will.

So I started having injections, medicines, doctors—two doctors from the world and Artemios here. And finally, with God's help, they brought me back. Fifty injections as well as other booster shots. Seven incisions from my thigh down to my foot. Blood flowed like a river. I had to change six times a day. I was immobile for five months; they had to turn me over on the bed sheet. We used up all the cotton in Daphni.

A huge wound! They drained the pus from my neck with a cup. A lemon could fit in the hole. And now, I still feel pain in that whole area. It was a great trial. I thank God very much that He showed me His great love. May His holy Name be glorified.

The sister you know was my only help from the world. Like a mother she frequently sent all things necessary for the sick. Our Panagia will reward her duly for her love.

I am well now. I can stand on my feet. I walk with canes. I am cooking again as I used to. But now, my beloved son, let us talk about you.

I wept when I read your letter. I remembered bygone days and meditated at night with my heart. Oh! Oh! Oh! Love of my soul! Do you remember that when you left, you said that everyone gave you his blessing to go out and return after eight days? And that you were sad because I was the only one that did not agree? And I told you that what you were saying would never come to pass, and that once you got there, you would break your promises to return. Do you see that I am more realistic than everyone else? Do you see that you have moved away instead of coming back?

Well even now, see to it that you come back and rest for good here beside us. There are many little houses, and you will be near your brethren, who love you and will look after you. And when I die, I shall see you by my side, and you, too, will leave your remains on the Holy Mountain, without the delusions of those people who led you away from your Repentance and handed you over to be tossed about once more in the salty sea of the world.

From now on, I don't want any more help from you. Only see to it that you come back, that you return to the garden of our Panagia. Thank you, thank you very much for everything.

We here, by the grace of Christ, are doing well. With the Divine Liturgies we are provided for sufficiently. People send us names and money for Forty-day Liturgies and we also do some handicrafts. Our young priest is sickly. Joseph is the "Superior" of the skete this year, so he is busy with the visitors; he provides no help to us. Athanasios stays by himself in a hut. Father Haralambos makes some stamps for *prosphora.** Elder Arsenios is the gardener, and I am the cook. Theophylactos is with Joseph. We had two little old men who died; you didn't know them. We also have a Nikodemos who washes the dishes for us. We live very pleasantly, by the grace of God.

This is how you will live, too. Don't give it a second thought. You will be fine. We also have a little boat to go fishing. They catch perches, pinnas, sea-urchins. Joseph is the captain of the boat.

But our main work is noetic prayer. Mourning and tears. Watchfulness and theoria. Abundant are Thy spiritual mercies, O Lord!

A good young boy came from there, but he didn't stay long enough for us to teach him noetic prayer. He went back. He is the one who told us about your health.

You have greetings and prayers from everyone.
I also greet you paternally,
Your most humble Elder Joseph.

Sixty-first Letter

O vain world! O deceived mankind!
You have nothing good in you!

y beloved child, Photini, my divine sacred love, I pray that you are well.

My little child, my small butterfly, I received your letter and saw what you wrote. I rejoiced that you are all well. But I am not well. Many expenses and medicines, but no health at all. Slowly but surely I am walking to the fatherland. "Here have we no continuing city."[1]

My synodia is trying with every means to turn me back, but unfortunately I am quickly walking towards the grave. I shall go there and wait for all of you.

My Photini,† my light, my Photini! We were once buds and became flowers. But then the leaves fell, the wind scattered them, and we were forgotten. We have dried up like grass whose flower has fallen. So what is left for us? If we have done and sent anything to the other life, only that remains intact. No one can take it. No one can steal it. So, my Photini, let us store up whatever we can for that life. If at this very hour death finds us and we leave some things here, others will enjoy them. You will be forgotten as if you never existed.

---

[1] Heb. 13:14

† Photini in Greek means "bright, luminous."

O vain world! O deceived mankind! You have nothing good in you. All lies. All deceit. You deceive us, you fool us, you toy with us. You show us years and talents and prolonged health, and then suddenly death finds us, and all these things burst like bubbles and tear like a spider's web. This, my beloved child, this is the enjoyment of the world.

So lay hold of instruction.[2] Weep and mourn. You have gotten to know God very well. Pray and cry out:

"My God, my God, look upon Thy Photini. Open Thy heavens once again, and let a drop of Thy divine grace fall. Enlighten the eyes of her soul, and have mercy on her. O my God! My God! Thou who seest the secret parts of our soul! Sweeten our heart which the evil one has embittered and which has forgotten Thy love."

This is the kind of prayer you should say and cry out.

This very moment that I am writing to you, the swelling has reached my navel. My priest went to Daphni, and without my knowledge, he contacted a doctor on the telephone and brought him here, and told me that the doctor happened to be passing by. So he looked at me, and told me that I have a heart problem caused by purulent tonsils. He gave me pills for the swelling, and stimulating injection for the tonsils, like those which John sent.

So, it was one thousand three hundred drachmas for one visit. Fortunately, I have spiritual children in America and they all write, "Take care of your health! Don't leave us orphans." And they send money. Another visit cost one thousand six hundred, including the medicines.

That's all. Whether I want to or not, they are not letting me die. So, be patient.

---

[2] cf. Ps. 2:12

Sixty-second Letter

I shall write a little composition for my son . . .

y beloved child, my divine and sacred love, I pray that you will always be well. Pay heed to what I am about to write to you. Have it as a keepsake. Study it, and I trust that you will benefit from it.

God, my child, formed man out of earth. That is, once He created all of creation like a garden, He made the luminaries and adorned the firmament. He made the moon to rule over all the stars of the night, which like a chandelier with many lights, small and great, adorn and beautify heaven. He made the earth with multitudes of trees both small and great, the beasts and creeping things, birds of all sizes flying beneath the heaven, the domestic animals and birds for the use of man, the sea with all the kinds of fish. Everything was made for man to feed upon and marvel at. And above all these things, He made the great luminary to rule over the day, to warm everything with its heat and to beautify and adorn all things with its light.

And man was created last as a king over all, as if called to be a spectator in a theater. What grandeur! What honor for man! Everything animate and inanimate sings praises to God. Some with their voice, others with the movement of their leaves: each one has its own voice. And even a small blade of grass, if you crush it, it shouts—the scent it gives off is its own voice.

So all these things that the Holy Scriptures mention were all made for man. He made man last of all, so that he would see that everything was very good and rejoice with delight beholding them.

But how was man formed? God took earth, the most humble material, so that he would always be humble; there is nothing more humble than earth. He designed a little clay house, breathed into it, and created man's soul…. That is, God placed the divine breathing as if within four walls of clay; He placed His breath inside.

O heavenly grandeur! O glory and honor of man! He is humble clay, but he is also divine breath! A time will come when he will change. "For dust thou art, and unto dust shalt thou return."[1] The words of our Creator shall be fulfilled. But what will happen to the divine inbreathing, the divine breath? Just as the dust will return to the dust, likewise the soul, which is the inbreathing of God, will return to God. Yes, but how? When it came forth from God, it was a fragrant divine breath, but is it so now? No, it is not. So, what will happen? Purification is necessary—tears, mourning, pain. For you have saddened God, your Benefactor and Father, Who is so good, Who glorified you—the clay—so much, Who gave you His divine breath. These deeds of repentance will purify you, by His grace. So then, weep and mourn so that He may restore you to your original state.

And when you weep with bitter pain of soul for having sinned against God and having saddened Him, then comfort

---

[1] Gen. 3:19

and consolation overshadow you, and then the door of prayer opens.

I know a man who while weeping wanted to hold back the tears because someone happened to pass by, but he could not restrain himself. For they flow with great impetus, as if one were mortally wounded.

When said with pain, the prayer gives birth to mourning. Mourning brings tears. Tears in turn give birth to purer prayer. For tears like a fragrant myrrh wash away the filth, and thus the inbreathing of God is cleansed, which like a dove is confined within four walls, as if made of the four elements.... And then, as soon as the walls break down and collapse, the dove immediately flies to the Father whence it came.

Saint Athanasios of Mount Athos

Sixty-third Letter

We do not have a wedding garment.
Therefore, we must purify ourselves.

ell, we have said that we are the breath of God. Since we have affinity with God, and God is present everywhere, we are always near God. We are His children. And considering the high position which He has given us, to be His breath, we must be careful not to sadden Him.

"I beheld the Lord at my right hand, that I might not be shaken."[1]

And since we have defiled our nous, heart, and body in words, deeds, and thoughts, we have no boldness now. We do not have a wedding garment. Therefore, we must purify ourselves: with confession, with tears, with pain of soul, and above all, with prayer, which purifies and perfects a person. The garment we hear about during Holy Week, "I see Thy bridal chamber adorned, O my Savior, but I have not a garment to enter therein," is the grace of God, which is obtained through arduous, pure prayer.

First, one prays with the simplicity typical of beginners and by shedding copious tears. All this is due to the grace of

---

[1] cf. Ps. 15:8

God which is called purifying grace, which catches us like a fish-hook, and guides us towards repentance.

For it is our God, Who is good in all and to all, Who finds us. He sees us. He invites us. He makes Himself known to us first. Then we get to know Him, after He anoints us with His divine mercy. Hence, repentance, mourning, tears, and everything that happens to someone who repents, is all due to divine grace. This is purifying grace which cleanses man.

There is no good thing that does not come from God, nor is there any bad thing that does not come from the devil. So don't ever get the idea that you have done something good without God, because as soon as you think like that, immediately grace will withdraw, and you will lose it so that you realize your weak condition and learn the adage "know thyself."

In order for one to realize his weak nature, he must encounter many great temptations. And then, through many trials he is humbled and learns true humility. But it takes time.

Humility does not consist of simple words such as "I am a sinner..." and so on. Humility is the truth. To learn that you are nothing. Nothing is what existed before God created everything: nothing. So this nothing is what we are. Your root, your existence began with nothing, and your mother is clay, but your Creator is God. "What hast thou that thou didst not receive? Now if thou hast received it, why dost thou glory as if thou hadst not received it?"[2]

It is a great gift of God for one to learn the truth. And the Lord said that this truth frees us from sin.[3]

Knowledge of God is vision of God, because spiritual knowledge, not natural knowledge, knows God. For natural knowledge is discernment which can tell good from bad, and all people have it, but spiritual knowledge comes from spiritual work, and coming to "know thyself." All these things

[2] 1 Cor. 4:7
[3] cf. Jn. 8:32

happen to us by the grace of God through prayer. The grace of God is beheld noetically and is known by the perception of the nous during prayer.

There are many ways to pray. All of them are good—if one does not know any better and prays with simplicity. But if one has a guide and yet is disobedient, then one regresses and falls into delusion.

Except for circular noetic prayer, all other prayers may undergo change with time when your simplicity is lost and you begin to have ideas about yourself. However, noetic prayer, the *single-phrased** invocation of the name of God, leaves no room for doubt nor can it be followed by delusion. For within the heart, the name of Christ is called upon, and He cleanses us from darkness and guides us into the light.

The Trans-   figuration

Sixty-fourth Letter

The heart does not tolerate divisions. Thou shalt bow down to thy God alone and Him shalt thou serve.

 oetic prayer, as we mentioned above, is the "Lord Jesus Christ have mercy on me." You should say this by lowering your nous into your heart with your breathing, as all the *Watchful Fathers** say. Restrain your breathing as much as you can, while paying attention only to the words of the prayer. In the beginning it is a lot of hard work, because the nous is unaccustomed not to wander, but with time it learns to stand still.

I know a brother who would keep his nous within his heart for six hours, without distraction for up to one hour, and sometimes longer.

The prayer is said initially with toil. But later, it is said effortlessly with wondrous exultation. Since we have affinity with God—not in essence, but as we said we are the breath of God—when we purify ourselves from sin through fasting, vigil, and this we are talking about, and through forcefulness and watchfulness, and by patiently enduring to keep the nous within the heart as if in confinement and not letting it escape, then our good God looks upon us and sends forth His refreshing grace. Like a radiant, luminous cloud it thoroughly illuminates him. And then he who was in darkness a moment ago clearly beholds the inner man. Grace remains with him as long as the Lord wills. This happens perpetually, and thus a person is constantly purified and perfected by divine grace.

For when grace overshadows and the breath of God (which is our soul, as we have said) is aflame with love, it is uplifted, a divine union occurs. Then, man is so assimilated with God that he can be neither recognized nor distinguished from Him, like the sun and its light, or fire and iron when they are united. For the inbreathing and grace spring forth from the same source: our sweet God.

Oh, how good our kind God is! How compassionate! He does not have any self-interest or any need of man, as the Most Perfect One. But since out of His great love He wanted to impart His most perfect gifts, He created all of creation. And having formed man, He made him king and bestowed everything upon him.

God seeks only one thing: that you honor Him, love Him, and keep His commandments, acknowledging that He is your Maker. He does not want you to divide His glory and to worship other things instead of Him. He does not want you to love anything more than Him. For this reason, when He gave His commandments to Moses through the divinely written law, He said, "Hear, O Israel: thou shalt love the Lord thy God with all thy soul, and with all thine heart, and with all thy might, and with all thy mind."[1]

So, my beloved child, do you understand? He has left no room for your love to incline anywhere else, but absolutely all the desire of your soul should be to love the

---

[1] cf. Deut. 6:5

Lord. In this manner, His grace will dwell upon you. The heart does not tolerate divisions. Thou shalt bow down to thy God alone and Him shalt thou serve.[2] Ah, then! Then Christ, Who is the Word with the Father and the Spirit, will come within you, and as He promised, They will make Their abode with you,[3] and you will be a temple.[4] Then the prayer will reign and will subjugate the nous. What a joy! What a joy for the miserable clay! How many good things the Lord gives us!

I know a brother with this kind of love who fell into ecstasy. He saw three identical children of the same age in boundless light. And they blessed, intoning, "As many of you as have been baptized into Christ have put on Christ. Alleluia."[5] They said this many times as they blessed. I marveled at how much love this brother had for God.

So don't look for any other way to approach God; just love Him with all your soul. Then you take no account of your body and torment it in order to overcome the passions. But it is the Lord Who gives you the strength to overcome them. And the more you are purified from the passions, the more peace you have, the wiser you are, and the more you understand God.

Postscript:

Well, my beloved child, my dear little child, I have begun writing to you. Copy my letters and send them back so that I can continue where I left off. In this way you will make a little book to have as a keepsake. I shall write wonderful things to you which you have never heard before. My own inspiration. Praxis and theoria.

I am near death. I am all swollen up, but I do not stop; I want to do something good—even if it means struggling until my soul departs.

---

[2] cf. Ex. 20:5

[3] cf. Jn. 14:23

[4] cf. 1 Cor. 3:16

[5] Gal. 3:27

The money you send goes to doctors, injections, the poor; not a penny is left over. The fathers here want flour now and are scolding me. But I am looking at the cypress trees—where they will open my grave.

Sixty-fifth Letter

I beg you to cast the grief away from your soul.

y very noble lady! For days I wanted to write to you and comfort your afflicted soul because of the misfortune that befell you, but I waited in case we would receive an answer from you, as you had written to my priest. But seeing that you were slow in writing, and feeling the pain of your soul, I entreat you to listen to my humble voice and cast the grief away from your soul. For excessive grief gives birth to other evils.

No one knows the counsels of God which He employs to save us. But anyway, no matter how things happen, they are for our benefit, regardless of whether we are sad or think that we have been abandoned by God.

It cannot be concluded that something bad happened to us because we sinned or transgressed, but it can be concluded that by means of grief, our transgressions committed since youth are forgiven.

Perhaps we had a little pride and through the sorrow we acquire great humility. Maybe the Lord wants to test us to see if we will be faithful to Him even after the misfortune. He wants to see the patience we have and our love towards Him.

Perhaps he was a bad person, although his parents were good. And with this accident his parents were helped by you. Although you suffered a material loss, you profited spiritually. Perhaps you would have been sad to do such a good deed of mercy under other circumstances, because maybe God wanted you to give more alms. Furthermore, it is possible that he was bad and God cut his life short to save him through pain.

God could have let the accident happen through someone else instead of through you. But through you, all these good things happen that we mentioned above. For this humility which you have, crying as if abandoned by God, could not have been acquired otherwise, even if you had lived ascetically for many years.

People commit sins from their youth: with words, with their eyes, with their mind, with consent, with deeds. Yet through one sudden shock, one misfortune, one great loss, all those sins are forgiven and one transforms from glass into a diamond.

And besides all of these causes, it could be due to the devil's hatred. When he sees that we want to be saved, he becomes an obstacle and stumbling block to hinder our good intentions, to give us despair, disbelief, despondency, and illness due to the grief and great pain, to dry us up like flowers suddenly hit by a gust of wind from the south.

So, for all the reasons we mentioned, we obtain a great reward, if we are patient.

And do not grieve, for intense sorrow can sometimes cause insanity. The Holy Forerunner will not abandon you. He has not forgotten your good deeds, but you will receive your reward many times over. The church we built is dedicated to the Forerunner.

So, I beg you to cast away this grief from your soul. Regain once more the gaiety which you previously had. Have love, and you will be forgiven everything. For it happened involuntarily and by the providence of God, as only He knows—He Who provides for our well-being and our salvation.

By all means, I am waiting for you to write me a few lines stating that you will do as we have written to you, and that you have found peace. We are sorry for everything that happened, and that is why you should write to us so that we may be at peace. My entire synodia and I are praying for you, and we are doing Liturgies every day for the health and peace of your soul and body. Likewise, we have a memorial service every day for the repose of the soul of that unfortunate boy who suddenly died.

Sixty-sixth Letter

**When a person confesses, his soul is cleansed
and becomes like a brilliant diamond.**

y good lady and your good and kindly husband, we all pray that the Lord gives peace, health, and longevity to your entire household and to your relatives.

I received your letter, my lady, and saw what you wrote. I commiserate with you on your trials and share in your pain, just as I share in your joy as well. The life of man, my lady, is leavened with afflictions and torments. When you see a little joy in your soul, know that it is a phone call telling you to endure the affliction that will come.

The one closest to man is God. No one else is closer than God. In Him we live and move;[1] we are continuously in His arms. So we are able at every breath to call out to Him with an inner cry: "My God, where art Thou? Help, hasten, help me, protect me! My Jesus, have mercy on me!"

Our Panagia is the Mother of mercy, the fountain of goodness, and Her grace anticipates everywhere. As soon as you open your mouth to call her, she hastens as a true Mother. Therefore, don't hesitate to call upon her at every moment,

---

[1] Acts 17:28

and you will find her an unmercenary helper and physician in your afflictions.

God, my child, is everywhere, and His eye observes everything, but He overlooks our sins because He awaits our repentance. When we are at fault, whether slightly or greatly, He sees it because He is present, but we do not see Him because we are infants in knowledge. And when He punishes us so that we may turn towards Him, we think that we are suffering unjustly. However, when we humble ourselves, then the eyes of our soul are opened and we realize that everything the Lord does is very good. Then we look upon Him as our Father abundant in mercy and overflowing with perfect love and kindness.

I don't know, my lady, if you have done a general and frank confession of sins starting from your childhood since you were seven. Clearly review your entire past, write your sins on a piece of paper, and take it with you to confession; you will find great benefit for your soul. Your husband should also do likewise. Write down not only those like the one you mentioned, but also lapses of all types, even the ones you don't consider to be sins. Even so, when a person confesses, his soul is cleansed and becomes like a brilliant diamond.

You will start from childhood: which sins happened from eight to ten years of age, which ones happened from ten to twenty and thereafter; sins of the *incensive aspect** and the appetitive aspect of the soul. The same for your husband: sins in accordance with nature, contrary to nature, sins at work, offenses, illegal deeds; everything openly, without bashfulness. But if a spiritual father has been guiding you and you have already confessed, then this is unnecessary.

If at some time, my lady, you want to give alms, give to that woman who lost her son. If you want to show mercy to that boy who suddenly died, don't forget to have a Forty-day Liturgy done for him, because as a youngster, he might have committed sins, and it will take him out of hell. Then you will be the reason why he was saved and went to paradise, because Liturgies save souls and pull them out of Hades. And thus, instead of doing a great evil, as you thought, a great good will come about. For through you, a soul will be saved and all of you will come closer to God through repentance.

As for your nervous condition—the anger you mentioned—say the prayer constantly. In this way grace will settle your nerves. And do not grieve, for the entire world suffers from such things.

St. Anthony the Great conversing with St. Paul the Simple in the desert

Sixty-seventh Letter

This shows that your life is pleasing to God.

y compassionate lady, I received your letter and greatly rejoiced to see the gifts that the Lord has given you. You are well taken care of and you don't need anything except patience and endurance for your soul to be at peace.

Now can I say with confidence that the envious devil saw your good and virtuous way of life, and in order to grieve you he caused that involuntary manslaughter. But with the Liturgies that you have done for him, I am sure that his soul is saved. So instead of something bad happening, something very good happened, for a soul was saved. For God looks for any reason to save a person.

When you say, "Everyone else is happy. Why are we the only ones sad?"—this shows that your life is pleasing to God. For the Lord sends afflictions only when a person does the will of God. For afflictions are a grace and gift from the Lord. So you are inadvertently confessing that you are elect children of God. "For whom the Lord loveth He chasteneth, and scourgeth every son whom He receiveth."[1] So take courage, or rather rejoice, because the Lord loves you very much. Don't be sad anymore.

---

[1] Heb. 12:6

Always advise your husband to go to confession. Those things he is telling you are not correct.

Confession is one of the seven Mysteries of our Church. Without confession, repentance doesn't count, and without repentance, one cannot be saved.

If you want to give alms to the mother of the child, it should be done in person, and not through someone else, so that her soul will be healed from the sorrow for her child. But give other alms anonymously.

You have had good spiritual fathers, and that is why they have led you on the right path. I am very pleased with them.

It was my responsibility to write to you because you have helped us, and I felt for your pain.

Now I rejoice with you, because I have come to know yet another good Christian family. Therefore, I shall stop writing to you. It is good enough that you correspond with my priest.

I continue to be your intercessor to God
The least among monks, Joseph.

Sixty-eighth Letter

If you don't give up sinning,
whatever you do will go to waste.

y blessed child, Panayiota, I pray
that you are well. I received your
letter, my little child, and saw what
you wrote and my soul hurt for you.
You are not in a very good position.
One of two things must happen:
either he must take you as his lawful
wife, or you must leave him and live
by yourself in repentance. As things are now, you aren't getting anything done; you can't even go to confession. If you
don't give up sinning, whatever you do will go to waste. As
soon as you separate and give up sinning, everything is forgiven, once you go to confession.

Are you unable, my child, to make a living? Go to the
house of some good Christians; do whatever work you can;
just flee from sin. Sin is separation from God. You will be
punished eternally. Whereas here in this life, no matter how
much affliction one might have, it passes.

Decide: if he marries you, it is no longer called a sin; it
becomes lawful. Then you will write to us and we shall work
out a penance for the past. If you leave him, still write to us

and we shall tell you what to do. But now, since you are living in sin, nothing can be done.

Force yourself, my child, because death comes suddenly, and it would be a pity to lose your soul. We shall do Liturgies and Supplicatory Services so that the Lord may help you.

I am praying for you—humble Elder Joseph.

Sixty-ninth Letter

***Do not doubt that it is time
for you to wear the holy schema.***

s is my duty, I continually send up prayers to the Lord, that He protect and guide you towards His holy will.

You asked, O child of our good God, if the Lord wants you to receive the holy schema. My sister, from the time you first saw the world, you have walked along the path of God, and you never sought anything but the will of the Lord. So, do not doubt that it is time to wear the holy schema, since even without the schema you are a nun. Now that you have grown old, what kind of works do you seek?

You already know your work. Give to the poor from whatever you have in excess. Give to poor nuns, and they are able to do what you are unable to do.

Find a good eldress, call a priest who is a Great Schema Monk, and become a nun in your house without letting anyone know about it. Then continue along your path. You will be very fortunate, because you will be reborn. All week long, don't leave your house. Stay inside and enjoy the grace which remains with you for eight days.

Don't be afraid. Don't hesitate. Christ came for us. He gave us His abundant love, and He said to us, "Love one another, as I have loved you."[1]

So don't wait. Don't postpone it. Don't miss this opportunity that Christ is giving you from above.

Give the note to Theophylact and I the humble one am praying for you, and by the grace of God I support you.

---

[1] Jn. 13:34

Seventieth Letter

The beginning and end of every good thing is Christ.

greatly rejoiced, my child, that you seek to hear a word of God for the benefit of your soul. So open your ears and I shall fill them with good things. Listen, my child:

Let your mouth continuously meditate on the prayer, "Lord Jesus Christ, have mercy on me!" Let your breath cleave to the name of our Savior. After a long time, the nous will grow accustomed to saying it with the inner voice. And when the nous has been purified with the prayer, it will draw the prayer down into the heart. Then there will be a union of nous, word, and heart. That is, through the constant invocation, the prayer finds a way into the heart through inhalation and exhalation, so that nous, word, and heart become one. And as the heart is continuously cleansed, it receives accordingly the overshadowing grace. And then, little by little, without your realizing it, it becomes heaven—paradise within you.

Up to this point is praxis; beyond this is theoria. Reach this point and we shall discuss the rest when the time comes.

Just know that everything—the beginning and end of every good thing—is Christ. By ourselves, we cannot do anything if Christ does not first assist us with His divine grace. He first made Himself known to us, and then we came to know Him. We love Him because He first loved us.[1] If He does not act, the good is not activated within us.

So become a little child with all its childlike simplicity, and throw yourself at the feet of our Panagia who carries the Great God as a small infant. Weep and cry out with much love (which He will give you):

"My dear, sweet Mother, help me, show me how I may be saved! Intercede, my dear Mother, with your Son that He may show me what He wants me to do and what I should seek from Him. May He open the eyes of my soul, which are closed, and thus I do not see Him—while He sees me at every moment—and I constantly grieve Him."

---

[1] cf. Jn. 4:19

Seventy-first Letter

Make a good beginning so that the end may be good.

isten, my child, hearken unto my words. Live very modestly. Be very humble. Don't speak idly about humility, but be like rubbish for people to step on, if you want Christ to visit you. Your heart needs to become as soft as cotton. Always yield to anyone you speak with: "You know best, my sister, forgive me!"

Whatever gentleness you use in speaking with others, that very same gentleness will Christ use with you. With whatever measure you measure out to others, with that very same measure will He apportion out to you.[1] Just as you forgive the failings of others, He forgives yours. With whatever love and gentleness you seek Him, likewise will He appear to you.

Don't say that you are pretending to be obedient, while you are really doing your own will. For you are not offending your eldress the abbess, but God Who is near you and sees your every movement. He is always with you; it is you who are blind and fail to see Him. You are always in His arms. You breathe Him, you eat Him, you wear Him, and you can never fool Him. He sees everything you do, even before you think of it.

---

[1] cf. Mt. 7:2

If you say, "The transgression is small; it doesn't matter!" then your small prayer doesn't reach God; it doesn't matter! If you say that you want your small prayer to be heard, know that even your small transgressions are recorded and they neutralize your small good deeds.

So, if you are punctilious and gentle so as not to grieve the Lord who sees everything, then be afraid of grieving the abbess and the rest of the sisters, knowing that you sin against God.

Never say, "I am right." Even if they gouge out your eyes, never seek justice, for you have put on Christ Who became man for our sake and suffered everything to save us. Just as He forgives transgressors, so must we.

When you are disobedient, my little child, do you know how much you sadden the eldress, and how much you resist the will of God, Who immediately withdraws His grace and leaves you bare? Your conscience is embittered and your nous becomes turbid, and for many days you remain like hard and barren earth. Oh, if you could only see how much damage it does to you! So, my child, be careful. Make a good beginning, so that the end may be good. Work now every day so that you may reap peace in old age.

Every morning at daybreak say, "My Lord Jesus Christ, make me worthy to pass my day without sin." Eagerly take hold of your work and keep the prayer on your lips. Be aware that the Lord is watching you and your angel is recording: your angel is recording your deeds, and the Lord is watching your thoughts. At every moment say with full knowledge, "My soul, collect your thoughts in fear, for the Lord sees you." Don't let your mind wander and don't daydream, but say the prayer with full attention. Do not look at what the others are doing, and do not wish others to think that you

know. What you need to know is to say the prayer continuously and to pay attention to your work. Become a fool for
Christ, so that the Lord may make you wise.

You will do good if you accomplish all that I have told
you, for you will become a good and virtuous nun, beneficial
to others as well.

May grace always be with you to protect you from every
influence of the evil one.

I pray for all the sisters and the abbess, that God grants the
abbess the grace and strength to bear your burdens, for the
burdens are great and the work she has is hard.

Seventy-second Letter

Everything must be accompanied by perpetual, unceasing noetic prayer.

Athos

rise, my child; follow the advice I wrote you. When you have any question or come across something you want solved and you can't find a way out, write to me and I shall write back to you with much love.

You said that many times by doing one person's will, another person is grieved. But if you want to grieve no one and to be in good standing with God, always ask the abbess, "What do you command, Mother? This is what so-and-so told me to do." Then do whatever she tells you unquestioningly, and no one will get upset. Let the others deal with the abbess later.

Obedience has a share in all things, and Christ weaves you a crown at every moment. But in order to develop the inner man, to find peace from the passions, and to have the fruit of your good work blossom, everything must be accompanied by perpetual, unceasing noetic prayer. While you work, say the prayer continuously, either with your mouth or with your nous.

When you say it constantly with the mouth, the nous will grow accustomed to saying it with the inner voice. Then the nous will bring it down into the heart. Thereafter follows the toilsome work of watchfulness: to keep the nous forcefully there, pure and without form, paying attention only to the circular movement of the prayer through inhalation and exhalation within the heart.

Then, since the nous does not have time to form any distracting thought, it is purified with time, thanks to the prayer. Then it no longer takes delight in evil remembrances, nor does it want to remain completely idle, but it becomes all aflame with the recollection of the divine name and with the love of Christ the Savior. So, my child, meditate on this God-inspired hidden work, and your soul will become paradise even before it leaves the body.

A monk who has not learned the prayer does not know why he became a monk. Reading enlightens the nous and helps the prayer. Bodily labor, when it is done in moderation and does not cause agitation, is very beneficial: it leads you to humility.

When you grow accustomed to saying, "Forgive me!" to everyone, and in everything you reproach yourself, and you never demand justice or seek your own will, then you will soon taste the fruit of humility, as long as you have patience in everything. With love and simplicity and without many thoughts, you will reach the heavenly harbor more quickly.

Embrace in your arms the icon of the Panagia as if she were alive, as you embraced your dear mother when you were little. Tell her all your pain, wet her icon with your pure tears, and you will derive constant consolation. She will intercede with her Son, Who is so good, Who loves the good, has mercy on the bad, and forgives repenting sinners. He will

open the noetic eyes of your soul and fill your heart with
love and divine eros. And then your eyes will become two
fountains of tears.

    I pray that you will attain this.

Seventy-third Letter

Christis is very merciful and does not seek much from you.

 y child, your modest letter moved me to tears.

Your humility moved my heart to love you very much, as the Lord loved the woman with an issue of blood, and to say to you the same words, "Take heart, daughter, thy faith hath saved thee. Go in peace, and grieve no longer."[1]

Paradise will open. The King of the ages will appear to you in that day, and you will be overjoyed and will leap like a deer from His great and infinite love.

Therefore, do not mourn your poverty, since the kingdom of Christ has compassionately dawned upon you. Do not lament for your transgressions, since the Son of God has come to earth and suffered as a man for us, and raises us to the heavens through pure repentance. It suffices for you to say, "I have sinned," with a fervent heart, and immediately grace opens the heavens to you.

Christ is very merciful and does not seek much from you. Only say with faith, confessing like the prophet, "I have

---

[1] cf. Mt. 9:22

sinned against the Lord."[2] And immediately you will hear, "The Lord also hath put away thy sin."[3]

Oh, how good the Lord is, how good! How fortunate we mortals are to have such a perfectly good Father!

So, take courage, my blessed child. With boldness write to me of your tribulations, and with much love I shall answer you with whatever the Lord gives me.

We are very thankful for the vestments, which took so much toil and money to send. When they get them, I shall tell my beloved priests to write you. They are filled with grace because they have ceaseless prayer.

See to it that you also say the prayer continuously, and then Christ, Who is joy, peace, love, and light, will enter within you. Now that you have already begun, exert yourself, and don't leave it.

When you see that the nous becomes tired of grasping the prayer, say it constantly with your mouth. In time, the nous will take it up again.

In the beginning it is hard work, but when years have passed, the prayer will cry out by itself from within. It continuously cleanses one from all the passions.

I forgot to tell you that we shall send you a little package soon. I have found a cross perfect for your little soul, and I am sending it to you as a blessing, as you wanted. And I pray that He will bless you—He who is blessed and glorified unto the ages.

2 2 Kings 12:13
3 Ibid

Seventy-fourth Letter

The more you love, the more you are loved.

 y divine, tender love, I pray that you are well.

May the grace of our Christ enlighten you, purify you, and make you like St. Mary Magdalene, whose sacred hand we have here at the monastery of Simonos Petras. Her hand is warm as if she were alive, and it exudes an ineffable fragrance. That is how much grace Christ gave her.

I greatly rejoiced, my child, to see how eagerly you seek your salvation. This is why I am certain that the Bridegroom of your immortal soul will give you His mercy abundantly.

Have our Panagia, His dear, sweet Mother, as your protectress and entreat her constantly. Embrace her holy icon as if she were alive, and wet it with tears as the myrrh-bearer did to Jesus' feet. And you will derive substantial consolation as if she were beside you.

Our Panagia hastens everywhere. She bestows her grace abundantly upon anyone who fervently cries out to her. She is a mediatress to Christ for everyone, because she was deemed worthy to give birth to the Lord and to become the Mother of God. She carries Him in Her arms and continuously entreats Him.

Since we sinners do not have the boldness to run directly to God from the start, we cry out to His Mother. She regenerates us; she intercedes; she anticipates all our afflictions. She is our protectress and helper, more honorable than all the angels, beyond compare more glorious than the Cherubim and Seraphim, second in rank only to the Holy Trinity. Oh, but she is so good, my good girl, so sweet, that you want to embrace her at every moment and obtain consoling grace. The more you love, the more you are loved.

Do not grieve about the package, my child. I care about your soul. I want to contribute a little bit with my words to build a little house for you in the heavens where everything is immortal and eternal. Everything here, whether or not they exist, does not harm our soul.

See to it that you clearly write down your confession since the time you were little. Write down everything very clearly. Do not hurry when you write, but send it quickly, lest I die. I want you to be benefited by me—not by someone else—so that I may say before Christ, "Behold, I and the children whom Thou, O God, hast given me."[1]

Don't spend any more money on us. Whatever you have done, you have done. Christ has accepted it as a fragrant myrrh. Whether or not it comes to us, you receive your reward; it has been recorded in the heavens.

Do not grieve, thinking that you have been deprived. From that very moment I numbered you among my spiritual children. I have been praying for you since your first letter, and every day we commemorate you in our Divine Liturgy. Take courage, for you will not undergo the death of your soul, but in repentance you will live unto the ages.

Send your letter quickly, and if you forget something, write it later in another letter. Have the beloved prayer on your lips:

[1] cf. Is. 8:18

"Lord Jesus Christ, have mercy on me!" He alone is the Savior, and we hope that He will save us. Just be patient.

Bear your daily cross and cry out to Him often, "My Jesus, where art Thou? Hasten, save me, for I am perishing!" And He will cry out to you, "Do not be fainthearted, my child. I am always here beside you. Be patient. The time will come for me to take you by my side to rejoice eternally."

So don't send any more packages, because they demand an outrageous tax for them. Just attend to your soul; take care that you save it since it is precious, immortal.

Seventy-fifth Letter

Put in your hundred mites,
and I shall put in my thousand gold florins.

 asiliki, my blessed child, I hope you are well.

I received your letter of confession, and I saw everything that you wrote. Everything is forgiven, my Vasiliki, except for the things that are not confessed: these things are not forgiven. But just one thing: the sin must not recur. So I ask this favor of you: do not fall into sin again, and all will be well.

The Liturgies will help you very much. And whenever you can, have them done again, for only they can take souls out of Hades.

Now, for the time being, you will abstain from Holy Communion. When you write to me that your bad habit has stopped, we shall work out a small penance analogous with what you deserve. I shall do the Supplicatory Canons you asked for—not just seven, but many; I shall keep doing them so that the Lord and His holy Mother will help you.

So don't be sad. The All-good God forgives everything; just don't repeat it. The Lord will make you bright and new, like a white dove. The only favor I ask of you is not to let it happen again.

I shall take care of you as long as I am alive. Take care. I am approaching death. I am very seriously ill. I await the hour. I want to put you in order. I fervently entreated the Lord and His golden Mother to enlighten you. Perhaps this is why that person saw what he saw as he was telling you.

So, make a good beginning. Put in your hundred mites and I shall put in my thousand gold florins, and arise from the mire. I am giving you my hand. Come out of the pit. Everything is vanity, a lie, and deception.

You are fine. Don't be sad. Don't despair. Take courage. Don't be afraid. Christ is good and compassionate, He forgives everything. I see His hand invisibly stretched out, and He calls out:

"My Vasiliki, don't cry! It was for your sake that I came to the earth and became man."

Do not lament your poverty. Christ the Master loves you. He is generous and has mercy on the first just like on the last. Shed two drops of tears with pain of soul, and all the filth is washed away. Give whatever you can to charity, for Liturgies, for Supplicatory Canons, whatever you can, to open the road to the heavens, where you will receive a hundredfold and eternal life. My joy will be to learn that you have made a start before death comes, because then it is too late.

Keep in mind that I love your soul more than your loving parents and children do. So don't let me leave this life sad.

Seventy-sixth Letter

Just be careful and apprehensive; flee from sin.

he Lord God liveth![1]

You are very good, my beloved child. This is why Christ loves you. An indication that He loves you is His divine grace which has visited you and counseled you since you were a small child.

So attend to yourself and do not embitter our God Who is so good for the sake of a small, bitter pleasure. It is Satan's jealousy, who hates anyone whose spiritual eyes Christ opens. Awaken, my beloved child, and attend to yourself, for He sees things that you do not see. Christ Who is full of mercy is trying to open the eyes of your soul.

Oh, how good He is! On the other hand, the evil one sees this and is trying to close your eyes with bitter pleasure. So, my child, do not cease crying out the name of Christ. At every breath meditate on His divine name. Even if your mind wanders, don't worry, because this continuous meditation and your constant longing to seek Him will draw Him to come on His own to see you. Then a refreshing spring will gush forth from within your heart crying, "Lord Jesus Christ, have mercy on me!" And then you will rejoice unceasingly at the voice and sweetness of Christ the Master.

---

[1] 1 Kings 25:34

Just be careful and apprehensive; flee from sin. It falls like snow and nips everything.

What you wrote about is a visitation of God. It is the first visitation for any sinner repenting and returning to God.

See to it that you cleanse yourself with frank confession. Don't leave the filth of sin inside you, so that the evil one will not find an opportunity to throw you down.

My child, man is unable to do anything on his own. He neither had, nor has, nor will ever have the power to do something good, unless God overshadows him from above. Every good thought, every good movement of the intellect is due to the operation of God's grace. If you accomplished a task without your body's participation, it is your own. However, if you did it with your body, it is God's, since your body is a creation of God. If you thought of something without your mind, it is yours. However, if you thought of it with your mind, it is God's, since your mind is a creation of God.[2] Therefore, man has nothing of his own—everything begins from God and ends in God.

I am writing these things to you through another's hand, my beloved child. But you must attend to yourself. And when I get well—for I am ill now—then I shall write to you with my own hand.

Convey my many prayers to your beloved spiritual father, and tell him that I am about to breathe my last. The doctor is sustaining me with injections and is telling me that I shall get well. But my synodia is crying. They are not letting me depart.

---

[2] cf. *The Ladder* 23:16

Seventy-seventh Letter

If you read lives of saints and toil a little at night . . .

our letter filled me with enthusiasm, my good child, and I hope that you will soon find the fountain of life. Your letters reveal that you are not far from the fountain. Grace has already opened the entrance for you. Walk straight ahead. Keep knocking a little longer through frequent prayer, and not just a spring, but waterfalls from heaven and the fountains of the deep will open, so that the feeling you have now of love towards Christ will be watered and grow. The enthusiasm you have is due to the purifying grace of God which compassionately purifies a person.

Grace is divided into three classes. Its first action is called purifying. After it purifies a person, he is given another greater gift, which is called illuminating grace, that is, he receives enlightenment of spiritual knowledge. And the third grace is called perfecting, which we shall talk about when you get there.

So behold, now you have your corresponding portion. Whatever good you do, whatever good you think of, it is all due to grace. As the saints write, "There is nothing good that is not from God, and nothing evil that is not from the devil."

So whatever good thing a person thinks, it is due to the grace of God.

And now, if you exert yourself in the prayer and pray continuously, if you read lives of saints and toil a little at night, you will quickly obtain what you seek, and your little soul will rejoice that Christ loves you so much. He is Love and He seeks love from us. It is when we love our neighbor that we show that we love Christ, too.

So exert yourself as much as you can, and I pray that you will quickly obtain Him Whom you desire.

The Holy Napkin

Seventy-eighth Letter

Without struggling very hard,
you can quickly reach great heights.

 rejoiced greatly, my child, because of your health and the many good deeds you do for our Christian brothers. This is the truth: the more a person runs to help his neighbor, the more the Lord's grace abounds in him, for love is the first and greatest commandment of God: "Thou shalt love the Lord thy God with all thy soul and heart." And the second is like unto it: "And thy neighbour as thyself. On these two commandments hang all the law and the prophets."[1]

So the more one thirsts for the salvation of his brother, the more his soul overflows with the love of God. And without struggling very hard, you can quickly reach great heights. For love has a share in everything. "It vaunteth not itself; it does not behave itself unseemly; it seeketh not her own; it is not easily provoked; it thinketh no evil,"[2] and so forth.

Do you see that it has a share in everything and quickly leads to dispassion those who attend to it? Our Lord's beloved disciple did well to say, "God is love; and he who dwelleth in love dwelleth in God, and God in him."[3] Do you see, my beloved child, that the Lord is always with you when you

---

[1] cf. Mt. 22:37-40

[2] 1 Cor. 13:4-5

[3] 1 Jn. 4:16

keep His commandments, and that a fragrant angel counts your steps and all your actions?

Read the Old Testament devoutly and you will extract the divine nectar of faith and love. In it God spoke directly to men, and the angels guided them.

God is everywhere. There is no place where God is not. The more you pay attention to Him, the more He pays attention to you. You cry out to Him, "Where art Thou, my God?" And He answers, "I am present, my child! I am always beside you." Both inside and outside, above and below, wherever you turn, everything shouts, "God!" In Him we live and move.[4] We breathe God, we eat God, we clothe ourselves with God. Everything praises and blesses God. All of creation shouts His praise. Everything animate and inanimate speaks wondrously and glorifies the Creator. Let every breath praise the Lord![5]

Always have the Holy Gospel in your pocket, and when you find a brief opportunity, read an excerpt. Thus Christ gives you light and guides you towards His commandments. He completes your love and guides you to imitate Him.

Cry out to His dear Mother constantly, read the Salutations, and she will protect you. She will always guard you from every evil.

Acquire copies of the book *The Way of a Pilgrim* and distribute them to our Christian brothers so that they may benefit spiritually.

Always have a little icon of the Panagia in your shirt, and venerate it when you go to sleep. The more you love her, the more she will love you. And whenever you cry out to her in difficult times, you will feel her help and consolation appreciably. She always intercedes unceasingly for all children who fervently cry out to her.

---

[4] Acts 17:28
[5] Ps. 150:5

Seventy-ninth Letter

All the yearning of the soul should absorb God.

 wave of joy filled my soul, my child, because of your wonderful letter telling about how the grace of our blessed and holy God visited you.

My beloved child, I have begun to recover now. For forty days I ate nothing. For three nights they did not sleep waiting for me to die, but my time had not come. My little children wept continuously and they served me like angels of God. Finally now, I am able once more to grasp things, to write, to answer all those who write and wait.

You wrote to me, my beloved child, about the grace you felt in your heart, so I shall begin writing about love:

Since God is full of love, and since everything He made, above and below, came to be out of His great love, He does not seek anything else from man but love.

When He gave the written law to Moses, the first and greatest of all commandments He cried out was: "Thou shalt love the Lord thy God with all thy soul, all thy mind, and all thy strength."[1] In other words, all the yearning of the soul should absorb God. Knowledge, perception, the mind, theo-

---

[1] Deut. 6:5

ria, radiance, and every motion of the nous, everything in all things should think of God. And man, that clay, should return "Thine own of Thine own."

Truly a great mystery!

All the virtues and divine gifts have perception of the divine and "action of grace." Divine love, though—when one reaches the point of loving Him Who loves—transcends perception. Thenceforth, divine love acts and theoria reigns. Then he who receives the action of divine love cries out:

"O my Jesus, sweet love! Before I saw Thee, Thou didst see me. O light of my soul! Before I knew Thee, Thou didst reveal Thyself to me. And before I loved Thee, Thou didst love me. O life and sweet breath of mine, I was in darkness and Thy sweet voice awakened me and called me. I saw Thee, when Thou didst make Thyself known to me. To know Thee is to behold Thee.

"O my joy and spiritual delight! O heavenly love! O love which burns yet does not consume!"

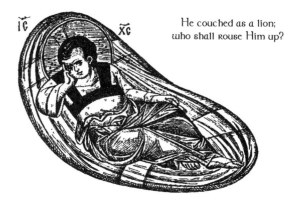

He couched as a lion; who shall rouse Him up?

Eightieth Letter

Once you love God,
then you will also love your neighbor as yourself.

o my beloved child, when this love begins to burn, then we begin fulfilling the second commandment of God. Once you love God, then you will also love your neighbor as yourself. Do you hear what the Lord says, my little child? So when you, my beloved child, thirst to benefit your brother and you go and tell him what you know, thirsting to help him, this is love towards your neighbor: you love your neighbor as yourself.

The feeling in your heart that you wrote about which causes joy and exultation, is the love of God, which is beginning to act in your soul. If you are vigilant and say the prayer constantly and help your little brethren, you ignite the fire of God's love in your soul. And the more you thirst and run to help your neighbor, the more God opens the torrents of love, and waters you.

When you hear the Apostle Paul saying, "Who shall separate me from love?"[1] it is not Paul saying it, but Love itself crying out to Love through the vessel of Paul. Therefore, "He who dwelleth in love dwelleth in God, and God in him,

---

[1] cf. Rom. 8:35

for God is love."[2] Wherever this love falls, it burns and does not consume. One thirsts, but this thirst cannot be quenched. The heart burns with love and cries out, "Where art Thou, my sweet love, my Jesus, the Light of my life?" And the heart burns even more, until the senses cease. So, my beloved child, seek nothing else but love. "Count me worthy, O Lord, to love Thee as much as Thou lovest me!"

But this is enough for now, my little child, because I am tired. My breathing problems torture me greatly. I had sent you another short letter that Father Ephraim wrote. I was unable to hold a pen then. But now, glory to Thee O God, I am beginning to write again.

Careful, my child; be very wary of heretics. You are admidst foreign races and languages.... Do not speak with them at all, because your pure, tender soul will be defiled by their blasphemous words. Our Orthodox Church has cut them off.

The Cruci-   fixion

---

[2] 1 Jn. 4.16

Eighty-first Letter

I will not leave. I shall fall asleep here with my Fathers.

 our days have not yet passed since I sent you a letter, my child, and I have begun to write you a little labor of love to have as a keepsake.

Since the time you left me, I have taken up the responsibility of being your spiritual father: to pray for you not as a stranger, but as my beloved child. And in addition to the Liturgies and the other prayers, I do six prayer-ropes for you every night.

Thank you for everything you have done for us. Don't worry now.

Have patience in your sorrows and illnesses, and cry out to Christ with the beloved prayer—it should never leave your lips. Cry out to His and our sweet Mother so that she shelters you from every evil.

I sent you another little pamphlet, the second one. Now I am sending you the third one. But I have become weak; I don't know if I shall be able to write another one. If not, I shall pray for you from the other life. My prayer will always be with you all.

Have Christ and the Panagia as helpers. Let their sweetest and most desirable name always be in your nous and in your heart. This suffices in place of many prayers.

Don't worry about not finding grace when you pray. It will come once again. This is why it withdraws: so that you seek it with greater longing. When it returns, you have to be more careful, in case you lose it. But again it will withdraw. In this manner one becomes perfect, practiced, and experienced to guide others also safely along the path of salvation.

So exert yourself and watch out for the devil's snares. For the violent take the kingdom of Heaven by force.[1]

As for the things you wrote to me, your spiritual brethren have taken care of everything. Today we had doctors and injections, but the hand of the Lord is above all. I wrote to you that my difficulty in breathing is caused by my heart condition, but deep down, the truth is that it is from God. When I was young, I struggled voluntarily. Now we must struggle involuntarily to have a greater reward.

I see it all, my child, but what can I do? Your brethren are not giving up. They are trying to revive me. But I see that the hand of the Lord is above me. I, the poor fellow, weep inconsolably and fruitlessly. I shout at them, "Let me die!"[2]

I will not leave. I will not go anywhere, lest I die on the road. I shall fall asleep here with my Fathers.

I bid you farewell,
humble Fr. Joseph

---

[1] cf. Mt. 11:12
[2] cf. Phil. 1:21-23

Part Two

An Epistle to a Hesychast Hermit

Part II

Epistle to a Hesychast Hermit

An epistle to an ascetic of the Holy Mountain, divided into chapters and containing in brief:

(a) practical advice how to pass a twenty-four hour day and a rule of food and prayer,

(b) answers to questions concerning delusion and grace, knowledge and prudence, humility and love, the dual warfare of the demons, the three states of nature, and perfect love, and

(c) some other things that he perceived, observed, and heard, which he wrote about to his spiritual children.

Prologue

My beloved child in the Lord. Greetings, and may the grace of God the Father, the Son, and the Holy Spirit be upon your soul. Amen.

ince I see you, my child, thirsting like a deer and longing for the heavenly springs of the waters of divine grace and seeking them with fervent love, although I am illiterate,[†] I am undertaking to write this to you, forgetting my own incapability and ignorance, and trusting in the prayers of my Fathers. And now, with God's help and with your holy prayers, I shall start from the beginning to expound on the monastic and ascetical way of life and the way in which a monk is made worthy of the heavenly kingdom and becomes a partaker of the eternal blessings by the grace and mercy of God.

Do not grow weary of studying these letters, my child, but read them diligently every day until they are engraved within your soul and produce good and fine fruits. Do not consider them to be just ordinary words, because they are not; they are words of experience from Holy Fathers enlightened by divine grace. I was taught by some of them and tasted their fruit in part. Since I am illiterate, it took me a great deal of hard work to write them down for you. For I even shed my blood in order to cultivate them. And now I present them ready before you

---

[†] Although the Elder did have only a few years of formal education, he was well read in Scripture and the Fathers, and he wrote in a very elaborate style of "katharevousa" Greek.

like a banquet with many different kinds of food and like a garden with various trees full of fruit.

So do not be negligent, but continually pick and eat them, so that you may have eternal life and avoid the fruit of knowledge of good and evil which Adam and Eve ate and then died.

O Lord, may we be thus protected from the forbidden fruit and enlightened with the truth by Thee, our sweetest God, to Whom belongs glory and dominion unto the ages of ages. Amen.

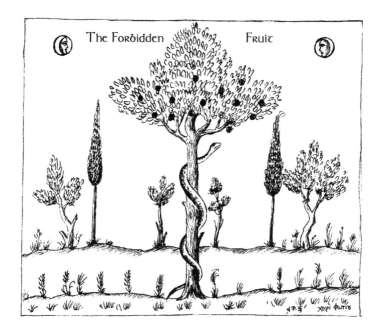
The Forbidden Fruit

Chapter I

On the monastic order and lifestyle;
namely, how to pass a twenty-four-hour day.

ehold, my child, I shall begin first of all by telling you how to live. Even though many times through countless counsels and letters I have already told you, behold once again I shall briefly explain in part the necessary subjects. Listen:

In the midday at seven [Athonite time, i.e., about 2:00 p.m.], eat your regular amount of food, and sleep for three or four hours. When you wake up, do Vespers on your prayer-rope. After you finish, make some coffee to help you in your vigil. And after you drink it, begin Compline. Quietly, without speaking, without light. Also say the Salutations to the Most Holy Theotokos. When you finish, be still, standing up if you are able, with your hands crossed and say this prayer noetically, without light, because light scatters the mind:

"Lord Jesus Christ, sweetest Father, God and Lord of mercy, and Creator of all creation: look upon my humility and forgive all my sins which I have committed all the years of my life up to this very day and hour. Send forth Thine All-holy Spirit, the Comforter, so that He may teach, illumine, and shelter me so that I shall not sin, so that with a pure soul and heart I may adore and worship, glorify, thank, and love Thee with all my soul and heart, my sweetest Savior, Benefactor, and God, Who is worthy of all love and worship. Yes, good eternal Father, co-eternal Son, and All-holy Spirit, count me worthy of enlightenment and divine spiritual knowledge, so that by beholding Thy sweet grace I may bear the burden of this vigil tonight, and render unto Thee my prayers and thanks, through the intercessions of the Most Holy Theotokos and of all the saints. Amen."

Afterwards, say some words of your own, as much as you can and as you know, inciting the holy compassion of God towards mercy and love. Once you get very tired, sit down. Bring to mind various salutary thoughts: death, hell, the judgment at the Second Coming, and weep as much as the Lord allows you to. Next, turn your thoughts to paradise, to the enjoyment of the righteous, to the eternal blessings, and thank our good Savior and benevolent God.

Then stand up and do your prayer rule. After that, sit down again. Read lives of saints, and other compunctious and beneficial books. If sleep comes upon you, stand up and begin the service. And after you finish everything (also the Hours and the Supplicatory Canon on the prayer-rope, as I have taught you) sit down and relax. Sleep a little, until daybreak.

When you wake up, drink something hot with 80 grams of bread or rusk, and begin your work while saying the prayer with your nous ceaselessly. If you have time, you may read and weep in silence. Cook your food by measuring with a milk can, as I taught you. So, a can like that filled with dry legumes or rice becomes two plates of food and suffices for two days, half each day. And after it boils well, eat it at 2:00 p.m.—together with 160 grams of bread or rusk. And when oil is permitted—Tuesday, Thursday, Saturday, and Sunday—put as much as 35 grams of oil on your plate. And if you have any, put some cheese, egg, a sardine, or ten olives. Also, eat a little of whatever fruits or sweets you have, partaking of everything for the glory of God. Eat and have humility, so that you do not judge others.

After noon, you do not have a blessing to receive or speak with anyone: neither a monk nor a layman. Whoever it is, let him come in the morning. This rule must be kept.

Even if it is Pascha, Nativity, or the day before Lent, you will always eat once a day. After Cheese-fare Sunday, do not fast for three days, but drink some tea with a little bread or rusk in the evening.

And in general, have moderation and discernment in everything. But since I have told you these things many times, and since you already know the order, I shall not say the same things over again, because practicing the virtues, after a long time with the help of grace, will make us wise concerning the rest.

Chapter II

Answers to questions of the same person.

ehold, my child, you have learned how to live. Learn now also about all that you asked and desire to know.

First of all, we shall speak about what you are hearing within you, "Holy—Holy..." and so on, as you wrote. I am telling you, my child, that you are actually sleeping when you hear such things. For there is a kind of sleep that befalls those who struggle, when the body is weakened, that is very subtle. While one is standing up or sitting down, it robs him without his realizing it. Then he sees these things in his sleep, and he thinks that he is awake, but he is not. He ends up sleeping all night without realizing it. So then, try keeping vigil at night by standing up and reading; walk around in your room; wash your face to wake up; and then you will realize whether or not what you are experiencing is from grace. All who struggle see such things in their sleep. Furthermore, if you see such things while you are awake, it is not an illusion. The devil does not say things such as, "I worship the Father, the Son, and the Holy Spirit."

You also wrote about the leaping of the heart that you feel. As for this, know that when a person purifies his soul, and when the new Adam, our sweetest Jesus, is conceived within, the heart is unable to contain the joy and the inexpressible pleasure that falls upon it, so it leaps, while very sweet tears flow from the eyes, and the whole man becomes like a flame of fire out of love for Jesus. His nous turns entirely into light and is astonished and marvels at the glory of God—not as you wrote, saying that you are darkened and don't know where you are. You misunderstand these things, so be careful.

Furthermore, you said that your body becomes paralyzed and as if dead. And I tell you, many times the body becomes paralyzed, but the nous becomes all eye, and the heart feels much sweetness and infinite joy. In any case, these things, even if they are the way I am writing to you, do not indicate great heights, but are characteristic of beginners. While the soul is being purified, it sees these things. When it has been completely purified, though, it sees differently. I shall not write about this stage to you now, because you would not understand. As for now, I shall tell you only this: pray to God to give you the knowledge of spiritual discernment—how you should think and what you should have in your nous—until you are counted worthy of the truth—and the real truth is Christ, to Whom be glory and dominion unto the ages. Amen.

Chapter III

On the spiritual work of the intellect, and how we must think.

ou have learned the specific answers to your questions, my child. Now listen how to fight the enemies. You should read this many times with attention as if it were a school lesson, so that you know what to seek and how to fight thoughts of pride when they tell you that you are a saint or that you have grace and you weep profusely.

This is how you should speak to the Lord:

"O my beloved, sweetest Jesus Christ, who was it that entreated Thee on my behalf, and who prayed for me to come into the world, and to be born by good and faithful Christian parents? While so many others are born to Turks, Catholics, Masons, Jews, pagans, and the rest,[†] who do not believe, but are as if they have not been completely born and end up being punished eternally. So how much must I love Thee and thank Thee for such a great gift and kindness which Thou hast bestowed upon me. And even if I were to shed my blood, I would not be able to thank Thee enough.

"And furthermore, whose prayers made Thee, my sweetest Savior, patient with me for so many years—for I have sinned

---

[†] In essence, what the Elder is teaching here is that we be thankful that God has brought us to a position where we can partake of the salvific life of the Orthodox Church.

since my youth—and not grow tired of seeing me acting unjustly, stealing, getting angry, being gluttonous, greedy, envious, jealous, and full of every evil, and insulting Thee my God with my deeds?

"But Thou, my Lord, didst not send death upon me to seize me in my sins, but readily Thou wast patient with me. If I had died, I would have been punished eternally! How good art Thou, O Lord!

"And who entreated Thee to bring me to repentance and confession, and to clothe me with the great and angelic schema? How magnificent art Thou, O Lord! How awesome is Thy great dispensation! How abundant are Thy gifts, O Master! How inexhaustible are Thine indescribable wonders! Who will not shudder, marveling at Thy goodness? Who will not be amazed, beholding Thine abundant mercy? I shudder, O Master, when I speak of Thine abundant gifts.

"My Master and Lord is crucified to save the crucifiers. With my sins, I crucify my Creator, and He Who fashioned me frees me! O sweet love of Jesus, how much am I indebted to Thee! Not only because of the eternal life which Thou hast promised to give me should I love Thee, not only because Thou wilt give me Thy grace, not even because of paradise; but I am obligated to love Thee because Thou hast freed me from the slavery of sin and passions."

What a great miracle! What slave that has been bought seeks payment because he works for his Lord? And how can he seek freedom, since he owes the money for his ransom? Behold, the King and Lord of all was crucified for you, and freed you from the slavery of the demons. He gave you commandments as an antidote for the passions, so that by keeping them you may escape from the passions that conquer you. He says to you, "Do not commit adultery."[1] So you work hard to

---

[1] Mk. 10:19

become chaste, because if you do not force yourself to become chaste, necessarily you will become a fornicator. "Do not steal,"[2] so that you become trustworthy. And if you do not force yourself to become trustworthy, you will become a thief without fail. "Do not love money," so that you will be charitable. And if you do not force yourself to become charitable, you will become a miser. "Do not be a glutton," so that you will be abstinent. "Have love," so that you will not become envious. This is how it is with all the virtues.

And so, after the Lord first freed us through Holy Baptism, He gave us His divine commandments as an antidote for the passions, so that we would not fall once again into the slavery of sin. Therefore, we do not work for God as if He owes us a reward, nor for eternal life, but as bought slaves we work so that we do not become slaves of the demons. We are obliged to work, because we have been redeemed. And since we are in debt, we should serve Him with great humility, keeping all His holy commandments. If we are found to be faithful servants, the Lord freely gives us His divine grace and delivers us from the passions. He also gives us His heavenly kingdom saying, "Come, thou good and faithful servant! Thou hast been faithful over a few things, I shall make thee ruler over many things."[3] Do you see, my child? He does not say to us, "Come, let me pay you for your hard work," but He gives us His sweet grace out of His loving mercy and out of His great goodness. He takes away from us the troublesome passions within us, and in general He counts us worthy of His kingdom.

So when you approach to fulfill your duty—to pray, that is—approach with great humility, seeking the mercy of the Lord: not because He owes it to you to give you grace, but because you are a captive seeking that He free you as a favor.

---

[2] Ibid
[3] Mt. 25:21

Say:

"O Master, our sweetest Lord Jesus Christ, send forth Thy grace and free me from the bonds of sin. Enlighten the darkness of my soul, so that I apprehend Thine infinite mercy and love and thank Thee worthily, my sweetest Savior, Who art worthy of all love and thanks.

"Yes, my good Benefactor and most merciful Lord, do not withdraw Thy mercy from me, but have compassion upon Thy creature.

"I realize, O Lord, the weight of my transgressions, but I also know Thine incomparable mercy. I behold the darkness of my insensitive soul, but I have good hope and await Thy divine illumination and the deliverance from my evil, foul, and destructive passions, through the intercession of Thy sweetest Mother, our Lady the Theotokos and Ever-virgin Mary, and of all the Saints. Amen."

Do not cease entreating God like this until your last breath. He is able to fulfill your request. To Him be glory and dominion unto the ages of ages. Amen.

The Prophet
David
praying

Chapter IV

On caution. Namely, how to wrestle with the thought of arrogance when divine aid comes.

ou have learned, my child, how to think; learn now also how to fight. If the good Lord visits us, frees us from the passions, and shows us His infinite love, do not think that you no longer need to be cautious. For as long as we are poor, we seek wealth, but once we become rich, we are all the more apprehensive, lest we fall asleep or become negligent and thieves break in and steal our treasure.

Now listen to an example about these thieves. After you pray, divine illumination comes upon you, and you feel joy and inexpressible sweetness. Immediately a thief—pride—comes and secretly tells you, "Oh! Now you are a saint!" Tell him, "Shut up, evil demon, for even if I ascend until the third heaven, it will not be of my own doing." Behold what Paul said: "I was caught up and heard unspeakable words."[1] Now then, did he ascend voluntarily? No. So since someone else takes him up, does he have anything of his own? No. Behold what he said as he was saving the entire world with his preaching: "Not by mine own will I do these things, but by Christ who worketh in me."[2]

---

[1] 2 Cor. 12:4
[2] cf. 1 Cor 9:17

Do you see, my child? So what did he have of his own, inasmuch as someone else led him? So then, you also should say to that evil pride, "If I ascend to the heavens and see angels and speak with the Lord, it will not be of my own doing. The King wanted to take some clay, mud out of the mire, and put it beside His throne. Isn't He a King? He can do as He pleases." But can the clay become proud because it is near the King? No. Rather, it marvels at the goodness and humility of the King: at how He did not abhor the filthy clay, but instead brought it near Him. So just as He raised you from the mud, likewise, whenever He wills, He can toss you down into your former state again. So neither when He raised you was it due to any progress of yours, nor should you grieve when He throws you back down to where He took you from, but say, "As for me, Lord, I am only worthy to be a son of hell and I do not complain, for I continue to commit deeds that merit torment. You willed it so, and raised me to the heavens. If You will it, You can throw me down into Hades. May Thy holy will be done."

You should only grieve when you sin and fall. And you should not grieve because you fell, but because you saddened God with your ingratitude after He showed you so much love. But once again you should resume hope and arise. Do not despair because you have sinned. Whereas if your spiritual state changed without committing a sin, do not be afraid, but rejoice because you have seen the good things of God and acquired more faith and a fervent hope that, by His mercy and benevolence, you will become an heir of those things you saw. Therefore, struggle to obtain more humility.

Furthermore, when the evil demon tells you that you are superior to the other monks, tell him: "Shut up, demon, because if the Lord wishes to pour out His divine grace upon all men, everyone would become the same. So, how is someone to blame if he does not have grace or has only a little?" Behold, the Lord gives five talents to one person and two to another. Is it perhaps his fault that he received two? No. The Lord knows what is best for each person. However, even though he was given only two, he heard the same words: "Enter thou into the joy of thy Lord."[3] He did not say to him, "Why didn't you make them ten as well?" Do you see, my child, that you have indeed received much from the Lord— and that He will ask much of you?

So neither can the one who received abundant grace scorn and criticize the one who did not, nor should the one who does not have the same grace grieve and grumble because God does not give similar gifts to him, too. But he who has grace must patiently bear with him who does not, putting up with all his bodily and spiritual illnesses, and must guide him with discernment along the spiritual path, until he, too, doubles his talent accordingly; or rather, until a ray comes and opens and enlightens the eyes of his soul so that he may see his deficiency and obey unquestioningly the person superior to him.

So this, my child, is how we must think: that without the help of our Holy God, we are unable to do anything, as the Lord tells us, "Without me ye can do nothing"[4] and "Except the Lord build the house, they that build labor in vain."[5] So we must seek to be granted spiritual knowledge along with discernment. For without these two, even things that seem good to our eyes can actually be bad and harmful, and where we think there is honey there can actually be poison. For discernment sees, measures, and weighs, while knowledge destroys and abolishes every evil and proud thought; humility collects thoughts, and grace and love keep them, as

---

[3] Mt. 25:21

[4] Jn. 15:5

[5] Ps. 126:1

love is the culmination of all virtues. It was out of love that our sweet Jesus came and was crucified to show us the infinite love He has for His creatures. To Him be glory and dominion unto the ages. Amen.

The Cruci-Fixion

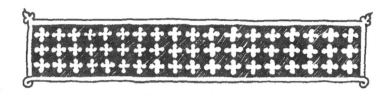

Chapter V

On how divine Grace comes,
and how it is distinguished from delusion,
and about the short path.

o, my child, listen also how divine grace comes and how it is recognized. We know that once someone has tasted wine, he can tell if they give him vinegar instead. This is how you should understand divine grace as well. One who has already tasted it recognizes delusion. For the demons imitate grace, but he who has eaten the fruit of truth, as we have said, knows the fruit of delusion. For, if his nous pays attention to the delusion even slightly, his heart is agitated and filled with disturbance. His nous is darkened and even his hairs stand on end. But also it blows him up like a balloon. Whereas divine grace is sweet, peaceful, humble, quiet, purifying, illuminating, joyous, and there is no room for doubt that it is divine grace.

Now pay close attention to learn how divine grace comes, and how we can recognize the path of truth from the path of delusion. We say that the monastic life is like this:

Once the grace of God enlightens a person and he leaves the world, he goes to a monastery, or somewhere else with many other brethren. He is obedient to everyone and is at rest keeping the divine commandments. And by fulfilling the spiritual responsibilities he has been given, he awaits with good hope the mercy of God Who loves man. Well, this is the common road many Fathers have walked. However, there is also a shorter road, which I shall mention here. This shorter road is not an invention of human knowledge, but is from the Master Himself, Who guides each one of us, as His holy will wants.

After the merciful and good God sends a ray of His divine grace into the heart of a sinner, he arises at once and seeks spiritual fathers to confess the evil deeds he has done. He also seeks the wilderness and caves for protection from the causes of the passions and to correct his previous sins—with hardships, hunger, thirst, cold, and heat and through other ascetical practices. And the Lord gives him even more ardor—which like a flaming furnace burns his heart with fervent eros for God—and immeasurable zeal towards fulfilling the divine commandments, and boundless hatred towards the passions and sin.

So he begins with great eagerness to give away all his belongings, whether he has many or few. Then once he becomes entirely destitute and keeps in part the divine commandments, he is no longer able to hold back his love and yearning for the wilderness, so he runs like a thirsty deer to the wildernesses, seeking a guide and leader for the ascent of the spiritual life.

Unfortunately, though, today all the eminent guides have vanished and there are very few who walk this path. So he cries and laments because he cannot find a guide as he desires, as in the old days. But what can he do since he has a great fervor for stillness? He inquires and seeks the most experienced guide, and puts himself under obedience, and with his guide's prayers and blessing, he begins his spiritual struggles.

Now, many who have this fervor would receive the holy schema and withdraw by themselves to a quiet place with the prayers and blessing of their elder, and every now and then they would go and receive his advice. Others would remain together and had permission at certain hours to be still and undertake every kind of virtue: to weep, to keep vigil, to fast, to pray, to read, to do metanoias according to their strength, and in general to give heed to purity and fight against the passions. And once he finds some quiet place, as we have said, he applies himself to ascesis even more.

However, one must be careful at this point. For many have withdrawn not out of a flaming love for Christ and a desire for struggles and afflictions, but they want stillness in order to serve their passions. For they cannot endure being obedient and insulted, but love their own will. And once they become slaves of the passions—anger and sinful desires— they serve these desires and completely fall into delusion.

But he who has truly withdrawn for Christ's sake has constant tears, weeps for his sins, and cultivates every virtue. And with fervent faith he dedicates himself to struggling until death. He puts his nous into his heart and forces himself to say the prayer while inhaling and exhaling, "Lord Jesus Christ... have mercy on me." Moreover, he collects his nous according to the directions of the Watchful Fathers.

By doing all this and painfully seeking the will of God, he begins little by little to perceive divine aid noetically, which spiritually cleanses him little by little, as a bath cleanses us physically. It softens his heart and moves it to feel compunction, to mourn, to be obedient, and to have greater zeal and ardor. And like a mother with her child, it supports him and educates him. Then when grace withdraws, he laments and seeks it, without understanding the wisdom of our Holy God. So he adds fast upon fast, standing and vigils, prayers and supplications, thinking that this will attract the grace of God. But by the dispensation of divine providence, temptations afflict him in many ways to test him so that with even more tears he seeks divine aid.

And then, when the divine visitation comes again, he cries out like an infant, "Ah! Ah! Why did You abandon me? The demons almost strangled me! Don't ever leave again! Ah! What can I do to keep You?"—thinking like an infant that his struggles bring this visitation. But as soon as he has a good taste of it, once again God withdraws immediately. Little by little, though, He returns more quickly and more intensely. But he who is still an infant in wisdom and knowledge begins to grow accustomed to it and grows bold, thinking that henceforth it has been given to him as a reward for his toils.

For three or four consecutive years he sees the grace of God continually training him and making him wiser, while his passions diminish and the demons are unable to fight him for long because divine grace protects him. When he is awake, he has tears to comfort him, whether he is walking or working. If he is praying noetically, he noetically perceives the radiant cloud, which occasionally visits him. And when he is sleeping, even if only a little, he sees beautiful dreams: gardens with brilliant, golden flowers and indescribable royal palaces shining brighter than the sun, and many other different things which the mind meditates on after he wakes up, and they rouse him to greater ardor and zeal. Then he marvels at the beauty of the eternal blessings and wonders when he will be made worthy to inherit them.

However, one must be cautious and discerning here, too, my child, and must not believe in dreams, but must recognize whether they are from God or from the demons. But since not everyone has this discernment, one should not believe in them at all. However, dreams from God can be recognized. Sometimes one sees them in deep sleep, other times in a light sleep, as if sleeping but not really sleeping and for a short duration. And when he wakes up, he is full of joy, and his mind meditates on them, and they bring him theoria. For years and years he brings them to mind, and they are unforgettable. On the contrary, dreams from the demons fill the soul with disturbance. When one wakes up and the mind tries to recall them, he is filled with fear, and his heart does not accept them. But even during sleep as he sees them, they are not stationary, but they change into forms and shapes, into places and ways, into actions and movements. From these changes and the disturbance and the unpleasantness, you are able to recognize where they are from. There are also other things proceeding from the imagination and from overeating, but it is not necessary to point them out. But, as we have said elsewhere, the heart of a struggler ceaselessly meditates on prayers even while he sleeps.

However, this spiritual infant does not have sufficient knowledge to understand and discern the providence of God, for until this stage he is still drinking milk and has not acquired clear eyes, but emanates both light and darkness, and his works are mixed with the passions. So when he sees all those blessings, he starts to think, "Behold what God has given me because of my struggles and afflictions."

Then an evil demon secretly sows the poison as of old with Eve, and this infant opens his ears. But this happens also by divine permission so that he learns humility. So the crafty demon starts telling him, "See? Nowadays they say that God does not give grace anymore. But just take a look at yourself. The truth is that they just don't want to struggle, so they hinder others and tell them: 'You will be deluded, you will fall, you will get weak.'"

The primeval evil one teaches him many other things. Without realizing the trap that the demon is weaving for him, he is plundered because he is inexperienced in battle and accepts a lie as the truth. But this may also occur by God's providence, as we have said, to make him wise so that he is not an infant forever.

Glory to the wisdom and knowledge of God, who arranges in various ways the cure of our soul: glory and praise always, now and forever, and unto the ages of ages. Amen.

The Giver of Life

Chapter VI

On how such strugglers fall into delusions when they have no guide, and what the remedy for their cure is.

ou have heard up to this point how grace comes. Listen now also how strugglers are deluded, for they must use great caution.

Many have fallen in the past, and still many fall every day. Because once a person accepts a lie as the truth, he is puffed up with conceit and begins saying and teaching that people do not want to struggle and that if a person merely wants to and exerts himself, he becomes a vessel of grace. Angrily arguing with those who object, he falls little by little into delusion and becomes a slave of the demons, saying that everyone else will be damned, because no one has knowledge except for him. He is no longer persuaded by those who tell him what is beneficial. Then he locks himself up in isolation, doing the will of the demon dwelling within him. And if he remains shut up, the demon will either strangle him or hang him, convincing him that he will die as a martyr. But if the demon does not do this, he will throw him into indifference and negligence so that he abandons everything and overeats and gets drunk. He does not realize that he has fallen so that he may seek his cure, but thinks that he is doing well and that this is the true and right path. But the Lord who loves man waits for him to realize why he has fallen. If he perceives his fall, he has his cure.

So then, my child, this is one delusion. And its remedy is for one to realize that he is deluded and to seek with tears an experienced physician able to save him, so that he gives him the appropriate medicines for the safety of his soul. But let us return to where we left off.

If a person does not go astray as the one we mentioned, he may instead go astray by thinking in his ignorance that he has acquired grace by his own efforts. So he argues that if one merely wants to exert oneself, one can receive grace. But since he has fear, he says with natural discernment, "How can I criticize the others and say that no one has knowledge and that only I am enlightened?" Thus, beating and being beaten, he wrestles with thoughts, while the grace of God moves away from him little by little, allowing him to fall into temptations so that he might learn humility. And since he cannot endure the bitterness of the thoughts and is afraid that he might be deluded, he runs off seeking an experienced elder to heal his wound.

Although all the fathers are good and holy, and each one gives his opinion, such a person is not healed because the hour has not yet come for God to reveal the physician and the medication. This is why he is not informed from above. Besides, he needs a word of praxis from someone higher than him to cast down his haughtiness. And since he does not find what he is seeking—because he does not have the patience for it to come when the Lord wants—he becomes even more puffed up. Then he is handed over to bodily illness. Grace departs. The body falls ill. He cannot do his regular duties as before. He is overwhelmed by negligence, despondency, heaviness of the body, limitless sleep, paralysis of the limbs, darkness of the nous, inconsolable grief, thoughts of disbelief, fear of delusion. And since he is unable to bear it, he runs seeking help. But as we have said many times, it is difficult to find a practiced guide today. Thus, one tells him to eat milk, eggs, cheese, and meat to regain strength. He is persuaded, since he is unable to do otherwise. For he has lost his patience, and his zeal and fervency of faith have cooled; he has become like a madman from everyone's advice. Others tell him, "You are lost." And others, "You are deluded. That's how others were lost, too." And everyone according to his own opinion says out of love whatever he knows. Then he starts eating, drinking, digging, and so on. So he who was once a man of watchfulness turns into a merchant, a viniculturist, and a gardener.

Yet, he is not content to remain even on the common path of the Fathers, but he will either throw away the schema completely and get married, or he will become, as we said, a slave of the flesh and an enemy of the other ascetics. And when he hears about someone who fasts, keeps vigil, weeps, and prays, he gets angry and agitated and says, "Those things are delusions. You will be deluded. God does not want these things today. I, too, used to do that and they almost had to tie me up with chains." Furthermore, he completely disregards his spiritual duties, lives with great insensitivity, and is at the threshold of hell, due to the sins in which he wallows at every moment. Moreover, he becomes an obstacle to salvation for the others. He wants everyone to become like him, who was at first a zealous fighter, but now a slave of the demons.

So this, my child, is another delusion that swindles strugglers. Its remedy is humility of heart; he must return to the place where he was and patiently await the mercy of God. And if divine help comes, fine. Otherwise, he should place himself under obedience and be humbled, following the common path of the Fathers. But let us get back to the subject.

If the one we mentioned endures the struggle with patience, awaits the compassionate mercy of God, and humbles himself, after he tries out the advice of the Fathers a little and sees that no cure is happening (because the medicines he is given are unsuitable and inappropriate— though certainly someone has what is appropriate), he begins humbly and in tears to seek it from God and men.

And our Holy God hides His grace even more and abandons him to temptations, until He humbles him completely and teaches him well how he must think, for he is still arrogant. Henceforth is the greatest struggle, and the true intentions of the struggler are tried as gold in the furnace. Since he is full of passions—most of all, pride—he is handed over to faintheartedness, dejection, anger, blasphemy, and every evil of the enemy. And every moment he tastes spiritual strangulation and drinks of the waters of hell; the demons stir all his passions day and night. Meanwhile, the Lord stands far off, not assisting him as before.

A true fighter, though, despite all these dangers, does not abandon his post, but stands defending himself and patching the parts of his vessel that were ruined in the fight with the demons. He sits weeping and lamenting his wounds. He tries to heal his own wounds and awaits in agony either the way out of the temptations or his utter destruction. With a small hope, he says, "It is better for me to die in the fight, rather than to give up and let the way of God be blasphemed, since I have so many testimonies that all the saints passed through this road. Abba Isaac the Syrian especially, the boast of hesychasm and the consolation of ascetics, assures and encourages us more than all the other Fathers do."

With such consolations, he heals his despondency a little and has patience. By eating a little humble food, he heals his body and is able to bear and endure the afflictions and the bodily struggles. And he puts all the powers of his nous on guard, lest he blaspheme the name of God in the turmoil from the demons and the passions.

So this great struggle lasts quite some time, according to one's patience and as long as God wills, until He thoroughly purifies him from the various passions and brings him to complete awareness to see clearly which things are from himself and which are from God. After he has been tempted enough, he begins to think correctly, saying to himself, "Vile wretch! Where are those things you used to say, that the others don't exert themselves, and that this is why they don't make progress? Woe to you, for unless the Lord builds the house of thy soul, in vain dost thou labor."[1]

He ponders this along with many other things and constantly fights with the demons. He gives one blow and receives ten. And the one blow he gives is patience, which God does not deprive him entirely of, but leaves him a little bit—just enough for him to stand on his feet. A secret voice tells him, "Be careful, do not move from your post, for you will fall and be utterly lost. Then your remembrance will be erased from the book of life and you will become worse than worldly people!" So he endures. But the malicious demons fight him so much that they nearly strangle him. In his sleep he sees entire battalions of them, and they torture him in millions of ways. And while he is awake, he sees all the turmoil of the passions.

---

[1] cf. Ps. 126:1

May the All-good God give us bravery and patience, so that we may safely pass this spiritual danger.

St. Makarios the Great

Chapter VII

On how divine Grace returns after it trains us well.

t would be good for you to hear how the wise Ruler arranges the way out of temptations and the return of His divine grace. Finally, after one fully realizes and sees the weakness of his human nature, and reaches a deep humility, then the Lord says, "His struggle and spiritual strangulation are enough now. Let us help this wounded person." But He does not send angels to help him, because the nature of men of the eighth millennium cannot endure it, nor does He give him His grace when he is alone, as in the beginning, so that he cannot say that he was given grace because of his own patience and struggle. Therefore, the wise God, Who arranges everything for our benefit, Who raises to the heavens and lowers to Hades, Who puts to rest and brings to life,[1] also does similarly here. He allows temptations to come upon him to cleanse and heal him, and when the time comes for Him to take them away, again He provides the way out with discretion and wisdom.

God enlightens a like-minded practiced elder, an experienced guide able to save souls—or, rather, God Himself dwells in him and speaks through him—to providentially

---

[1] 1 Kings 2:6

meet with him. And as they talk: behold the return of divine grace. The elder speaks, and his words penetrate like lightning to the depth of his heart, and divine light encompasses his soul, and the demons flee far away from the elder who has become unbearable to them. For at that moment, the holy elder is all divine fire, his words are filled with divine illumination, his advice is keen, with great wisdom and understanding and full of holy thoughts, for it is accompanied by divine grace. And as soon as that advice enters his heart, his nous is moved to amazement and wonder, for the elder supernaturally teaches him everything necessary to lift the huge burden of the demons' evil. Then, once the elder revives him and gives him enough soul-saving guidance, they separate. That whole winter night of struggling miraculously passes in a moment, without his realizing how it passed.

After they separate and he returns to his cell, he who was previously an infant has now become tried through experience with the demons. And he cries out, shedding streams of sweetest tears of love and shouting, "With patience I waited patiently for the Lord, and He was attentive unto me,"[2] and "Had the Lord not helped me, my soul had well nigh sojourned in Hades,"[3] and many other things. And once he returns to his hut and puts to practice the guidance he received, he is freed at once from everything that had previously overpowered him.

Shortly thereafter, through the prayers of that holy elder whom he would see even at night and be strengthened by him, he is entirely healed. Then he is filled with the love of Christ, his passions have quieted down, and he has peace of thoughts. Moreover, he is given a strong faith caused by theoria—not like the faith in the beginning which comes from reading and

---

[2] Ps. 39:1
[3] Ps. 93:17

the secret hope we have from Holy Baptism and correct dogmas—but faith caused by theoria, when one sees and believes. Likewise, all the other gifts from God come together like a chain: grace and mercy, without his seeking them. Furthermore, when he stands at prayer, he cannot say, "Give me this or that," because the Lord gives him more than he asks for. And his prayer is that the Lord's will be done. From time to time, while he prays, he is captivated by the love of Jesus. As he unceasingly thanks the Lord for the multitude of benefactions, his nous is seized by amazement and wonder, and the air of divine grace stops his mouth. Then Christ reigns. Once the theoria passes somewhat, he becomes as if bodiless. And in amazement he cries out:

"O the depth of the riches both of the wisdom and knowledge of God![4] How inscrutable are Thy mysteries, O Lord! Who is able to trace out the immeasurable riches of Thy grace? And what tongue can explain Thine incomprehensible mysteries? O Lord, if Thou dost not hold back the waves of Thy grace, man melteth like wax."

Saying these things, he considers himself even worse than the reptiles of the earth. And if it were possible, he would like to put all the people into his heart, for them to see and be saved, even if he himself were to lose the grace of God. But since this has been tried already, he knows that it is impossible for someone to save others. Therefore, he is satisfied remaining in his stillness and praying that God will save them all.

So this, my child, in short is the way of divine grace, and he who has reached here is able to tell us what else he sees, if he has not met any other obstacle. For he eats divine love and drinks the wine that all the Holy Monastic Fathers drank who walked this path and forgot the sorrows. Moreover,

---

[4] Rom. 11:33

grace does not leave anymore, as it did in the beginning. Unless some change occurs—God forbid!

So, if you, my child, are obedient, without a doubt you, too, will experience all this. And I shall end this discussion here to tell you about another kind of delusion. I am only telling you now that all those temptations he suffered, all the storms and shipwrecks he went through, all the fears and the enormous difficulties, he had because he did not have a guide to support and direct him. And since there is a lack of these practiced guides, barely one in a thousand is found to pass through this dangerous path, which, as we have said previously, is the short path of God which raises one to eternal life. And, since there is a shortage of such guides, various delusions have followed.

For it is absolutely necessary for the grace of God to leave, once a tried struggler has acquired a good taste of it in the beginning, so that he may be tested and become a practiced soldier of Christ. And without such temptations, no one has ever ascended to perfection. This stage that we mentioned where many fall into delusion is the stage where the grace of God withdraws in order to make us, as we have said, practiced soldiers of war, so that we are not infants forever. But the Lord wants us to become worthy men and brave fighters able to guard His riches. That is why He allows us to be tempted.

The Holy Fathers who teach us to abide in obedience, the highest of virtues, thus imitating Jesus, do so for a purpose. Namely, to purify us through it from the various passions of high-mindedness and complacency with one's own will, so that we may receive divine grace. But when grace withdraws to test you, the elder, like another grace, supports you and gives you guidance out of his own practical experience. He warms up your zeal to the point that, by God's grace and the prayers of your elder, you, too, are freed from the struggles. Then God's grace lays hold of you once more and our sweet Jesus entrusts to you His precious treasures as to one perfected.

So there is no other purpose for one to place himself under obedience. Today, however, everyone thinks that he receives a disciple to teach him a craft to make money, or to dig his vineyard, or to become a merchant and make him an heir to his house or cell or shop or whatever else he has, or even to serve him.

We are not saying not to do things that are necessary, but that the main purpose that a disciple attaches himself to an elder and is perfectly obedient is this: the elder, who is flaming with the love of Christ, transmits the talent of the riches of his virtue. The disciple, in turn, enjoys abundant grace from his spiritual father, because he cuts off his own will and has perfect self-denial and obedience. Then, of course, he will complete all the household tasks as needed.

And so, because this true purpose of monasticism has disappeared from thousands of monks, only a few are barely visible, like sparks. But these few are called deluded by all the thousands of other monks. And since they do not have anywhere to pass on their spiritual treasure, they hide it and pretend that they are fools and deluded.

And this is why when strugglers reach this point where grace inevitably leaves, they cannot find the appropriate medicine for their therapy. So they fall, they are deluded, and thousands of souls are lost which had shown great eagerness and godly zeal in the beginning. And today, those who out of ignorance do not understand call the path of God, which the sore feet of the saints walked, a path of delusion. Thus they sin out of ignorance and revile the path of God and hinder those who want to walk it. And when asked, they do not say at least, "My child, I am weak and unable to walk this path. But since you have zeal, see to it that you find such a guide. And if you find one, follow him faithfully. But if you don't, follow the common path of the Fathers where you will have many fellow travelers and guides and where there is no fear of delusion."

This is the plain and dispassionate truth of God, and whoever speaks like this is shielded from many snares.

But if, when asked, one says that this road is delusion and that all who walk on it are deluded, such a person should realize that he is in the trap. And let him know it so that he seeks God's mercy, before death catches us and we are locked up behind the bars of Hades. Then no one will be able to deliver us from the eternal condemnation which we suffer because of our foolish tongue.

And even though the Father of Lights has given all judgment to the Son, we fools seize it and judge our neighbor without discernment, without realizing his work and God's divine providence for him—to Whom be glory and dominion unto the ages. Amen.

The Garden of the Panagia

Mount Athos

Chapter VIII

On another delusion.

ear, my child, about yet another delusion so that you will be on your guard. Many monks attended to a single virtue and applied all their strength to accomplish it. For example, consider fasting; that is, not to eat oil or cooked food or other such things. They bound their freedom by believing that everything depends on fasting. While practicing this virtue they advise others that this is the only way, the fullness of all virtues, and that it secures the soul's salvation. They rely on the fact that they have lived so many years without eating oil or cooked food or whatever else.

But we say that such a person has become a slave of his willful fasting and thinks that whoever does not do likewise will not be saved or is off the right path. Let us ask such a person, "O man of God, tell me: in your many years of fasting, what have you gained? Show me the fruit of your lengthy fast, and I shall be convinced. Through your fasting you have excluded the mercy of God from others who cannot fast as much. So where have you put the infinite mercy of the Lord's goodness? Or do perhaps all men have the same temperament and physical strength as you do, so that you can demand that all should become like you? Well then, since you can't rule yourself well, you strike the anvil of fasting for so many years without any results, because you have no discernment." The cure for such a person is to abandon his so-called fasting and to seek from a spiritual father guidance how to live.

Likewise, another person counts on his vigil and teaches about it alone. He counts the years that he keeps vigil and thinks that anyone who does not live like him is walking in the darkness. Such a person should give up his vigil and follow a spiritual guide.

And yet another person trusts in his tears, and he teaches others as though it were his own invention: "Woe to him who does not weep!" He thinks that if he only weeps, that is perfection. His remedy is to recognize that tears must be accompanied by humility, and not to presume that he is doing the work of God, or that God owes him grace. But then again, even if he weeps properly, let him know that he is practicing only one virtue, and that he still lacks ninety-nine.

Similarly, another one trusts in his prayer and teaches others that if one behaves like him, one will keep one's nous from wandering. He, too, asserts this as an invention of his own knowledge. And another one trusts in his hesychia, that all perfection lies therein. He thinks that if someone wants to, he is able to have hesychia. But what can I say? There are people who hope merely in the number of years that they wear the monastic schema and boast of them.

Now, concerning all these virtues, we certainly say that these are the tools without which we cannot reach perfection. However, we must work at all of them along with all the other virtues that we have not mentioned until we shed our blood.

Hesychia is the best aid that helps us accomplish all the virtues. But we say that no one is able to withstand the burden of hesychia in knowledge and discernment unless the Lord sends the grace of hesychia as a gift and mercy. So he who practices hesychia must recognize that it is a gift of God and must thank Him.

Likewise, we would say to him who prays: "The Apostle says, 'No man can say that Jesus is the Lord, but by the Holy Spirit.'[1] Now, how can you say that you pray purely and keep your unrestrainable nous from wandering, and teach that if a man exerts himself, he can keep his nous from wandering and pray purely?" So we remark that prayer is the best aid that assists in purifying the intellect, and that without it we are unable to live spiritually. However, no one is able to keep his nous from wandering and pray purely if the grace of divine and spiritual knowledge, or a good and divine supernatural thought, or another action of divine grace does not come. So he should realize that it is not he, but divine grace that keeps his nous, and according to the amount of divine grace, he prays purely. Such a person should know that this is not from himself but from God, and so he should thank Him. And let him teach others that we ought to use whatever methods and ways we can to show God our good intentions and our desire to pray purely, but for grace to come is up to God.

Likewise, we would say to him who has tears that tears are the best weapon against the demons, and a bath that washes away sins, if one weeps cognitively. However, they are not from him. Although he exerts himself showing his intention and will to weep, whether or not tears come depends on Him Who "bringeth clouds up from the uttermost parts of the earth."[2] Let practice teach him that he does not weep when-

---

[1] 1 Cor. 12:3
[2] Ps. 134:7

ever he wants but whenever God wants, and let him thank God Who gives. He should not judge those who have no tears, for God does not give to all equally.

Similarly, we say about vigil that it assists in the purification of the nous, if it is done with knowledge and discernment. However, if the Lord does not help, there is no fruit from it. Therefore, he who is able to keep vigil should ask for knowledge from God and conduct himself with discernment. For without divine aid he will remain without fruit.

The same holds for him who fasts and all the others, if they govern themselves well. These are virtues that we strenuously cultivate. In this way we show God our good intentions and also wrestle with the desires of the passions. For if we do not force ourselves in these virtues, we will commit sins without fail. This is the plain truth, our duty, our human effort. As with the farmer: he digs the earth, clears, sows, and awaits the mercy of God. But if God does not send rain and favorable winds at the appropriate time, the farmer loses all his labor as well. Since his field fills with thorns, he reaps nothing, and what he sowed becomes food for irrational animals. It is the same with us. If the Lord does not send the purifying waters of His divine grace, we remain without fruit, and our works become food for the demons. For our passions choke them, and we reap nothing. Moreover, the virtues that were not practiced properly turn into vices.

So then, above all we need spiritual discernment, and we must arduously seek it from God, to Whom be glory and dominion unto the ages of ages. Amen.

Chapter IX

On a different aspect of the same delusion.

 y child, hear about another delusion. There are also other monks who work on all the virtues together, and trust in their works. And when they pray and ask something from God, they do not seek it with humility, but with insolence and pretension, as if they have obligated God with their toils and therefore He owes it to them. When they are not heard and the Lord does not do their will, they are troubled and greatly grieved. Then when our enemy the devil sees them with this ignorance, he attacks them with twisted thoughts and teaches them saying, "See? You are struggling so hard even until death to work for Him, and He doesn't even listen to you! So why do you work for Him?" Then he pushes him to blaspheme the name of God, so that he may enter inside him and possess him, and then people bind him with chains.

But if the devil is unable to accomplish this, he comes around differently. He transforms himself into an angel of light, saying that he is the Archangel Gabriel or some other angel, and that God sent him to be near him, since God is pleased with his works. Or similarly, he transforms himself into the form of our Lord Jesus Christ, while another demon goes earlier and says, "Since you have gladdened God with your toils, He has come to visit, so go and venerate Him to receive grace." Or he says that he has come to raise him like the Prophet Elias to the heavens. And in closing, to make a long story short, with such methods he has deluded many both in the past and today. Some were thrown upon the rocks, others into wells, others were slaughtered in various ways and were utterly destroyed. And all this happened because from the beginning they had no discernment and were doing their own will, without being under obedience.

But you, my beloved child in the Lord, since you are obedient, and confess everything openly, do not be afraid. Since you have an elder who guides you and prays for you day and night, God will not allow you to be deluded. But even if some such fantasy in the form of an angel appears to you, do not be afraid but tell him with boldness, even if it is in the form of the Lord, a saint, or an angel, tell him:

"I have an elder who guides me. I don't want the teachings of angels! I want to see my Lord, the angels, and the saints in the other life. I don't want to see them here." And turn your face elsewhere. Do not look at him. And since he is unable to endure such boldness, he will disappear. But even if the vision is true, the Lord will not get angry with you, but at once your fear is transformed into joy and things will turn out as the Lord wills.

But we should never request or want such things from God, that is, to see angels or saints, because this is delusion. We should seek—as we have written many times—God's mercy for the remission of our sins, and should attend to the purification of our soul. Then things from God come by themselves without our seeking them.

And even if we ascend to the heavens by theoria, nothing is due to us. But if after a little while we undergo a change without wanting to, and great sorrow and unbearable distress come upon us as if we were in Hades, and it seems to us that it will never leave but will afflict us till death, once again we should remain composed. And just as we were happy when we were raised to the heavens, likewise, when some change occurs and grief overtakes us, we should have patience, without being agitated and without grumbling. But in peace tell your thoughts, "The Father has two places for us to dwell: one of joy and pleasure in the heavens, and one of sorrows down in Hades. And whenever He wants He raises me to the joy above, and whenever He wants He takes me below, so that I learn that as long as I wear this earthen body, I am subject to change. So I have nothing to say. Only let the will of the Lord be done in all, to all, and through all. But even if He leaves me below forever, I would say:

'My sweetest Savior and God, I have done nothing good or pleasing before Thee, but as a diligent worker of sin I am worthy to be a son of hell. So even if I am punished, I rightly deserve it. Only do not be grieved with me, but rather look upon me with a happy face, and then even Hades will become a brilliant paradise for me!'"

When you say such things, the sorrow departs and joy returns. But you should not say it so that joy comes back, but you should say it from your heart. And as long as you are in this life—as we have already said—you should never become cocky, even if you ascend to the seventh heaven and see all kinds of mysteries. Since you bear a body, there is danger and caution is needed. Only once you have departed from your dead body should you rejoice, because then you are not subject to change anymore, but whatever the Lord bestows upon you is yours and no one can take it from you—to Whom be glory and dominion unto the ages of ages. Amen.

Chapter X

On the double warfare of the demons and how they fight skillfully against strugglers.

o now, my child, learn now also about the double warfare of the demons. We say that the demons fight skillfully against strugglers. When an evil demon sees that a monk is running with great momentum and fervor but has no guide, he follows him closely and secretly plots against him. He conceals his traps and pushes him onward. And the struggler, not suspecting that the enemy is with him, goes to extremes without discernment: fasting, keeping vigil, praying. The demon completely cuts his appetite for food so that he does not desire anything, even if he has the best foods.

Likewise, he lets him keep vigil freely, so that the monk thinks that he has already reached dispassion and that he is able to live without food. Then, once the demon sees that he has reached the extreme, he abandons him and he falls. Since he does not have lofty wings of theoria to lift and raise his body, he grovels on the ground like a snake. For just when he thought that he had been raised from the earth to the heavens, he suddenly found himself in the sea without weapons, without realizing it. For the body, which carries the weapons and fights, was exhausted and collapsed due to the excessive starvation. Then the bloodthirsty dragon, rejoicing and exulting, hastily falls upon that poor monk, dragging along with him thousands of other evil spirits as well. They will completely strangle him, if he does not immediately seek an experienced and practiced guide. From here, the demons have thrown many strugglers into various filthy passions. For the demons excite carnal passions more than the rest when the body is exhausted and has collapsed.

But if this struggler has a sharp mind, struggles with discernment, and is cautious not to fall forward, the demon leaves him alone. But as soon as he sees that the monk's fervor and great zeal flag, that his momentum has decreased somewhat, and that he begins to be negligent, the demon pulls him back and throws him into indifference so that he abandons everything, and in this way becomes the demons' slave.

This is why the warfare is double. A monk must either have a guide with the same spiritual work and be obedient to him, cutting off his own will completely, or, if he is alone, he must guard himself from extremes and walk the middle way: he must incline neither to the right nor to the left. And he should fully know that only when he receives lofty wings of theoria can his body bear illnesses in proportion to this divine grace. For the body, being corruptible, changes many times, becomes ill, and falls. But since the nous has other, heavenly, supernatural wings, it flies high and does not care about the heaviness of the body, but supports it, however weak it may be. This is why many saints who had this grace passed many years without bread or food. Holy Communion of the immaculate Body and Blood of the Lord alone was sufficient for them.

But since the Holy Fathers do not teach us not to eat at all (even if we have received this grace and know that we are able to live without food in truth and not in our imagination), we should still eat cheese and eggs and milk and fish, too, if we happen to have any. We should eat a little of everything allowed by our monastic profession for two reasons: first, we crush the root of arrogance and pride and trample down every proud thought that goes against God, and second, we appear to be just like everyone else, without anyone knowing our God-pleasing work; thus we avoid human glory and praises. Furthermore, we should not think that this meager amount of food eaten with knowledge and discernment deprives us of divine grace, or that if we fasted we would have more grace. No. For God does not look at the quantity of our struggles, but examines the intention and the discernment with which we work, and He pours out His good, great, and abundant mercy accordingly, to Whom be all glory, honor, and worship, always, now and ever, and unto the ages of ages. Amen!

Chapter XI

On the three states of nature that man ascends and descends: according to nature, contrary to nature, and above nature. And on the three modes of divine Grace by which it acts when human nature is constrained, namely: purifying, illuminating, and perfecting grace.

o, my child, let me tell you also about the three states of nature that man ascends and descends.

The natural state of man, since we have transgressed the commandment of the Lord and have fallen out of paradise, is the divine Law which was given to us in writing after that exile. Every man desiring salvation has to fight with the passions: thrashing and opposing, fighting and being fought against, winning and suffering defeat. And in general, he has to struggle in order to stay within the divine laws of nature.

When we abide by the divine law given to us in the Bible— we are not fornicators, murderers, thieves, liars, gossipers, and are not unjust, proud, vainglorious, gluttonous, greedy, avaricious, envious, taunting, blaspheming, irascible, peevish, complaining, hypocritical, and so on—then we are in the state natural for us after the Fall.

Whereas the state contrary to nature is when one is outside of the divine law and behaves like the irrational animals that do not have a law. The prophet says regarding such people, "Man, being in honor, did not understand; he is compared to the mindless cattle, and is like them."[1] So whoever lives like this outside of the divine Law, wallowing in various sins as we mentioned, is in the state contrary to nature.

But the state above nature is dispassion, which is what Adam had before he transgressed the commandment of God and fell out of this divine grace and innocence.

So these, my child, are the three states through which, if we make progress, we ascend from the contra-natural to the supernatural state. But if we live insensibly and neglect our salvation, then we feed swine and try to get our fill from husks like the prodigal son.[2]

As we mentioned, the three modes of divine grace that the nature of man is likely to receive when he has good intentions and exerts himself are: purifying, illuminating, and perfecting.

Once a man comes to repentance from his previous sinful life, he forces himself to stay within the divine Law. And due to his passionate habits, he undergoes great struggles and suffers sharp pains. Then divine grace secretly gives him comfort and joy, mourning, delight, and sweetness from the divine words he reads, as well as strength and boldness in his spiritual struggle. This is called purifying grace which mystically helps the struggling penitent to be purified from sins and to remain in the state according to nature.

So if he remains there, in the state according to nature, and does not stop struggling, does not turn back, is not negligent, and does not fall from his post, but endures and forces

---

[1] Ps. 48:21
[2] vid. Lk. 15:15-16

himself to bear good fruits, being patient and accepting the continuous changes of nature, and awaiting the mercy of God; then his nous receives divine illumination and becomes entirely divine light, by which he noetically perceives the truth and discerns how he must proceed until he reaches love, which is our sweet Jesus.

However, here too, one must be very cautious. When you hear me saying "light," do not think that it is fire or light from a lamp or lightning or some other kind of colors. Away with such absurdity! For there were many who did not understand and accepted some kind of lightning as something divine, and thus were deluded and miserably ruined. But the noetic light of divine grace is immaterial, formless, colorless, gladsome, and peaceful. This is, and is called, illuminating grace which illuminates the nous and knows the safe roads of the spiritual journey, so that the traveler will not get lost and fall.

However, since the body is commingled with changes, and since there is plenty of time, grace does not abide permanently, but comes and goes. Light is followed by darkness and then darkness is followed by light.

Now listen carefully to understand:

Our natural state is darkness in comparison to divine grace. How much more so when the gloomy demons approach us, which are dark by nature! So when the light of grace comes, everything evil disappears—just as when the sun rises the darkness leaves, and we can clearly see even the smallest details that escaped notice before dawn. But once the sun sets, the darkness overtakes us naturally once more, and whoever walks in the darkness suffers great damage and grievous incidents.

Likewise, the same thing happens to us in our spiritual journey. When we have divine light, we can see everything clearly, and the demons flee far away, as they are unable to stand before divine grace. But once divine grace leaves again, the darkness remains, that is, our natural state. Then the thievish demons come and fight us. And so, since our nature is subject to so many changes, and since in a time of darkness we, without the discernment of divine grace, work many deeds that harm us, and since many times we are mortally wounded by the enemies, because it is dark and we cannot see the enemies that are hiding. Therefore, we must never grow bold and think that everything we do is pleasing to God, nor should we trust in our weapons and our skill. But we should call upon divine aid and trust only in it, and should say with great fear, for we do not know, "I wonder, is what I say pleasing to God, or do I perhaps sadden Him?" And in times of change, we must be patient.

If, then, we remain in this state and are not harmed by the continuous wars and turmoil from the passions, then we are given the gift of God, perfecting grace, which perfects us. It is called supernatural, because he who has it walks above nature. In the first two stages of grace, a person forces himself with good thoughts and spiritual recollections to keep the virtues: love, humility, abstinence, and so on. Thus by thinking pious thoughts and by opposing demonic thoughts, he destroys the passions' malice and keeps the virtues. But when the perfecting, supernatural grace comes, all the passions are wiped out. Then all the virtues are kept as though they belonged to his own nature, without needing to use his own devices and methods, because he has been given that dispassionate state that existed before the Fall. For the passions entered the nature of man after Adam's disobedience, whereas the natural state in which man was created by God was passionless. For this reason when the nous is freed from the passions, it walks above nature like a king by means of divine knowledge.

So when you, too, my child, see that without artifices and spiritual thoughts all the virtues remain naturally and do not change, know that you are living above nature. But if you keep them with good thoughts and they change, know that you are living according to nature. And when you commit sins, know that you are living contrary to nature and feed the swine of the citizens, as in the Holy Gospel: so struggle to free yourself. As for those things beyond what we have already mentioned, the All-wise and All-good God knows, as well as he who abides in God, to Whom be glory and dominion unto the ages of ages. Amen.

St. Nikephoros of Mount Athos

Let us zealously pursue noetic prayer

Chapter XII

On love.

ince we have written about many and diverse things, my child, moved by your ardent faith and piety, I considered it good also to write a few things about love that I have learned from the Holy Fathers who lived before me and from reading the Scriptures. However, fearing the height of this supernatural grace, I am overcome by awe, lest I am unable to bring the discourse to an end. All the same, warmed by the hope of your holy prayers, I shall begin the discourse. For how can I, my child, with my own strength write about such a great charisma which exceeds my strength? And with what tongue can I tell of this heavenly delight and sustenance of the holy angels, prophets, apostles, righteous, martyrs, monks, and every category of those listed in the heavens?

Truly, my child, even if I had all the tongues of men since Adam to help me, it still seems impossible to me that I would be able to extol Love worthily. What am I saying, "worthily"? A mortal tongue is entirely incapable of even remotely expressing something concerning love, unless God, Who is truth and Love itself, gives us the power of speech, wisdom, and knowledge. And through the human tongue, this God Himself, our sweet Jesus Christ is both called and praised as God. For Love is nothing but the Father and the Savior Himself, our sweet Jesus, together with the Divine Spirit.

Of course, all the other divine gifts of the loving God, such as humility, meekness, abstinence, and so on, have divine sensation when they act upon us through divine grace. For without the action of divine grace all these in general are simply virtues that we keep to heal our passions because of the commandment of the Lord.

Before we receive grace, we undergo changes all the time: towards humility and towards pride; towards love and towards hatred; towards abstinence and towards gluttony; towards meekness and towards anger; towards forbearance and towards indignation, etc. However, once we are acted upon by divine grace, these continuous changes and alterations of the soul cease. Although the body continues to have its elemental and natural changes (namely: cold, heat, weight, fatigue, hunger, thirst, illness, and so on), the soul, fed by the action of divine grace, remains unchangeable in the natural, divine gifts it has been given.

What I mean by unchangeable is this: due to the grace abiding in us, the soul does not change in the divine gifts it has been given by God. Not that it does not change when grace withdraws, but it changes with difficulty due to the soul's firm resolution—it is not completely unchangeable, though.

For we have written also elsewhere in this epistle that as long as we carry about this earthen garment, no one should believe that there is an advanced spiritual state free from danger, except in the presence of divine grace. Then one senses well every divine gift, and unerringly comprehends them. However, when he reaches the sensation of divine love—which is God Himself, according to him who said, "God is love; and he that dwelleth in love dwelleth in God, and God in him,"[1]—how can a tongue, which is mortal and has no divine action, suffice to converse about God and His holy gifts?

Today, many virtuous people who live good lives, who please God with their deeds and words, and who benefit their neighbor, think they have (and are thought of having) attained Love through their insignificant work of mercy and compassion they show towards their neighbor. But this is not the truth. They are only fulfilling the commandment of love for the Lord, Who said, "Love one another."[2] He who keeps this commandment is worthy of praise as a keeper of the divine commandments—but this is not an action of divine Love. It is a road towards the fountain, but not the fountain. It is stairs towards the palace, but not the gate of the palace. It is a royal garment, but not the King. It is a commandment of God, but not God.

Therefore, he who wishes to speak about Love, must have revelation of the mystery of Love. Only then, if the fountain of Love, our sweet Jesus, permits, should he impart to others some of the fruit he received; then he shall surely benefit his neighbor. For there is a great danger for us to speak erroneously, to think turbidly, and to believe we know things that we do not.

So then, my beloved child, know this for certain: fulfilling the commandment of love through works done for mutual brotherly love is one thing, and the action of divine Love is another. All men are able to fulfill the commandment of brotherly love if they want to and if they force themselves. Divine love, though, neither results from our works, nor does it depend on our will—if we want, when we want, and how

---

[1] 1 Jn. 4:16
[2] Jn. 13:34

we want. But it depends on the fountain of Love, our sweetest Jesus, Who gives us if *He* wants, how *He* wants, and whenever *He* wants.

When we walk in simplicity, keep the commandments, and patiently and persistently seek divine love with tears and pain, guarding Jethro's sheep like Moses[3]—that is, guarding the good and spiritual movements and meditations of the nous during the heat of the day and the frost of the night of continuous battles and temptations, which we crush with our struggle and humility—then we are counted worthy of seeing God and the Bush in our hearts, burning with the divine fire of Love, burning but not consumed. And having approached it through noetic prayer, we hear the divine voice in a mystery of spiritual knowledge saying, "Put off thy sandals from thy feet!"[4] That is, put off from yourself every self-will and worry for this age as well as all childish thoughts, and be subject to the Holy Spirit and His divine will, "for the place whereon thou standest is holy ground."[5]

And once such a person puts off everything, he is entrusted with the responsibility to protect the people and inflicts wounds on Pharaoh—that is, he discerns and governs through divine gifts, and conquers the demons. Then he receives the divine laws—not on stone tablets, as Moses did, which wear out and break, but rather in divine engravings of the Holy Spirit which act in our hearts. And not only ten commandments, but as many as his nous, knowledge, and nature can contain. Afterwards, he enters into "that which is within the veil."[6]

When the divine cloud descends in a pillar of fire of Love, he becomes all fire as well. He is unable to endure any longer, and the divine action of Love within him cries out to the fountain of Love through human lips, "What shall separate

---

[3] vid. Ex. 3:1
[4] Ex. 3:5
[5] Ibid
[6] cf. Heb. 6:19

me from Thy sweet Love, O Jesus?"[7] And when the breeze
blows even more—whether in the body or out of the body,
God knows; whether within the hut or out in the open air,
God knows—he who has experienced this knows only this:
that he has totally become fire with the fire, and shedding
tears of love, he cries out in amazement and astonishment,
"Stop, O sweet Love, the waters of Thy grace, for the joints
of my body have come apart!" As he says this, and while the
wind of the Spirit is blowing upon him with His marvelous
and ineffable fragrance, his senses cease, not permitting any
bodily action at all. And entirely captivated and enclosed in
silence, he can only marvel at the riches of the glory of God
until the divine cloud passes.

He remains as one crazy
As from wine all ecstatic.

For neither his tongue nor his mind nor his heart
Permits him to speak any words except these:

I beg Thee, my Jesus, my Love that is sweetest!
My Father and Savior, O sweetest pure eros!

My God and Creator and the All-holy Spirit,
O Trinity Holy in a heavenly Oneness!

O life of my soul and my heart's delectation,
My intellect's brightness, O Love that is perfect!

O fountain of Love and my hope and my faith,
Teach me how I must seek Thee in order to find Thee.

Yes, my Love that is sweetest, my Jesus and Savior;
Just tell me the way, for I want nothing else.

---

[7] cf. Rom. 8:39

I desire to find Thee and to fall at Thy feet
And to kiss with much sweetness Thy wounds
and the nails;

To weep without ceasing out of pain that is heartfelt,
And wash Thy divine feet as Mary once did.

And let not any powers or dominions detach me,
Nor Belial the rival with his unholy angels,

Nor temporal pleasures of this age which is passing,
Nor all of the world with its fleeting enjoyments.

But just as I am now, come take my poor soul there
However Thou knowest, and Thy feet shall I wash then.

I yearn to behold Thee and worship forever
My God and Creator, my Love and my Savior,

Together with all of the Righteous and Prophets,
Apostles and Martyrs, with the Monks and Saved Women,

And all hosts of the heavens: Archangels and Angels,
With the Cherubim, Seraphim, Thrones, and the Powers,

And our sweetest true Mother Panagia the Virgin,
The Lady of all, our most pure Theotokos.
Amen.

So my child, blessed is the hour in which—if we are worthy—we present our soul clean to the Lord and rejoice together with all of those we mentioned, where for all, in all, and over all reigns Jesus Christ, the sweet Savior; God the Father; the Beloved, Holy, Good, Peaceful, Life-Giving, Life-creating Spirit—the Holy, Indivisible Trinity, now and ever, and unto the infinite ages of endless ages. Amen.

Epilogue

y child, unceasingly turn over in your mind and heart everything that I have written to you. Know well that the beginning of the clear way of God, and the coming of all good things, is for a person to realize his own weakness. For him to realize it, though, he must undergo great temptations above his strength. Without undergoing such extraordinary temptations above nature, it is impossible for him to realize the weakness of his nature. Once he realizes it, he knows everything and everything will fall into his hands. Then true humility is near. Within it is also patience. He has also laid hold of the knowledge of mysteries and is sheltered by discernment. From Love he has received the fruits of the Spirit: joy, peace, long-suffering, faith, meekness, abstinence.

Question: But where do all of these good things come from?

Answer: All these come about when one sees in plain sight—not visions and fantasies, but the whole, bare, plain truth—that man is nothing.

Question: But what is nothing?

Answer: Nothing is what existed before God made the earth and all of creation: nothing. And after He made the heaven and earth, He named it earth—which came into being from nothing. Furthermore, when God took clay from it and formed man, he was just lifeless clay. But after He breathed on him with His breath, he received a living spirit, a reasoning soul, and named him man "in His image and likeness."[1]

"In His image" refers to the spirit which He gave him through His breath, the reasoning soul. "In His likeness" refers to the good virtues: love, kindness, charity, and the rest that we have written above. So whoever has these natural good virtues is "in His likeness." Whoever does not have them is not "in His likeness," but as the prophet has said about him, "Being in honor, he did not understand; he is compared to the mindless cattle, and is like them."[2]

Question: So what is the fulfillment of all good things and the end of all, so that we may conclude our discussion?

Answer: The fulfillment of all good things and the termination of all is God: good, compassionate, merciful, through Whom everything came into being out of non-existence, and without Whom nothing whatsoever came into being. So to Him belong all glory, love, honor, worship, and veneration, together with His beloved Son our sweetest Savior Jesus Christ, and with His All-holy and Good and Life-creating Spirit, now and forever, and unto the infinite ages of endless ages. Amen.

The End.
And Glory to our God in Trinity.

---

[1] cf. Gen. 1:26
[2] Ps. 48:21

Glossary

Antidoron (ἀντίδωρον):

Antidoron is the blessed bread distributed in pieces to the faithful after the Divine Liturgy. These pieces are cut from the *prosphora* remaining from the *proskomede* after the "lamb" (the piece to be used for the Eucharist) has been cut out. It is called antidoron, that is, "instead of the Gifts," because those Orthodox Christians who did not receive Holy Communion receive this piece of bread as a blessing instead of the Holy Gifts.

Appetitive aspect of the soul (τὸ ἐπιθυμιτικόν):

The appetitive aspect of the soul is the soul's desiring power. It is one of the three aspects or powers of the soul, the other two being the *intelligent aspect* (τὸ λογιστικόν) and the *incensive aspect* (τὸ θυμικόν).

Ascesis (ἄσκησις):

Ascesis is man's struggle to keep the commandments of Christ. It encompasses not only his bodily and spiritual effort, but also the method by which he passes through the three stages of the spiritual life, namely: *purification* of the *heart*, *illumination* of the *nous*, and *theosis*. Thus, it is an essential tool for one's sanctification. According to St. Gregory Palamas, it is primarily "the evangelic life which is based on repentance. It is man's preparation for his union with Christ." See also *praxis* and *theoria*.

Assault (προσβολή):

Assault is the name given to the first stage of a temptation. See *consent* for more details.

Athonite (ἀθωνικός):
Athonite means relating to, or of *Mt. Athos.*

Athos (Ἄθως):
Mt. Athos, or the Holy Mountain, is a self-governed monastic community on a peninsula in Northern Greece. The term can also refer to the mountain at the tip of this peninsula.

Blessing (εὐλογία):
Besides its usual meanings, a "blessing" can also mean the permission given by one's spiritual father for a particular action.

Circular prayer (κυκλικὴ προσευχή):
Quoting St. Nicodemos the *Hagiorite*: "St. Dionysios the Areopagite refers to three forms [of prayer]: direct, spiral, and circular—which alone is without deception. It is called circular prayer because as the perimeter of a circle returns to its starting point, so also in this circular movement, the *nous* returns to itself and becomes one. This is why St. Dionysios, that superb theologian, said, 'The movement of the soul is circular because it leaves the externals, enters into itself, and unites its *noetic* powers in a circular movement which keeps the soul from deception.' (*Divine Names*, ch. IV) St. Basil also noted, 'A nous that is not distracted toward externals or scattered through the senses to the world, returns to itself and through itself rises to the understanding of God.' (Epistle 1) St. Gregory Palamas has also mentioned in his letter to Barlaam that deception can enter into direct and spiral prayers, but not into circular prayer. According to St. Dionysios the Areopagite, direct prayer is the activity of the nous based on external perceptions that raise it to a simple intellectual activity. Spiral prayer occurs when the nous is

illumined by divine knowledge, not entirely noetically and changelessly, but rather intellectually and by transitions, combining direct and some circular prayer. Therefore, whoever wishes to pray without deception must occupy himself more with the circular prayer of the nous, which is accomplished by the return of the nous to the *heart* and by *noetic prayer* in the heart.

"This prayer is very arduous and toilsome, yet correspondingly fruitful because it is free of deception. This is the most important, the most sublime activity of the nous, for it unites the nous with God Who is above all things. In short, this circular movement of the nous purifies, illumines, and perfects the nous more than all the algebra, physics, metaphysics, and other sciences of secular philosophy. This noetic prayer makes man spiritual and a seer of God, whereas those other intellectual disciplines make him only a natural (ψυχικός) man. But as St. Paul says, 'The natural [unspiritual] man receiveth not the gifts of the Spirit, for they are folly to him.' (1 Cor. 2:14)"
—*A Handbook of Spiritual Counsel*,
St. Nicodemos the Hagiorite, pp. 116-117 (Greek ed.).

Consent (συγκατάθεσις):
Consent is one of the stages of temptation. St. John of the Ladder describes the stages as follows: Assault is a simple conception or an image encountered for the first time, which has entered the heart. Coupling is conversation with what has been encountered, accompanied by passion or dispassion. And consent (συγκατάθεσις) is the yielding of the soul to what has been presented to it, accompanied by delight. But captivity is a forcible and involuntary abduction of the heart, or a permanent association with what has been encountered which destroys the good condition of our soul.

Struggle "is power equal to the attacking force, which either wins or loses according to the soul's desire. Passion is primarily that which nestles with persistence in the soul for a long time, forming a habit in the soul, by its long-standing association with it, since the soul of its own accord clings to it. The first of these states is without sin, the second not always, but the third is sinful or sinless according to the state of the struggler. Struggle can earn crowns or punishments. Captivity is judged differently, according to whether it occurs at the time of prayer or at other times; whether it happens in things neither good nor bad, or in the context of evil thoughts. But passion is unequivocally condemned in every situation, and requires either corresponding repentance or future punishment. Therefore, he who regards the first assault dispassionately cuts off with one blow all the rest which follow"

—The Ladder of Divine Ascent, Step 15:73

Contemplation (θεωρία):
    The Holy Fathers use the word θεωρία (theh-oh-ree'ah) in three different ways. Its first meaning is simply "seeing" or "beholding" physically. Its second meaning metaphorically refers to intellectual perception, that is: "consideration," "speculation," and "philosophical contemplation." In this case, we chose to translate θεωρία with the word "contemplation." Its third meaning refers to *noetic* contemplation which is the highest state of prayer. When used in reference to this noetic contemplation, we merely transliterated the word as "theoria," instead of using the term "contemplation," to avoid confusion with the second meaning of the word, i.e. intellectual contemplation. See also *theoria*.

Discern, discernment (διακρίνω, διάκρισις):
Discernment is a spiritual gift pertaining to the *nous*. Through discernment, one discerns the inner states of the spiritual life, distinguishing between uncreated and created things: between the energy of God and the energy of the devil. Through discernment, one is also able to distinguish between the energies of God and the psychosomatic energies of man, thereby distinguishing emotional states from spiritual experiences.

Disciple (ὑποτακτικός):
Taken in the broad sense, the word "disciple" refers to every Christian who receives spiritual guidance from his spiritual father. In the monastic life, though, it applies to a monk who obeys an elder so that his soul may be healed from the *passions* and attain *theosis* by the grace of God.

Dispassion (ἀπάθεια):
Dispassion is achieved when all three aspects of the soul (i.e., the intelligent, *appetitive*, and *incensive* aspects) are directed towards God. It is the transfiguration of the *passionate* aspect of the soul (i.e., the aspect of the soul which is more vulnerable to *passion*, namely, the appetitive and incensive aspects), rather than its mortification. Thus dispassion in this context does not signify a stoic indifference, but rather, a transfiguration and sanctification of the powers of the soul and eventually of the body also.

Ecstasy (ἔκστασις):
One experiences ecstasy when, with the synergy of grace, one detaches his *nous* from reason and the surrounding environment and brings it back to the *heart*. Then, "through the

heart the nous ascends to God," according to St. Gregory Palamas. During ecstasy, the nous is found in a different, spiritual realm. It is not a respite of the actions of the soul and nous, but a respite of physical actions, such as eating, sleeping, etc.

Eighth Millennium (ὄγδοος αἰών):
The eighth millennium, according to the Church Fathers, is the end times that immediately precede the advent of the Antichrist.

Eros (ἔρως):
Although "eros" can mean sensual love in other contexts—as the Ancient Greeks used it—the elder uses it in the *patristic* sense, which denotes exclusively the burning or intense longing or love (completely void of any sensuality) that impels man towards union with God.

Fantasy (φαντασία):
In the *patristic* sense, a fantasy is a mental image formed in the *nous* either by oneself or by the demons. Fantasies are the chief instruments of the demons to lead man into sin. As St. Hesychios the Priest writes, "It is impossible for sin to enter the heart without first knocking at its door in the form of a fantasy provoked by the devil." (*Philokalia*, vol. I, p. 173) Fantasies created in one's own nous, though, can be either beneficial or harmful. For example, it is helpful to *contemplate* death, heaven, hell, etc. with our nous at the outset of prayer, because in this way one's *heart* is predisposed to prayer. However, it is also possible with one's nous to meditate on worldly or sinful things. Nevertheless, all fantasies are an obstacle to pure prayer, which requires an undistracted *nous*.

Flesh (σάρξ):
In addition to its literal meaning, the word "flesh" denotes the carnal *passions* or a carnal way of thinking.

Forty-day Liturgy (σαρανταλείτουργον):
A Forty-day Liturgy is the celebration of the Divine Liturgy for forty consecutive days.

Geronda (Γέρων):
A geronda (pronounced "yeh'-ron-da") is a *hieromonk*, priest, or monk who, ideally, has reached *dispassion* by the grace of God. Thus, because of his own experience, he is able to lead his spiritual children to dispassion as well. In a broader sense, though, it is used as a respectful title for any spiritual father and any elderly hieromonk, priest, or monk.

Heart (καρδία):
In *patristic* usage, the heart is both spiritual and physical. The spiritual heart is: "deep," (Ps. 64:6) an "immeasurable abyss" (*Philokalia*, St. Makarios, vol. III, pp. 321,83), the "inner man" (*To Xeni*, St. Gregory Palamas, Gk. Philokalia, vol. IV, p.109), the "hidden person" (1 Pet. 3:4), the "battleground of the spiritual struggle" (*Saint Silouan*, Archimandrite Sophrony, p. 10), identified with *nous* (St. Maximus the Confessor, *Philokalia*, vol. II, pp. 109, 73), into whose depths the grace of God enters through baptism (St. Diadochos of Photike, *Philokalia 1,* p. 279, 77), where God may be made manifest (*Writings*, St. Theoleptos, Metropolitan of Philadelphia, pp. 385f, 8. Greek Philokalia IV, p. 6) and may dwell (Eph. 3:17) and writes His laws. (Rom. 2:15 and *Philokalia*, St. Maximus, vol. II, pp. 158, 81) It is located in the physical heart as in an organ (*Triads*, St.

Gregory Palamas, 1, 2, 3, CWS p. 43), which is man's "natural, para-natural, and supernatural center" (*St. Nicodemos the Hagiorite—a Handbook of Spiritual Counsel,* CWS p.154-157), and is the path for the nous to return to the spiritual heart. (*Saint Silouan,* Archimandrite Sophrony, p. 47)

Hesychast (ἡσυχαστής):
A hesychast is someone who lives a life of *hesychia* in seclusion from the world and is wholly dedicated to God. His chief struggle is to bring his *nous* into his *heart.*

Hesychia (ἡσυχία):
The term ἡσυχία can mean either external stillness or internal, *noetic* stillness. In the former instance, the word is translated as "stillness," whereas in the latter instance, it is transliterated in this book as "hesychia."

Hesychia is the ascetical practice of noetic stillness linked with *watchfulness* and deepened by the unceasing *Jesus prayer.* Hesychia is an undisturbed *nous* and a *heart* with peace, freed from *thoughts, passions,* and from influences of the environment. It is dwelling in God. The only way for man to achieve *theosis* is through hesychia. External stillness can help one achieve hesychia. Hesychia can also mean noetic stillness itself.

Hieromonk (ἱερομόναχος):
A hieromonk is a monk who has been ordained to the priesthood.

Holy Mountain (τὸ Ἅγιον Ὄρος):
See *Athos.*

Icon (εἰκών):
An icon is a two-dimensional sacred depiction of Christ, of His saints, or of a holy event. Icons are to be venerated, not worshipped, as worship is due to God alone. As St. Basil the Great has stated, the reverence given to icons is transferred to their prototype, that is, to the one portrayed.

Iconostasis (τέμπλον):
An iconastasis is the partition with *icons* on it that separates the altar from the nave in an Orthodox church.

Illumination (φώτισις):
Closely connected with *noetic prayer*, illumination of the *nous* occurs when the *heart* is purified from the *passions*, the nous returns within the heart, and *the prayer* operates unceasingly. At this stage, one weeps tears of *repentance* daily.

Incensive aspect of the soul (τὸ θυμικόν):
The incensive aspect of the soul is the power of the soul that is manifested as anger.

Inner voice (ἐνδιάθετος λόγος):
St. Nicodemos the Hagiorite explains the "inner voice" or "inner reason" in this manner:
"Once you have brought your *nous* into the *heart*, it should not just stay there, looking and doing nothing, but should find reason, that is, the inner voice of the heart through which we think, compose essays, make judgments, analyze, and read whole books silently, without saying a single word with the mouth.
After the has found this inner voice, do not let it say anything else except this short, *single-phrased* prayer: 'Lord Jesus Christ, Son of God, have mercy on me.' But this is not

enough. It is also necessary to activate the soul's will so that you say this prayer with all your will and power and love. To put it more clearly, let your inner voice say only *the prayer*, let your nous pay attention through its spiritual vision and hearing to the words of the prayer alone and especially to the meaning of the words, without imagining any forms, shapes, or any other perceptible or intelligible thing, internal or external, even if it is something good. . . . Let all your will cleave to the same words of the prayer with love, so that the nous, the inner voice, and the will—these three parts of your soul—will be one, and the one three, for in this way man, who is an image of the Holy Trinity, is united with the Prototype, as St. Gregory Palamas, that great practicer and teacher of *noetic prayer* and *watchfulness*, has said."

—*A Handbook of Spiritual Counsel*,
Nicodemos of the Holy Mountain, pp. 117-118 (Greek ed.).

Intellect (διάνοια):

The word διάνοια means the reason of man, that is, his discursive, conceptualizing, and logical faculty of conscious thinking and cogitation. It draws conclusions and formulates concepts from information either obtained by revelation or by the senses.[1]

Jesus prayer (εὐχὴ Ἰησοῦ):

The Jesus prayer is a short prayer which is continually repeated, consisting of the words: "Lord Jesus Christ, have mercy on me."

Knowledge (γνῶσις):

Through the process of *theosis*, man attains to a knowledge of a higher order than any human knowledge and beyond any

---

[1] See footnote at end of glossary.

other natural knowledge. It is neither an intellectual speculation about God nor knowledge about God, but it stems from personal experience of God, first through undistracted prayer accompanied by peace and love of God or joyous *mourning*, and later by means of *theoria* of His uncreated light.

Meditation (μελέτη):

The term "meditation," as used by the Holy Fathers, indicates a thoughtful reflection or pondering upon a certain aspect of the faith, e.g. the Incarnation, God's mercy, the Crucifixion, the Transfiguration, one's sinfulness, etc. This is quite different from what is known as "Eastern meditation," which is the use of various psychosomatic techniques intended to bring about self-identification with a "supreme being" (or so-called "deity"), an "impersonal reality," or even nothingness. On the other hand, for an Orthodox Christian, meditation brings about humility, gratitude, and love, and is a preparation for prayer, which is a personal experience of the one, true, living God.

Metanoia (μετάνοια):

In its primary sense, μετάνοια (pronounced "meh-tah'-nee-ah") means *repentance*, literally, "a change of mind." However, it can also mean the specific act of making the sign of the cross, followed by a bow either down to the ground or to the waist. It is a gesture of reverence, worship, respect, or repentance. A typical *prayer rule* includes a number of metanoias done while saying the *Jesus prayer*.

Mourning (πένθος):

The elder always uses the word "mourning" to mean godly

mourning. Godly mourning is caused by grace and gives rise to repentance and sometimes tears. Godly mourning, as well as "joyous sadness" (χαρμολύπη), has a positive effect on the soul, bringing it peace and a determination to struggle harder to live a Christian way of life. Merely human mourning, though, is a destructive sorrow that leads one to despair and causes psychological and psychosomatic abnormalities.

Noetic (νοερός, νοητός):
Belonging to, characteristic of, or perceptible to the *nous*.

Noetic Prayer (νοερὰ προσευχή):
Noetic prayer is prayer done with the *nous* without distraction within the *heart*. Another name for it is *"prayer of the heart."* It is contrasted with the prayer of the *intellect* which is done within the reason.

Nous (νοῦς):
The Church Fathers employ the term "nous" with several meanings. They mainly refer to the nous as the soul (the "spiritual nature" of a man—St. Isaac the Syrian) and the *heart* (or "the essence of the soul"—vid. *Philokalia*, vol. II, p. 109, 73). More specifically, it constitutes the innermost aspect of the heart (St. Diadochos §§79,88). However, they also refer to it as the "eye of the soul" (*The Orthodox* Faith, St. John of Damascus, FC vol. 37, p.236) or "the organ of theoria" (*Makarian Homilies*) which "is engaged in pure prayer" (St. Isaac the Syrian). When referring to the energy of the nous, they call it "a power of the soul" (*On the Holy Spirit*, St. Gregory Palamas, 2,9) "consisting of thoughts and conceptual images" (*On the Hesychasts*, St. Gregory Palamas, p. 410,3). However, it is more commonly known

as the energy of the soul, whereas the heart is known as the essence of the soul.

Panagia (Παναγία):
This is a title of the Virgin Mary which literally means, "the all-holy one."

Pascha (Πάσχα):
Pascha is the celebration of the Lord's Resurrection, known in the Christian West as Easter.

Passion (πάθος):
A passion is a spiritual disease that dominates that soul. When one repeatedly falls into a certain sin, it becomes second nature—a passion—for him to keep falling into this sin. Thus, one who misuses the God-given powers of the soul of desire and anger, or one who continually succumbs to temptations of lust, hate, malice, or jealousy, or one who succumbs to pride and vainglory, acquires those passions. It is primarily through obedience to an experienced elder that one is cleansed or healed of the passions and reaches *dispassion*.

Passionate (ἐμπαθής):
The word "passionate" in this text is not used in any of the secular senses of the word, but is used to describe someone or something subject to the *passions*.

Patristic (πατερικός):
This adjective is used to describe something of, or relating to, the Holy Fathers of the Church.

Praxis (πρᾶξις):
Praxis is the practice of the virtues, in contrast with *theoria*. It refers to the external aspect of the ascetical life (namely, purification, fasting, vigils, *metanoias*, etc., and in general the keeping of the commandments) and is an indispensable prerequisite of theoria.

The prayer (ἡ εὐχή):
The *Jesus prayer*, "Lord Jesus Christ, have mercy on me," is usually referred to as simply "the prayer."

Prayer of the heart (καρδιακὴ προσευχή):
"Prayer of the heart" is the highest form of prayer in which the *nous* is kept in the *heart* by the grace of the Holy Spirit, and prays there without distraction. Beyond this form of prayer is *theoria*.

Prayer-rope (κομποσχοίνι):
A prayer-rope is a cord with many knots (usually thirty-three or one hundred) which is used in prayer to help the *nous* concentrate. At each knot, one prayer (usually the *Jesus prayer*) is said.

Prayer rule (κανών):
A prayer rule consists of the prayers and *metanoias* which one does daily, under the guidance of one's spiritual father.

Predisposition (πρόληψις):
Predisposition is "the involuntary presence of former sins in the memory" according to St. Mark the Ascetic. This state is caused by repeated sinful acts which predispose a person to yield to particular temptations. Even though in principle he

retains free choice and can reject provocations from the demons, in practice the force of habit makes it progressively harder for him to resist.

Proskomede (προσκομιδή):

The Proskomede is the service of preparation for the Divine Liturgy in which the portion to be used for the Eucharist is cut out of the *prosphora*, and during which the living and the dead are commemorated.

Prosphoron (πρόσφορον):

A prosphoron (plural: prosphora) is a specially-prepared loaf of bread to be used in the *Proskomede* in preparation for the Divine Liturgy.

Purification (κάθαρσις):

In *Patristic* Theology, purification refers to three states: (1) the rejection of all *thoughts* from the *heart*, (2) the ascetical effort by which the three powers of the soul are turned towards God, thereby moving in accordance with and above nature, and (3) the ascetical method by which man overcomes selfish love and achieves unselfish love.

Rebuttal (ἀντιλογία):

Rebuttal is the repulsing of a demonic thought at the moment of *assault*. See also *consent*.

Repentance (μετάνοια):

The Greek word for "repentance" does not mean merely regret or contrition, but it literally means a "change of mind" through which one directs his entire life towards God.

Schema (σχῆμα):

The schema, usually called the "great schema" or "angelic schema," is the habit of a monk of the highest level of monasticism. It is called the "angelic schema" because its bearer strives to live angelically in purity and devotion to God alone.

Single-phrased (μονολόγιστος):

This is an adjective used by St. John of the Ladder and other Church Fathers to describe the *Jesus prayer* because of its short content.

Skete (σκήτη):

A skete is a small monastic village, usually consisting of a central church and several "cells." "Cells" are monastic houses, each with its own chapel and its own *synodia*.

Synodia (συνοδία):

A synodia (pronounced "seen-oh-dee'-ah") is a group of monks living together, consisting of the elder and his *disciples*. This word is often translated as "brotherhood."

Theoria (θεωρία):

Theoria is the "vision of the spirit" or "a non-sensible revelation of the *nous*" (St. Isaac the Syrian) through which one attains spiritual *knowledge*. That is, through theoria, the Holy Spirit grants one understanding of the mysteries of God and creation which are hidden to the rational human *intellect*. Knowledge stemming from theoria is revelation from above. Theoria is not intellectual work, but an operation of the Holy Spirit which opens the eyes of the soul to behold mysteries. The Church Fathers often contrast it with *praxis* which is an indispensable prerquisite of theoria. In the first stage of theoria, *the prayer* is said without distraction and with a sense of the presence of God with love, peace, *mourning*, etc. In the next stage, the nous proceeds to feel what Adam felt in paradise before the Fall, and it sees spiritually how all nature glorifies God. Furthermore, it sees His omnipotence, omniscience, and providence therein. By St. Maximus the Confessor, this is called perceiving the inner essences or principles of created beings (*Philokalia, vol. II*, p. 69). In the final stage of theoria, one beholds God Himself in uncreated light. (*On Prayer, Philokalia, vol. I*, Evagrios the Solitary, p. 61). See also *contemplation*.

Theosis (θέωσις):
    Connected with the *theoria* of uncreated Light, theosis, or divinization, is a participation in the uncreated grace of God. At this stage of perfection, one has reached *dispassion*. Through the cooperation of God with man, theosis is attained through the action of the transfigurative grace of God.

Theotokos (Θεοτόκος):
    This is a title for the Virgin Mary, the Mother of God. Literally, it means, "God-birthgiver." This title was approved of by the Third Ecumenical Council because it declares that Christ even before the incarnation was truly and fully God.

Thoughts (λογισμοί):
    In the *patristic* sense, "thoughts" refers not merely to thoughts in the ordinary sense, but also to evil thoughts provoked by the demons. Only with *watchfulness* can we prevent the demons' *assaults* of thoughts from developing into sins.

Tonsure (κουρά):
A tonsure is the rite in which a novice becomes a monk or nun. It is called a tonsure because during the rite, some of the novice's hair is cut.

Typikon (τυπικόν):
The "typikon" can mean: (a) a brotherhood's system of rules regulating the life of a monk in general; or (b) the set of rubrics governing the order of liturgical services.

Watchful Fathers (Νηπτικοὶ Πατέρες):
The "Watchful Fathers" or "Neptic Fathers" are the Church Fathers who wrote about *watchfulness*.

Watchfulness (νῆψις):
Watchfulness is unceasing attentiveness, alertness, or vigilance whereby one keeps watch over one's inward *thoughts* and *fantasies*, so that they do not enter the *heart*; it is only the *nous* which must be within the heart.

---

† We chose to translate διάνοια (dianoia) as intellect, because it is the word closest in meaning to the Greek term. For, according to the Oxford Dictionary of the English Language, the intellect is: "that faculty or sum of faculties of the mind or soul by which one knows and reasons (excluding sensation, and sometimes imagination; distinguished from feeling and will); power of thought; understanding. Rarely in reference to the lower animals." (vol. IX, p. 369)

The word "mind" could be used to translate "dianoia" because one of the meanings of the word "mind," according to the same dictionary, is: "the cognitive or intellectual powers, as distinguished from the will and emotions. Often contrasted with heart." (vol. XIII, p. 461) However, this word also has other meanings which render it ambiguous. In particular, the primary sense of the word is: "the seat of a persons consciousness, thoughts, volitions, and feelings; the system of cognitive and emotional phenomena and powers that constitutes the subjective being of a person; also, the incorporeal subject of the psychical faculties, the spiritual part of a human being; the soul as distinguished from the body." (Ibid) This meaning of the word "mind" is not only different than the meaning of the word "dianoia," but it is also remarkably similar to the meaning of the word "νοῦς" (nous). Furthermore, the word mind is needed to translate the term nous in phrases such as "keep in mind," "the mind wanders," etc. Thus, if the word "mind" were employed to translate the term "dianoia," it would be unclear whether dianoia or nous is meant. Therefore, in order to avoid this confusion, we decided to use the clearer word "intellect."

Unfortunately, though, the word "intellect" has been used with a new meaning in recent years. Some Orthodox books published today have translated the word "nous" as "intellect" and the word "dianoia" as "mind." As explained above, it is not wrong to use the word "mind" for the term "dianoia," given that the reader understands that it is the limited sense of the word "mind" which is intended. However, to use the word "intellect" for the term "nous" is inaccurate—or at best, innovative (if one bears in mind that the meaning of a word in a language is not static, but develops according to usage).

Index

charity 165, 207, 210, 319, 391
chastity 23, 34, 63, 171, 173, 174, 182
circular prayer 186, 394, 395
coldness 77
communion 139, 145, 197, 232, 318, 377, 393
compunction 41, 54, 86, 142, 353
conceit 357
condemnation 88, 368
confession 52, 80, 116, 162, 180, 218, 232, 247, 262, 286,
    297, 300, 301, 316, 318, 321, 344
conscience 25, 100, 110, 145, 154, 184, 238, 267, 308
consent 176, 196, 294, 393, 395, 407
contemplate 34, 137, 203, 253, 398
contrition 407
courage 34, 68, 71, 72, 84, 106, 107, 118, 120, 128, 129, 161,
    176, 215, 244, 299, 314, 316, 319
cowardice 180
cross 53, 61, 65, 71, 104, 105, 140, 150, 151, 198, 199, 200,
    207, 242, 314, 317, 403
curiosity 223
damnation 168
Daniel, Elder 86, 93, 196
David 93, 123, 124, 149, 276
death 14, 25, 26, 34, 91, 92, 118, 137, 138, 140, 156, 157,
    158, 160, 165, 203, 209, 219, 238, 243, 250, 281, 282,
    302, 339, 344, 368, 398
delusion 21, 46, 96, 186, 187, 188, 189, 261, 262, 263, 279,
    288, 351, 353, 357, 358, 359, 366, 367, 368, 369, 373,
    374
desert 29, 30, 46, 62, 109, 110, 137, 181
desire 30, 63, 75, 120, 121, 264, 396, 405
despair 106, 116, 122, 125, 156, 169, 180, 195, 214, 222,
    294, 319, 348, 404

humility 32, 34, 49, 50, 51, 56, 60, 61, 62, 74, 103, 128, 151,
    169, 172, 173, 183, 263, 287, 293, 294, 307, 311, 356,
    358, 359, 363, 370, 403
icons 23, 209, 225, 226, 401
idle talk 146
ignorance 51, 60, 113, 115, 167, 200, 208, 216, 253, 336,
    358, 367, 373
illnesses 67, 159-160, 271, 278-279, 281, 282
illumination 22, 33, 45, 78, 83, 129, 136, 138, 174, 181, 182,
    206, 207, 346, 347, 364, 381, 393, 401
impatience 167, 168, 169, 192
incensive aspect 297, 393, 397, 401
indifference 357, 377, 397
inner voice 44, 305, 311, 401, 402
intellect 58, 72, 90, 138, 188, 197, 206, 252, 321, 343, 371,
    388, 394, 395, 396, 402, 403, 404, 408, 410, 411
jealousy 212, 320, 405
Jesus prayer 130, 146, 232, 400, 402, 403, 406, 408
Joseph, Elder
    as a layman 64, 192
    first years on Mt. Athos 39, 139, 192-193
    as a monk 20-24, 65, 66-67, 87, 88, 113-115, 132-135,
        136-137, 144-145, 157-158, 160, 192-200, 234-244,
        245, 255
    illness 45, 75, 141, 143, 157, 160, 161, 170, 182, 242,
        243, 244, 247, 255, 294, 330, 349, 352, 353, 358,
        365, 377, 385, 400
    repose 25-26
    visions 70-71, 134, 153, 157, 166, 193-194, 195-196
        197-200, 228-229, 291
joy 28, 44, 54, 62, 63, 69, 71, 82, 83, 91, 109, 118, 128, 129,
    134, 136, 138, 142, 148, 149, 160

Glory be to God
for all things.